Edited by Helene Cooper

At Home in the World

by Daniel Pearl

The House at Sugar Beach

IN SEARCH OF A LOST AFRICAN CHILDHOOD

Helene Cooper

Simon & Schuster

New York   London   Toronto   Sydney

 Simon & Schuster
1230 Avenue of the Americas
New York, NY 10020

SIMON & SCHUSTER and colophon are
registered trademarks of Simon & Schuster, Inc.

Designed by C. Linda Dingler

Manufactured in the United States of America

ISBN-13: 978-1-60751-639-2

For my parents,
John Lewis Cooper Jr. and Calista Dennis Cooper,
and the family they raised at Sugar Beach:
Vicky, Janice, John Bull, Marlene, and Eunice.

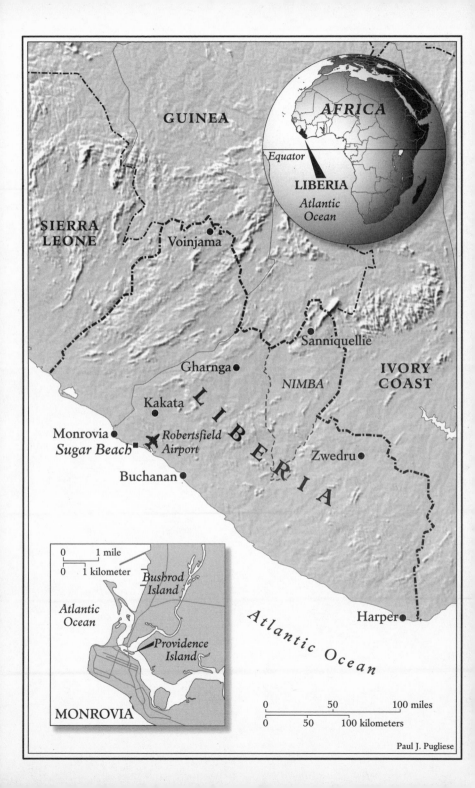

GUINEA

SIERRA
LEONE

Voinjama

AFRICA

Equator

LIBERIA

Atlantic
Ocean

Sanniquellie

Gharnga

NIMBA

IVORY
COAST

Kakata

L I B E R I A

Monrovia
Sugar Beach   Robertsfield
Airport

Zwedru

Buchanan

0   1 mile
0   1 kilometer

Bushrod
Island

Atlantic
Ocean

Providence
Island

MONROVIA

Atlantic   Ocean

Harper

0   50   100 miles
0   50   100 kilometers

Paul J. Pugliese

THE Public have been already informed of the strenuous exertions of the United States Government, in enacting numerous laws for the purpose of suppressing the Slave Trade; and of the successful vigilance of our naval officers, in detecting those desperadoes, the slave-traders, and bringing them to justice.

The Public have also been informed of the benevolent operations of the American Colonization Society, in endeavouring to form a settlement on the western coast of Africa, composed of those free people of colour who choose to emigrate thither. It is moreover known that this settlement, if established, may prove an asylum for those Africans, who shall be recaptured by the United States cruisers, and sent to the coast.

There is reason to hope that these acts of mercy will contribute to meliorate the sufferings of a large portion of the human race, by the final abolition of the Slave Trade, that scourge of Africa and disgrace of the civilized world; by introducing the arts of civilization and the blessings of the Christian religion, among a race of beings who have hitherto lived in heathen darkness, destitute of the light of the Gospel, or knowledge of a Saviour, by teaching the children of Ethiopia to stretch forth her hands unto GOD.

—Abstract of a Journal: Ephraim Bacon, Assistant Agent of the United States to AFRICA, 1821

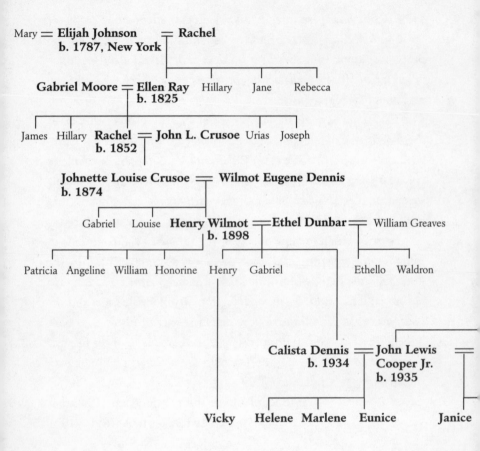

Mary = **Elijah Johnson** = **Rachel**
b. 1787, New York

Gabriel Moore = **Ellen Ray**   Hillary   Jane   Rebecca
b. 1825

James   Hillary   **Rachel** = **John L. Crusoe**   Urias   Joseph
b. 1852

Johnette Louise Crusoe = **Wilmot Eugene Dennis**
b. 1874

Gabriel   Louise   **Henry Wilmot** = **Ethel Dunbar** = William Greaves
b. 1898

Patricia   Angeline   William   Honorine   Henry   Gabriel   Ethello   Waldron

Calista Dennis = **John Lewis** =
b. 1934   **Cooper Jr.**
b. 1935

Vicky   **Helene   Marlene   Eunice   Janice**

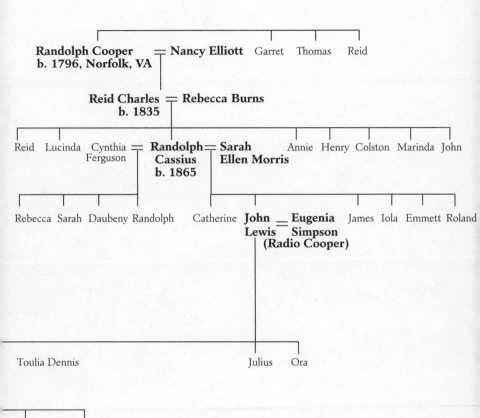

Randolph Cooper = Nancy Elliott   Garret   Thomas   Reid
b. 1796, Norfolk, VA

Reid Charles = Rebecca Burns
b. 1835

Reid   Lucinda   Cynthia = Randolph = Sarah   Annie   Henry   Colston   Marinda   John
                  Ferguson   Cassius   Ellen Morris
                            b. 1865

Rebecca   Sarah   Daubeny   Randolph   Catherine   John _ Eugenia   James   Iola   Emmett   Roland
                                                      Lewis   Simpson
                                                            (Radio Cooper)

Toulia Dennis   Julius   Ora

John   Ora
Lewis III

Part One

SUGAR BEACH, LIBERIA, 1973

$\mathscr{T}$his is a story about rogues.

Burglars are "rogues." The word *burglar* is not in the Liberian-English vernacular. I occasionally used "thief," though only for two reasons: (1) to impress whoever was listening that I knew proper English, and (2) to amplify "rogue," like when yelling out "Rogue! Rogue! Thiefy! Thiefy!" to stop a fleeing rogue. But rogues and thieves were very different ani-

---

Helene at Sugar Beach

mals. Rogues broke into your house while you were sleeping and made off with the fine china. Thieves worked for the government and stole money from the public treasury.

Our house at Sugar Beach was plagued by rogues. From the time we moved into the twenty-two-room behemoth my father had had built overlooking the Atlantic Ocean, they installed themselves as part of daily life. It wasn't hard to figure out why: we were a continent away from civilization at eleven miles outside of Monrovia, my mother was hell-bent on filling up the house with ivory, easily portable if you're a rogue, and our watchman, Bolabo, believed that nights were meant for sleeping, not guarding the house.

Bolabo was an old man. His hair, which he kept cut very short, was almost white. He had nine teeth, at alternating places on the top rim and bottom rim of his mouth, so that when he talked you could see the holes, but when he smiled, which was a lot, it looked like a perfect set. He didn't have a gun, he had a nightstick. He walked with a bounce and always seemed cheerful, even when he was getting reamed out by my mother in the mornings after the discovery that rogues had once more gotten into Sugar Beach and made off with her ivory.

The first time it happened—within a week of our arrival at Sugar Beach—I woke up and stumbled out of my bedroom to the sound of my mother yelling at Bolabo outside. Jack was leaning against the wall, enjoying the proceedings. He winked at me. Jack was technically our houseboy, but none of us ever dared call him that because he grew up with Daddy.

"Rogues came here last night," Jack reported.

Mommee had hauled Bolabo to the kitchen porch for his dressing down. She was in the doorway, her arms punctuating the air with her grievances. She wore her usual early-morning attire: knit shorts that stopped just above her knees, a T-shirt, and slippers. Her hair, originally piled on top of her head, had come undone as she paced angrily back and forth on the kitchen porch, arms flailing. Before her stood Bolabo, his entire demeanor one of remorse.

Bolabo: "Aya Ma, na mind ya."

Translation: Gosh! How awful! Never you mind, Mrs. Cooper, please accept my apologies.

Mommee: "You hopeless seacrab! I should sack you!"

Translation: Bluster. "Seacrab" and "damn" were as close as Mommee ever came to cussing. History would show Mommee sacked Bolabo every month and always rehired him when he came back and "held her foot."

Bolabo: "I hold your foot, Ma."

Translation: An exclamation point that punctuates this heartfelt entreaty. When begging a Liberian's pardon, you can't get much lower than telling them you hold their foot.

This went on for about fifteen minutes, until Mommee slammed the door in disgust. Bolabo was extra vigilant for the next few days, making a big show of closing his bedroom door in the boys' house during the day so we would know that he was getting his rest for the night ahead. Then, at around six p.m., he came outside with his nightstick and strutted around the yard, inspecting the coconut trees that surrounded the estate, presumably for signs of imminent attack. He peered down the water well near the fence, as if rogues were treading water thirty feet down, waiting for the family to go to sleep before jet-propelling themselves out like Superman.

Bolabo settled into his chair by the laundry room, then jumped up self-importantly when a car drove into the yard, as if the rogues might just drive up at seven p.m. for supper. Invariably, he was asleep before my bedtime at eight p.m.

I, on the other hand, was not.

Who could fall asleep way out in the bush like that? I went

to bed at night wishing we were back at our old house in Congo Town.

Liberia is nowhere near the Congo River, but the term *Congo* is endemic. We are called the Congo people—my family and the rest of the descendants of the freed American slaves who founded Liberia in 1822. It is a somewhat derogatory term invented by the native Liberians back in the early nineteenth century, after Britain abolished slave trade on the high seas. British patrols seized slave ships leaving the West African coast for America and returned those captured to Liberia and Sierra Leone, whether they came from there or not. Since many of the slave ships entered the Atlantic from the mouth of the massive Congo River, the native Liberians, many of whom happily engaged in the slave trade and didn't like this new business of freeing the slaves and dumping them in Liberia, called the newcomers Congo People. Because the newly freed captives were released in Liberia at the same time that the freed blacks arrived in Liberia from America, all newcomers became known as Congo People. Monrovia is full of Congo this and Congo that. Congo Town, where our old house was, is a suburb of Monrovia. It was filled with Congo People like us.

We got the native Liberians back by calling them Country People, far more derogatory, in our eyes.

Daddy moved us to Sugar Beach because he thought the old house in Congo Town was too small. It only had three bedrooms, three bathrooms, a TV lounge, a living room, a den, an office, a kitchen, a palaver hut outside, and a huge lawn, where I learned critical social skills from Tello, my favorite cousin and role-model supreme.

"Jus' kick your foot de same time you jumping!" Tello, short for Ethello, yelled at me one Sunday afternoon on the Congo Town lawn. It was a typically heavy, soupy day, and my ponytail, drenched in sweat, glued itself to the back of my neck. Next door, the Baptist church people, who spent hours in that church singing their holy ghost songs, had quieted down—it was time for their midafternoon snack of check-rice with crawfish gravy. The sharp, intense smell of the fish gravy wafted to our yard from the back of the church, making my stomach rumble with hunger.

Tello was teaching me how to play knock-foot, a girls' game where players hop on one foot and kick toward their opponents with the other foot. Knock-foot involved intricate maneuvers that need rhythm and balance. The Country People had thought it up. Knock-foot is sort of like rock, paper, scissors with feet. A good knock-foot session between two girls who know what they're doing looks like dancing, with each girl bobbing, kicking, and clapping to a precise beat.

There were many variations of knock-foot; one, called Kor, required such precision I knew I'd never be able to do it. All I wanted was to be able to do basic knock-foot. Hop, hop, kick. Clap, hop, kick. Except the clap was on a half beat and the kick was on a half beat.

Beads of sweat collected on my forehead as I tried again. Hop, hop, kick. "Not like that!" instructed Tello. She was four months older than me and very sure of matters of correctness. "You kicking before you jumping!"

"Aye, I tryin," I whined.

Hop, hop, kick. I raised my foot slightly higher, and when I kicked, got her full in the knee, good and hard. She stomped the grass, then turned around, and, with a sucking of her teeth—that social skill I had mastered at last—walked back to the house. I chased after her.

My escort into high society was mad at me. "Tello!" I said, trailing her into the house. "Na mind."

She forgave me when we entered the living room and we

automatically headed for the black leather couch to pretend to be our mothers.

"I say, it's too hard to find good help these days," Tello said, crossing her legs as she sat on the couch with her doll propped in her lap. "I told Gladys to make up the bed, and you know wha' she did? Cleaned the cupboard instead!"

I sighed, in what I hoped was a long-suffering way. "Ma people, I got' de same problem m'self, I tell you," I replied, flicking some imaginary dust off my pants. "I asked Old Man Charlie to cook palm butter and he cooked cassava leaf!"

I loved the Congo Town house. It was close to town and Tello visited all the time. There was always stuff to do and people to see, even if it was just picking fights with the Baptist people next door.

But Daddy said we were crowded there. I shared a bedroom with my little sister, Marlene, and Marlene's nurse, Martha, a tall Kru woman. There were way too many people in my bedroom at night. "Don't worry," Daddy said. "When we build the house at Sugar Beach, you're going to have your own room."

My own room! Wouldn't that show the world how grown I was!

"What color do you want it?" Mommee asked me before we left Congo Town.

I thought for days and days before finally deciding. "I wan ma room be pink."

And so, bought off with the false notion that I actually wanted my own room, I followed my family to Sugar Beach and our grand new home.

This was our house at Sugar Beach: a futuristic, three-level verandahed 1970s-era behemoth with a mammoth glass dome on top, visible as soon as you turned onto the dirt road junc-

tion a mile away. The house revealed itself slowly, like a co-
quettish Parisian dancer from the 1920s. Emerging from the
road's first major pothole—big enough to swallow a small European car—your reward was a glimpse of the house's sloping
roof and glass dome, shining in the equatorial sun. Rounding
the bend between the dense bush of plum trees and vines, you
next got a glimpse of the house's eastern wraparound second-
floor porches, painted creamy butter, with a roasted red pepper trim hand-selected for tropical contrast. Driving by the
two huts that formed the outermost edge of the nearby Bassa
village of Bubba Town, you then caught another tease: the
sliding glass doors that formed the perimeter of the second-
floor living room.

But nothing could prepare you for the final disrobing as
you crested the hill that opened up to the panoramic view of
the house, back-lit by the thunderous waves and pounding
surf from the Atlantic as far as the eye could see. Shangri-la,
Camelot, the Garden of Eden—the Cooper family's perfect
and perfectly grand paradise, where John and Calista Cooper
could raise their perfect family, cosseted by well-paid servants,
and protected from the ravages of West African squalor and
poverty by central air-conditioning, strategically placed coconut trees, and a private water well.

The upper level had five bedrooms and three bathrooms
and a TV lounge and an indoor balcony that looked down onto
the children's toy room on the first floor. The middle level had
an enormous kitchen with adjoining dining room, the two separated by double swing doors. There was a music room with a
rock wall on one side, housing a baby grand piano that over-
looked the ocean. There was the sunken living room with its
rich velvet couches the color of cognac and its wraparound
glass doors, from which you could view the ocean to the south
and the bush to the north.

The lower level had two bedrooms and three bathrooms and a huge recreation room with a full bar. There was a playroom and a toy room and my father's office. And there was a nook under the stairs for storing our plastic Christmas tree.

With the exception of the bedrooms, all of which had wall-to-wall carpet, all floors were marble. A nine-foot-tall grandfather clock stood in an atrium halfway down the marble staircase separating the middle level from the lower level.

The five-acre grounds had a lush green carpet grass ringed by hibiscus and bougainvillea plants, and coconut trees. The two-car garage housed the favorites of the moment; the older cars and Daddy's pickup truck were relegated to a parking area by the boys' house.

In moving to Sugar Beach, eleven miles out of Monrovia, we were supposed to be suburban pioneers. If the world had worked out the way it was supposed to, Monrovia would have followed us out there, as housing developments, businesses, cafes, and restaurants overran the city and pushed its boundaries farther east from Providence Island, where the first Congo People—the freed black Americans—built their houses and established their capital city. My parents, especially Mommee, had both grown up in houses in what was now the heart of inner-city Monrovia. Mama Grand, Mommee's mother, still lived "across the bridge" on Bushrod Island, an area near the port that was now completely overtaken by shops and business.

By contrast, Sugar Beach was in the bush on the edge of the sea. Our closest neighbors who weren't Country People were the people at the mental hospital Catherine Mills, about five miles away. There were plenty of Country People living in Bubba Town and other Country villages nearby. Uncle Julius, Daddy's brother, built his house right next to ours at Sugar Beach, so we at least had our cousins—Ericka, Jeanine, and

Juju—next door. Together, the two houses made up the Cooper Compound.

Our house at Sugar Beach was a source of pride and of pain. It was a testament to the stature of my family in a country where stature mattered, sometimes above all else. Liberian society rivaled Victorian England when it came to matters of social correctness. In Liberia, we cared far more about how we looked outside than about who we were inside. It was crucial to be an Honorable. Being an "Honorable"—mostly Congo People, though a smattering of Country People were sometimes pronounced educated enough to get the title—meant you were deemed eligible to hold important government posts. You could have a Ph.D. from Harvard but if you were a Country man with a tribal affiliation you were still outranked in Liberian society by an Honorable with a two-bit degree from some community college in Memphis, Tennessee. Daddy was an Honorable with a proper college bachelor of science, but being Hon. John L. Cooper Jr. was a hell of a lot more important than whatever degree he got in America.

But the Cooper Compound was far from Monrovia. It didn't take more than two days out there for me to realize that I'd been had. Eleven miles is a continent when you are seven years old and all of your friends live in town and rogues and heartmen rule the nighttime. Radio Cooper, my grandfather, wired Liberia, but his telephone lines didn't reach Sugar Beach, where his two sons had decided to build their houses.

"How much longer until we get a phone?" I whined to Daddy on the first day we moved there.

"You're seven years old. Who you plannin to call?"

"Tello 'them."

In Liberian English, saying " 'them" after someone's name is a shortcut for including a whole group. "Tello 'them" meant "Tello and her sisters."

"Ain't nothing you and Tello got to talk 'bout every day. You can talk to her when your Mommee carry you to church Sunday."

I knew not to argue too much with Daddy. He sat at the top of the Sugar Beach hierarchy, with Mommee. Together, John Lewis Cooper Jr. and Calista Esmeralda Dennis Cooper, represented three Liberian dynasties: the Coopers, the Dennises, and the Johnsons.

Hon. John L. Cooper's ancestors dated back to one of the first ships of freed blacks that immigrated to Liberia from America in the early 1800s.

Mommee's ancestor, on the other hand, was on *the* first ship. If Elijah Johnson hadn't existed, Liberia might not exist. He and sixty-five others survived the trip to Africa back in 1820. The three white men sent along with the group, along with twenty other blacks, all died within weeks of landing in West Africa. Elijah Johnson lived, and ostensibly founded Monrovia after disease ravaged the group of freemen settlers.

When native Liberians attacked the newcomers, Elijah Johnson led the fight back. A British gunboat came ashore and its commander offered to send help if Elijah Johnson would cede to the British flag. "We want no flagstaff put up here that will cost more to get it down again than it will to whip the natives," Elijah Johnson said, in a phrase we memorized in school.

Elijah Johnson's son, Hillary Johnson, became Liberia's sixth president. His great-great-grandson, my great-uncle Gabriel Dennis, was secretary of state and secretary of treasury. Cecil Dennis, the minister of foreign affairs, was my cousin, although we called him Uncle Cecil.

Mommee took great pride in the fact that, as one of the heirs to Elijah Johnson, she received a $25 check from the government every once in a while. It was his pension, divided up among his descendants. Sometimes jealous people—Country and Congo—complained about why a poor third-world country was still doling out money to Elijah Johnson's heirs more than a century after he died. To which Mommee replied, "Excuse me, there wouldn't be a country if it weren't for Elijah Johnson."

Daddy had clout, but Mommee ruled Sugar Beach. She was tall and thin and light-skinned, and had the ultimate symbol of beauty in Liberia: long, silky, soft, white people's hair. She had long legs and a long neck and she never went out without her Christian Dior sunglasses propped on her nose. She had the first Lincoln Continental Mark IV ever to show up in Liberia. She could order Old Man Charlie, one of our cooks, to make sure he put enough raisins in the cinnamon rolls one minute, and then turn around the next minute and give $100 to the market women who came to the house to beg for school tuition for the children.

Daddy's side of the family, the Coopers, made their mark in business. The four brothers arrived from Virginia as freemen in 1829—newbies by Mommee's standards. They bought up land left and right and quickly became one of the most powerful and wealthy families in Liberia. My great-great-great-granduncle, Reid Cooper, became a Liberian navy commodore who helped to fight the Country People and rescued one batch of early settlers up in Maryland County from a group of angry native Liberians. Radio Cooper, my grandfather, was chief of the Liberian Telephone Exchange. My uncle Julius was minister of Action for Development and Progress. My father was deputy postmaster general.

There is a photo of the cabinet of former Liberian president William V. S. Tubman, taken just after his inauguration in 1944. My great-uncle, Gabriel Dennis, secretary of state (Mommee's side), stands next to my grandfather, Radio Cooper. I see my mother's, and my own, flat mouth in my uncle Gabriel. I see my father's, and my own, deep-set eyes in my grandfather Radio Cooper.

Their pedigrees matched on paper, but in reality, Mommee and Daddy were from different planets. Daddy took nothing seriously. He drank like a true Cooper—beer with raw eggs for breakfast, gin for lunch, whiskey for supper; Mommee thought a sip of brandy was deliciously naughty. Mommee went to church religiously; Daddy treated church like it had a black snake inside. Mommee was hypersensitive and quick to take offense: her college epitath was "Calista Dennis, Lah to us; Nice and friendly, willing to fuss." Daddy was an incorrigible jokester who prized his wit and whose favorite brag was: "I lost a million dollars by the time I was thirty."

Daddy was light-skinned, too, with those big round fat Cooper cheeks. He had a beard and a goatee mustache and deep-set eyes. Mommee called him a shorty, because they were the exact same height and he was always trying to stop her from wearing high-heeled shoes when they went out together.

After Mommee and Daddy in the family totem pole, at least as far as I was concerned, came me. "Helene, the great," I called myself. "The Joy of my Heart," Mommee called me. "Hard-time Biscuit," my brother, John Bull (same Pa) said. "Cracky Cooper," my cousins said.

I was darker than Mommee and Daddy but still light-skinned by Liberian standards. I weighed eleven pounds thirteen ounces when I was delivered by cesarean on April 22, 1966, at Cooper Clinic in Monrovia. When the doctor whacked me to check out my lungs, I growled like Barry White. Mommee, who only weighed 118 pounds at the time, was too tired to get a good look at me after the operation. "Is it okay?" she said, then fell asleep. When she woke up, the nurse said: "Are you ready to see your monster?"

I was living proof that Mommee could conceive. She was thirty-two when she had me, a full two years after she and Daddy got married. That's old age in West Africa, where girls are married off as soon as they come back from the Grebo bush. We were civilized Congo People with *American roots,* so nobody was sending Mommee off to the Grebo bush when she was fourteen to get circumcised and to learn how to be one of umpteen wives to some husband. But even in civilized Congo Liberian society, thirty-two was old to be having your first child.

She swaddled me in wool before taking me home, bundled warmly to protect my mocha-latte infant skin from the African sun. And the mosquitoes. "You are the joy of my heart," she told me, again and again. No question about it. I was special. Nobody was more special than me.

But I came out with Mommee's flat Dennis mouth. That's what we called white people's lips: "flat mouths." African lips are full and juicy. Daddy had full juicy African lips. His lips wrapped around a forkful of palm butter and rice, and he chewed, and his lips moved up and down, with moist palm oil oozing out before he licked it back in with his tongue. I loved watching him eat. It made me hungry. Nobody would watch me eat like that, because I had a flat mouth.

Five years after me came Marlene. Marlene and I are same Ma, same Pa, a critical distinction in a country where men routinely father children by multiple women. If a Liberian asks about your relationship to a sibling, you can always just answer "same Pa" meaning "we have the same father, not the same mother" or "same Ma."

"Same Ma, same Pa" implies you share the same blood from both parents.

Marlene was a chubby, white, green-eyed, silky soft hair, Chinese-looking Buddha-baby. We were all lined up in the upstairs TV lounge at the Old House in Congo Town on the day she was born, waiting to hear whether Mommee had had a baby girl or boy. Daddy came trooping up the steps. I held my breath. I didn't know what I wanted, a boy or girl? I already had two sisters through Daddy's first marriage—Janice and Ora—and one brother, John Bull.

Daddy looked at us and grinned. The suspense was too much and Janice finally yelled. "What Aunt Lah got?" Daddy looked at me. "Your Mommee had a baby girl."

We erupted into whoops and cheers and took off out of the house and down the street, chanting: "Baby girl again! Baby girl again!" The original baby girl was me, but now there was another one, who would always be the babiest baby girl. The people who lived near our house in Congo Town came out into the streets. Some of them danced with us and some just stood on the side of the road observing our antics. "You see how these Cooper people crazy?" one woman said.

Daddy took us to Cooper Clinic to see Marlene the day after she was born. "Wha' she look like?" I asked him excitedly, as we marched up the steps to the second-floor maternity ward.

"Like a Cooper," he said. Translation: fat and white.

Marlene could easily be taken for white if it wasn't for her African features. She had a big wide African nose and Daddy's lips. Those fun-to-watch-eat-palm-butter lips.

She was always hungry. Marlene ate things that I wouldn't consider putting in my mouth, like kernels from the palm trees, which she dug out of the yard. She had two nicknames, both given to her by the servants at Sugar Beach: one was "PlurTorTor," which meant pepperbird, and the other was "Mrs. Palm Kernel," except in Liberian English we don't say "palm kernel" we say "pam-kana."

I didn't immediately adjust well to being usurped as the

reigning baby girl. One time Daddy caught me standing over her crib pinching her fat butt. I got spanked, and was banished from my parents' room, where Marlene was sleeping.

Fortunately, there were other distractions at Sugar Beach.

Janice (same Pa) was Daddy's oldest daughter, five years older than me, from his first marriage. She was the shortest one in the family, with a smile that always somehow looked fake.

Janice could sit for hours on the floor cross-legged, each leg on top of the opposing knee like some kind of deranged yoga instructor. Then she smiled that fake smile at you and you knew that whatever had been going on in her head was a matter best left alone.

She spoke with a British accent because she went to boarding school in England: the Queen's Park School for girls in Oswestry, Shropshire. She was geeky before she went to boarding school, but once she started going, she became a "been-to."

A "been-to" in Liberia meant you'd been to America or Europe. Going to visit for a month or so didn't count; you had to have lived there. When longing to be a "been-to," I never really considered the part about actually living away from home. It was always much more about arriving back in Liberia, to great fanfare, after an extended stay "abroad." In my fantasy, I looked fresh and hip and American or British as I swept off the plane after a year living in the States or London. Everyone would greet me at Robertsfield airport like I was a celebrity, and I would speak with an American accent, just like Janice spoke with a British accent whenever she came home from boarding school in England.

I wrote Janice letters telling her how boring life was at Sugar Beach, so far from town. She wrote me back that she had a white girl for a best friend, Jane, and how they ate four times a day in England because of tea. We only ate three times a day at Sugar Beach. How could anyone eat four times, I thought, shaking my head in wonder. When Janice came home to Sugar Beach during her summer vacations, Marlene and I followed her around the yard mimicking her British accent. "Whatever are you up to!" we said in high-pitched voices. "Bloody hell!"

John Bull (same Pa) was Daddy's only son, also by his first marriage, and four years older than me. We called him John Bull because he was thirteen pounds twelve ounces at birth and he ate and ate. His only rival when it came to eating was Marlene. John Bull's favorite game was Boofair. If he said "Boofair," while you were eating and you didn't have your fingers crossed then John Bull got your food. John Bull hid cans of corned beef in his room and at night, Marlene went in and the two of them snacked right out of the can. Marlene was in love with him and wanted to marry him. She told everyone she could find that she planned to marry her brother.

John Bull was husky and tall and had the Cooper round cheeks. When he went to boarding school at Ricks Institute up-country, we sent him care packages: cardboard boxes filled with Spam. Eventually he switched to the St. Patrick's all-boys Catholic school in Monrovia. He flirted briefly with teenaged cavorting around, before he became a born-again Christian at age fifteen and stopped going to movies and dancing parties. He started hosting Bible study classes in the TV lounge at Sugar Beach. I asked if I could attend but after a while I got bored and stopped going.

Victoria Yvette Nadine Dennis added the "Nadine" herself because she liked it. Vicky was Mommee's niece, the daughter of Mommee's oldest brother, whom we all called Bro. Henry, short for Brother Henry. You run the two words together "BrHenry."

Vicky's mother was a Gio woman named Season, who was Bro. Henry's girlfriend while he worked briefly up in San-niquellie, up-country in Nimba County. He didn't own up to Vicky until she was two years old, when his brother, Bro. Ga-briel, discovered Season and Vicky in a shop in Sanniquellie.

Vicky had the trademark flat Dennis mouth, which quickly gave away what Bro. Henry had been up to while in San-niquellie. Faced with the obvious, Bro. Henry confessed. The whole extended family trooped up to Sanniquellie to ask Sea-son if they could raise Vicky and send her to school.

Vicky moved to Monrovia to live with my grandmother, Mama Grand. Soon thereafter, Bro. Henry, still a bachelor, was appointed deputy consul to the Liberian embassy in Rome. The job came with a nanny, so he took Vicky. When they came back, Vicky went back to live with Mama Grand—a single man in Liberia couldn't raise a child. Mommee was liv-ing with Mama Grand at the time, rapidly approaching old maid status at thirty. When Mommee finally got married to Daddy, she brought with her into her marriage a trousseau, a lot of land from her father, and seven-year-old Vicky.

Vicky was cursed, as far as I was concerned, because she saw spirits. Late one night at the old house, the first year my parents were married and before I was born, my father was eating dinner by himself in the dining room downstairs. Vicky and Mommee were upstairs watching TV.

"Who's that man there?" Vicky, seven years old, asked my mother.

My mother looked at the doorway, where Vicky pointed. No one was there.

Mommee decided not to answer Vicky. But Vicky per-sisted.

"Does he live here?"

Mommee started screaming, jumped from her chair, and

raced downstairs yelling: "John! John! The child's seeing spirits oh!" Vicky ran behind my mother. Neither of them would go back upstairs until my father accompanied them, and Vicky spent that night in my parents' room.

Vicky continued spirit-spotting at Sugar Beach. She saw them playing in my hair. She saw them dancing outside the dining room. It got to the point that whenever we saw her getting that faraway look, we'd all jump and run.

Vicky often wore her hair in an Afro, and platform shoes and bell-bottom pants. Her skin was the deep brown color of milk candy after you fry the sweetened condensed milk. Sleeping was her favorite hobby.

And that—Mommee, Daddy, Marlene, Janice, John Bull, Vicky, and I—made up the family half of the house at Sugar Beach.

In Liberia, servants are called "boys." Occasionally you might call them "old men," like with Old Man Charlie, the cook. But most of the time, they're called boys, no matter how old they are. At Sugar Beach, all the men who served our family lived in the boys' house, about two hundred yards from the main house.

Fedeles, the driver, had the most clout because he drove the cars. Mommee and Daddy could both drive so Fedeles mostly drove us, the kids. He was from Ghana: tall, thin, and always wearing tight jeans. He was my first crush; I was fascinated with how he looked in his tight jeans. In Liberia we called butts "boneyhinds."

Jack was the houseboy, but that was too disrespectful a term for him so he was just Jack. Handsome and from the Kpelle ethnic group that populated the area around our family farm, Kakata, he grew up with Daddy and had been with the Cooper family all his life. Jack always wore skinny black pants that stopped right before they got to his feet, so you could see his white socks. He looked like Sidney Poitier. He vacationed in Spain with us. Jack nursed me with bottled milk when I was a baby and cleaned my room and made my bed. He always reminded me not to give him cheek because he "used to clean my poopoo drawers." He organized the household and saw to it that Mommee's orders were carried out by the other boys.

After Jack came Old Man Charlie and Tommy, our two cooks. Why did we have two cooks? One came from Daddy's side of the family (Old Man Charlie) and one came from Mommee's side (Tommy). Old Man Charlie, grumpy and irascible, also worked for Uncle Julius, next door. But Uncle Julius's house was often empty when my cousins, Ericka, Jeanine, and Juju, went and stayed with their mother, Aunt Millie, since Uncle Julius and Aunt Millie had divorced. So Old Man Charlie would come and cook for us, which was a good thing, since Tommy, our other cook, who had worked for Mommee's family for decades, often disappeared for weeks at a time. Tommy's disappearances usually came after paydays. We never knew where he went, and Mommee always vowed not to let him come back. But eventually, Tommy would come back and "hold" Mommee's foot, and he'd be our cook again.

Old Man Charlie was grumpy and irascible, and was always throwing people out of the kitchen. He made the best cinnamon rolls. I was the only person he didn't kick out of the kitchen. He let me help him make biscuits, dipping the top of the water glasses in flour and making the round biscuit-circles.

After Old Man Charlie came Sammy Cooper, the yardboy. Also Kpelle. I liked hanging out with Sammy Cooper because he knew, and told, stories about Daddy from when Daddy was younger. Old Sammy Cooper, who I always thought was Sammy Cooper's father but who was apparently not technically, used to work for my grandparents. He helped Radio Cooper plant the Cooper family farm up in Kakata, and believed Radio Cooper should have given the farm to him when Radio Cooper died, instead of leaving it to Daddy 'them.

It was the common belief in our household that Old Sammy Cooper, who was Kpelle, witched Radio Cooper, and that's why Radio Cooper got sick and died. When we first moved to Sugar Beach, Old Sammy Cooper brought a chicken to the house, and asked Mommee if he could sacrifice it and bury it in the yard so that we'd have good luck at the new house. Mommee didn't trust him but was too afraid to antagonize him so she let him do it, but then spent the next seven years trying to figure out where the chicken was buried so she could have it dug up.

Galway, the washman, was Bassa, and had his own room in the Sugar Beach house, next to the laundry room, where he slept away from the boys' house. Galway couldn't see out of one eye. He was also a grump.

And after Galway came Bolabo, the watchman. Bassa. Asleep by eight p.m.

Unlike me. I had demons to wrestle with.

The first night at Sugar Beach, I eagerly reported to my bed at seven forty-five, a full and shocking fifteen minutes before my scheduled bedtime. I couldn't wait. It was going to be so great, sleeping in my own room, all by myself.

Mommee went in with me and closed the curtains. She knelt beside me and we said my nightly prayers: "Now I Lay Me Down to Sleep, I Pray the Lord My Soul to Keep."

I was antsy to rush through and finish so I could get into bed. We recited, "If I Should Die Before I Wake, I Pray the Lord My Soul to Take."

A small shiver of premonition shot through me. If I died, I would be all by myself in that room. I hadn't thought about that.

I crawled into bed and Mommee leaned over and kissed

me. "Good night, joy of my heart," she said, and left the room, flipping off the light behind her.

I was immediately engulfed in an impenetrable, malevolent blackness.

Vicky's spirits were in the room with me. There were three of them, one man and two women. I could feel them; each was standing in a separate corner of my pink room, looking at me silently. They were trying to decide what they were going to do to me. I started to shake, and curled tightly in my bed, putting the blanket over my head. But then I couldn't breathe. Was that how they were going to get me, by scaring me into suffocating myself? That's how I would die before I woke?

Slowly, so the spirits wouldn't notice, I drew the blanket down and stuck out my nose, ever so carefully. Cold air-conditioned air filled my nostrils. I could breathe again.

But the spirits were still in there, edging closer to me, especially the two women. I clutched myself tighter and squeezed my eyes even tighter. *If I should die before I wake, I pray the Lord my soul to take.*

This was not a good prayer. I was accepting death as a fait accompli, without appealing up high for a different outcome. *Please God don't let me die before I wake. Please please. I promise to be a good girl. Please please please. I'nt want die before I wake.*

I was still praying when I finally fell asleep. Every night for two weeks, I prayed myself to sleep in sickly fear.

In those same two weeks, Sugar Beach had three nighttime visits from rogues. They took one of Mommee's favorite paintings, a pastoral scene of a Kpelle village by the river, with two women washing clothes, their babies on their back. Mommee had hung that painting up on the wall next to the music room; it was one of the first things you saw when you walked into the upstairs part of the house. The rogues took it, along with a giant elephant tusk in the living room.

They didn't pick the place clean, only taking a couple of things each visit. In the morning, an empty shelf or bare wall taunted us: the rogues could come in and do whatever they wanted.

The night after the rogues' third visit, I realized that the rogues were actually heartmen. That's why they were only taking a couple of things at a time; they weren't really coming for ivory and paintings. They wanted me!

Heartmen are witch doctors who kidnap people and cut out their hearts while they're still alive and use it to make medicine. Now that I was sleeping in my own room at night, they had the perfect opportunity to come and get me and cut out my heart and I would die before I woke.

They floated into the room that night as I slept, two of them, their cutlasses strapped to their waists. Long gleaming knives that curved at the tip, the better to carve out your heart—a paralysis came over me and woke me up. I lay on my back with my eyes open but I couldn't move, as the heartmen floated closer.

If I should die before I wake, I pray the Lord my soul to take.

They closed in on me, and I tried to scream. Nothing, no sound. I tried and tried, but no sound came from my locked throat.

If I should die before I wake, I pray the Lord my soul to take.

Just as they were about to pounce, a scream burst out of my throat and I almost fell out of my bed as I ran out the bedroom door as fast as I could, straight in to Mommee and Daddy's bed, refusing to leave until morning.

The next day, the Mandingo men came to sell Mommee more ivory, to replenish her reserves, which were being rapidly depleted by the nightly visits from the rogues.

Any private detective worth his two cents could have immediately figured out that the Mandingo men who sold Mommee the ivory had the most to gain from the constant burglaries, but Mommee welcomed them in anyway.

They came, in their customary long white flowing robes and their white pointy slippers. Two tall statuesque haughty men, with skin the color of a Hershey's chocolate bar. They walked up the dirt road to Sugar Beach, carrying barley bags, the sharp end of one of the elephant tusks poking out, gleaming in the sun.

Marlene's dogs, Happy, Blackie, and Christopher, started barking as soon as the men entered the yard, rousing themselves from their usual slumber under the kitchen steps and running around the men furiously. They were all mutts, distinguishable by color: Happy was light brown, Blackie was black, and Christopher was white. Happy, in particular, was yipping around the Mandingo men's ankles.

But the Mandingo men didn't even flinch. They walked right up to the steps and asked for "Ma."

I didn't understand how they could wear those long robes in the heat. It was the height of Liberian summer—January— and there wasn't the slightest breeze, not even from the ocean right at our backs. I was in shorts and my favorite Wonder Woman T-shirt, which the men eyed disapprovingly. "How they looking at people so?" I muttered to Old Man Charlie, standing next to me on the kitchen porch.

"That Muslim people, wha' you expect?" Old Man Charlie replied, not bothering to whisper.

Old Man Charlie eyed the Mandingo men. He was Kpelle and Kpelle people didn't really like Mandingos. The Mandingos had been in Liberia for about as long as anybody else, but somehow Liberians still thought of them as outsiders. Mandingoes worked hard and saved their money—a definite cause for envy and suspicion.

Just after he became president in 1971, William R. Tolbert, in an attempt to be inclusive, permitted the Mandingos to celebrate Ramadan at Liberia's Centennial Pavillion, which set God-fearing Christian Liberians muttering. It was bad enough the Lebanese people were all flocking to Liberia to take over the shops and stores, because of the fighting in Beirut, but at least they weren't pretending to be Liberian. The Mandingo people, on the other hand, loved reminding everybody that they had been around since way before us Congo People first began to return from America on ships.

Mommee liked the Mandingo people because her grandmother, Ma Galley, used to hide them in her basement whenever the police came looking for them to hit them up for bribes. She liked that they knew where to find good ivory, because she had a house to decorate.

Mommee took the Mandingo men into the living room to inspect their wares. I trailed behind them, observing as they visibly blanched upon walking into the cool, air-conditioned house. I sat on the brown velvet love seat in the corner to watch the proceedings.

One of the men had a glass eye. He put one elephant tusk on the glass coffee table and started to describe it to my mother. "This came from a great African elephant from the Serengeti," he said. "You see how it da' form like this? If you put two of them together, one on each side o' de' table, it will be fine, so."

The whole time he talked, his glass eye kept looking at me. I bolted from the living room and locked myself in my room.

That night there was a thunderstorm, and the electricity went out. The air conditioner rattled and wheezed and stopped. The porch lights went out. Lightning crackled through the air, and I quickly took off my gold bracelet so I wouldn't get struck. I burrowed as deep as I could under the covers, but I was still scared. I knew this was all the doing of the Mandingo man with the glass eye, who was clearly in cahoots with the rogues, who themselves were actually heartmen. And they were angry that I had gotten away from them the night before, but they would be back, I knew.

I just knew the elephant tusk was witched. I was whimpering under the covers when the door opened and Mommee came in with a candle. She already had a crying Marlene in tow. She looked at me and shook her head, and before she could motion toward her bedroom, I was out the door and climbing into bed with Daddy.

The next morning we had a family meeting. We always had family meetings in the living room, because it was more formal. I tried to sit in "my" corner by the sliding doors—the same spot I used the day before to watch the Mandingo men—but Daddy just eyed me and pointed to the love seat.

"She's too scared to sleep by herself," Mommee began. This was technically true but not something I, at the age of seven, wanted discussed so brazenly by the whole family.

"No I'm not!" I said, hotly.

"You're too old to be sleeping with us," Daddy said, Marlene on his lap sucking her pacifier.

That was it. I felt my ears get hot with embarrassment and I stomped out of the room—though I stopped in the kitchen to eavesdrop on Mommee and Daddy. I couldn't hear all they said because Old Man Charlie was singing "Old Yellow Woman" in the kitchen.

"Old, yellow woman . . . you want make trouble for me . . . every day you come to my house . . . I don't want trouble, no . . . you are somebody's wife . . . go away, yellow woman . . ."

It was Old Man Charlie's fault I didn't hear Mommee and Daddy making their decision. I didn't know it at the time, but the house at Sugar Beach was about to get one more resident.

Crossing the Atlantic

NEW YORK, 1820

*Today while we were up on deck John Fisher
whipped his wife. I think that this is a dull lamp
for us to carry into a dark land, but I have not
lost confidence in my God.*

—Elijah Johnson, writing in his journal,
aboard the ship *Elizabeth*, February 1820

The Elizabeth

*A*bout 150 years before Eunice came to Sugar Beach, two men set in motion the series of events that would lead to the day that I, a privileged almost-eight-year-old Congo girl, acquired my new sister, Eunice, a not-so-privileged eleven-year-old Bassa girl.

The chain started by those two men would eventually separate me from most black people in America, at the same time separating me from most black people in Africa. Their names were Elijah Johnson and Randolph Cooper. They were my great-great-great-great-grandfathers. At the turn of the nineteenth century in pre–Civil War America, they both belonged to that nebulous class of freed-blacks-once-removed from southern plantations.

When presented the choice between America and Africa, they chose Africa. Because of that choice, I would not grow up, 150 years later, as an American black girl, weighed down by racial stereotypes about welfare queens. Nor would I have to deal with the burdens of a sub-Saharan African girl, with a life expectancy of about 40 years, yanked out of school at the age of eleven so I could fetch water and cook over a coal pot and bear babies barely younger than myself.

Instead, those two men handed down to me a one-in-a-million lottery ticket: birth into what passed for the landed gentry upper class of Africa's first independent country, Liberia. None of that American post–civil war/civil rights movement baggage to bog me down with any inferiority complex about whether I was as good as white people. No European garbage to have me wondering whether some British colonial master was somehow better than me. Who needs to struggle for equality? Let everybody else try to be equal to me.

Elijah Johnson was born free in New York in 1787; Randolph Cooper in Norfolk, Virginia, in 1796.

Elijah Johnson's parents are believed to have been mulattos who had been freed from plantations because they were half-white, which was the case with many people in the growing class of freed blacks in America at the time. Many of them were light-skinned; some could even pass for white. Southern plantation slave-owners impregnated their female slaves, and, either out of guilt or some misbegotten sense of paternity, freed the kids, most likely to get them off the plantation and out of the visual range of the missus.

Elijah Johnson could read and write. When he was twenty-four, he joined the American Army, and fought against the British in the War of 1812 as part of a regiment of colored and black soldiers. After the war, he married a former slave from Maryland named Mary.

Not as much is known about the parents of Randolph Cooper and his four brothers, three of whom joined him in abandoning pre–Civil War America for Liberia. No one has managed to track down the man who fathered the five Cooper brothers. Many questions remain unanswered, like how they came to be freeborn to the same mother in Virginia at the turn of the century.

Elijah Johnson and Randolph Cooper, confronted with the same choice—Africa or America—made the same decision.

Elijah Johnson went first.

Elijah Johnson was on Liberia's version of the *Mayflower*— the very first ship of freed blacks to sail from New York Harbor, in 1820. After years of debating the back-to-Africa movement—the notion was that you couldn't have both freed blacks and enslaved blacks living in the same country, so the best fix was to send the freed blacks back to Africa—America's ruling white men were finally ready to launch their experiment. They designated and funded the American Colonization Society to send black Americans to Africa to establish a colony.

Since you could only go back to Africa if you were freed, the majority of people who got on those ships were light-skinned. That's light-skinned by African standards, not American ones. The difference is less distinct today, because in the ensuing years, Africans as a whole have gotten lighter skinned, courtesy of the Europeans who colonized Africa. There are still plenty of Africans with that gorgeous deep bark look that can only come from thousands of years of pigment in the equatorial sun. But today, there are probably just as many Africans who look like Nelson Mandela.

Many white people don't notice the difference. They don't see the difference between Will Smith and Djimon Hounsou.

But 150 years ago that difference was as distinct as black and white. So on that freezing blustery winter afternoon of February 6, 1820, when Elijah Johnson boarded the good ship *Elizabeth* in New York Harbor, it might as well have been a white man boarding that ship bound for Africa. He was tall with huge eyes that seemed to take up his entire face. He and his wife, Mary, set sail alongside eighty-six other black Americans. Thousands of people, both white and black, crowded the wharf to wave good-bye to what would be America's first, and only, attempt at colonization.

The passengers could smell the oil-soaked timbers of the ship. The quarters were spare, and even on this maiden voyage to pioneer a new country, class and race lines were observed strictly. The mostly white crew slept in their own quarters. The three white agents of the American Colonization Society shared a generous-size cabin. The eighty-eight blacks were back in steerage, sleeping on mildewed mattresses made of corn husks.

Still, the atmosphere as the *Elizabeth* pulled up its anchors and left the New York port was buoyant and festive. And God-fearing. The passengers spent a lot of their time praying. Before the *Elizabeth* pulled away from the port, one of the white agents, Rev. Samuel Bacon, a Boston Episcopalian minister and lawyer, assembled all the other passengers before him and read from the Good Book, Deuteronomy 11, the part where Moses gives the Jews the Ten Commandments to prepare them for the promised land. Reverend Bacon told the settlers they were pilgrims, new explorers, paving the way for other blacks to follow. They were also missionaries, he told them, going forth to the dark continent of Africa to convert the heathen Africans.

Elijah Johnson wrote in his journal regularly during the voyage across the Atlantic. Some of his writing was lyrical, like when he wrote of a tempest that rose one night early on. "But now there is a long storm in the seas; I hope that it will soon be over," Elijah Johnson wrote. "After the raging angels it became calm. In the afternoon we saw a ship which had lost her mast, which caused both Agents and people to rejoice that it was not us."

Mostly, though, he wrote about the passengers bickering and fighting with one another. They stabbed each other with cooking knives, threw pots overboard, whipped their wives, and generally acted the way people do when they're scared and stuck at sea for weeks. There was a big argument with the white agents of the American Colonization Society over how land would be distributed once the group actually found some land to call home in Africa. Elijah Johnson, in particular, didn't trust the agents at first to give the blacks their fair share, and refused to sign a letter saying that he had "full confidence in the judgment and sincere friendship of the agents." He confronted one of the agents, and disliked what he heard, writing in his journal that "I saw there was an evil in it."

But eventually all the adult males on the ship signed the letter, and Elijah Johnson was the only holdout. He decided to cast his lot with the white agents, for better or worse.

That night, he wrote: "I came out with the Agents and I will stand by them, unless they do something more than they do now."

On the morning of March 9, 1820, they made land at Sierra Leone.

Africa.

Arriving on West African soil for the first time is unlike any other arrival in the world. The first thing that hits you is the smell: a combination of coal fires, dried fish, humid air, and the sea. After smell comes the feel of the air. It is heavy, even when the sun is shining and there is not a cloud in the sky. You can never escape the humidity of the West African coastline, and in the interior, even more so. It is air so heavy that it weighs on your tongue, as if you can open your mouth and take a sip. It is a soup, a big hot pot of soupy air, fetid under the equatorial sun.

Finally, after air you can taste and smell and feel, the sights before you are almost anticlimactic: dense rain forest that ends just before the sea. Red earth. Palm trees that gleam, almost roasting, in the sun.

And then, there are the people.

Africans. For the first time, Elijah Johnson was seeing the people who originally sold his great-great-great-grandparents into slavery. These were his distant cousins, descended from the women who had wailed into the air when his ancestors were stolen from them. These were the men who had bartered—who still bartered—with Europeans over the price they wanted to sell their own brothers and cousins.

Freetown, Sierra Leone, was a bustling mass of people with sheep, pigs, chickens, and dogs adding to the cacophony. At the market, the new colonists saw all kinds of tropical produce, from plump mangoes to juicy pineapples to butterpears and breadfruit and pawpaws. The native West Africans stared at the motley group from the *Elizabeth*: black men dressed in Western garb, quoting the Scriptures.

In the afternoon, two of the passengers walked up to a group of native West African men playing a game. The men welcomed the two, and eventually offered them cane juice—a sweetish rum made from fermented sugarcane.

The Americans saw this as the perfect time to start converting the heathens. "We no drinkey rum," one colonist replied. Then he pointed his finger toward the sky. "God no likey dat."

Britain had recently outlawed the slave trade, establishing Freetown as a haven for slaves who had been captured and then released. But there was still plenty of trading in human cargo. It was hard for the new colonists from America to stomach, since they all thought they had left slavery behind for good when they left America. Instead, they saw captured Spanish and Portuguese slave schooners being hauled in, one after another, by the British. The captured schooners anchored right next to the *Elizabeth,* and smelled foul, like a mixture of human waste and oil. The hold of the ships, where the slaves were kept, looked impossibly small.

This was not what the colonists had come to Africa to see. Why were Africans still selling their brothers and sisters to European slave traders? The new settlers took this as another sign of their superiority to the native Africans, which would persist for decades to come.

Within a month of their arrival in West Africa, twenty-five of the passengers from the *Elizabeth* were dead, struck by virulent malaria. For the next year, lacking a permanent home because the American Colonization Society had yet to find a suitable site, the group sailed from one unhealthy malaria-infested swamp to another.

From Sherbro Island, where they were attacked by mosquitoes, parasites, and waterborne diseases, back to Freetown; to Cape Mount; Cape Montserrado; Grand Bassa, and points between. The first three white agents sent with the original group of settlers all died within weeks of setting foot in West Africa. Since the American Colonization Society couldn't conceive of entrusting black people with the money and negotiating authority to purchase land, it sent new white agents to do the job.

Elijah Johnson and the other black colonists waited aboard the ship, while the white agents called on various regional African kings and chiefs. They were turned down left and right. The kings and chiefs didn't want the new black colonists interfering with their slave trade. They had already gotten wind that this was a pious, Bible-quoting bunch, though they had yet to find out that these settlers also had brought guns, cannons, and ammunition with them from America, and knew how to use them.

One African king, King Peter, point-blank refused to meet with the white agents looking for land, because on the very day the agents were requesting a meeting in Cape Montserrado, a ship flying the French flag was waiting nearby to pick up some newly captured slaves, courtesy of King Peter.

The Americans then traveled up to Grand Bassa, several miles southeast of Montserrado, and traded tobacco, pipes, and beads with some of the Bassa people, receiving chicken, fish, oysters, and palm oil in return. During the transaction, the Americans met with Jack Ben, a prominent Bassa slave-trader. They gave him "gifts"—one gun, some gunpowder, tobacco. He accepted them, but when the Americans stated their objective—to purchase land for the colonists to settle—he started acting skittish.

The group sailed back to Freetown, exasperated and still landless. One white agent wrote in his journal: "It indeed requires much patience to deal with these children of the forest."

Still, the colonization movement plowed on. The American Colonization Society sent another ship, with fresh agents and more settlers. On December 12, 1821, they returned to King Peter for another go, sending him a bottle of rum as an inducement.

Again, the African chief refused, saying he would not sell Cape Montserrado to the Americans because "his women would cry aplenty." But he made the crucial mistake of agreeing to meet with the agents the next day.

The meeting came on December 15, 1821, in a palaver hut in King Peter's village in Cape Montserrado. There were several other African kings, representing the Dey, Mambe, and Bassa groups there as well. The African gathered in the hut, prepared to refuse the Americans again.

Not this time. The white agents walked into the palaver hut, pulled out their pistols, cocked them, and pointed them at King Peter's head. The deal was struck twenty-one months and six days after landfall on the African continent. Cape Montserrado, stretching from the Atlantic Ocean to the inland tropical bush, about 130 square miles in all, was sold to the Americans for guns, gunpowder, beads, mirrors, and tobacco.

The net value was less than $300.

A century and a half later we had a house in Spain, multiple houses and farms in Liberia, and our palace at Sugar Beach. We were Congo royalty.

And I, princess that I was, could not be allowed to whimper alone in my room all night hiding under my bedclothes from imaginary spirits and real-life rogues. And so Mommee and Daddy went to the Country People and found me a sister.

3

Eunice

SUGAR BEACH, 1974

$\mathcal{E}$unice came to Sugar Beach on a hot, muggy afternoon. After Mommee put out the word that her eight-year-old daughter needed a live-in playmate, Eunice's mother, a Bassa woman of little means, was quick to respond. The rickety yellow taxi, its front covered in rust, came clattering down the dirt road to our house, hesitating briefly at the gate before driving up to the front.

"Wha' you mean some girl just coming here to stay w'people?" I had demanded of Mommee earlier, after she let it drop that I was getting a new sister. This was not happy news. I did not appreciate, at all, the idea of having my turf invaded by a foreigner. Having Marlene around was bad enough.

So I was sulking in the TV lounge, with one ear cocked for the sounds of vehicles approaching Sugar Beach, when I heard the clackety-clack of a car engine as it rattled into the yard. I raced to Marlene's window. From my perch there I saw three people getting out of the taxi.

First there was a woman in full Bassa attire: lapa skirt and with a bright red shirt and a head-tie scarf. She looked nervous. Next was a nondescript man wearing gray wool trousers and a shirt. He reached into the taxi and pulled out a gangly looking girl also wearing a lapa. Long skinny legs. *She* looked terrified.

Mommee came out onto the porch to welcome them, and I immediately followed to investigate, peering at the girl. On the way out, I grabbed an orange, with its top cut off, from the bowl where Old Man Charlie had them. I squeezed the rest of the orange into my mouth, massaging the skin to coax out the juice. It gave me something to do while I looked at my new sister.

She stood with one arm behind her back, holding the other arm. She looked to be about eleven years old. She had a high forehead and huge eyes; between the pair of them you could hardly see anything else on her face. She stood with her legs slightly apart, but even so I could tell that she was bowlegged, a plus in my mind, since I longed to be bowlegged, too. She didn't look happy to be there.

"My name is Helene Calista Esmeralda Esdolores Dennis Cooper," I announced, finally taking the depleted orange out of my mouth. I was wearing Wrangler jeans that my father had bought for me in the United States.

"My name is Eu-u-u-u-unice Patrice Bull," she stuttered.

We inspected each other while Mommee and Eunice's mother and uncle talked. For Eunice's mother, this was one of those things you did because you love your child. She knew that Eunice would have a better shot at life with us than she would living in her zinc shack with her, where there was no electricity, no running water, and no inside toilet. She was struggling to come up with the money every year to send Eunice to school. She had another son, and numerous adopted children—strays picked up along the way—to feed.

For all she would miss her daughter, this wasn't really much of a decision. Native Liberians routinely jumped at the chance to have their children reared by Congo families. And in Liberia in 1974, it was the chance of a lifetime to leave a poor Country family and move in with the Coopers.

Eventually, Mommee turned to me. "Show Eunice her room," she said.

I had no idea what it was like to live in a shack, or even that Sugar Beach's opulence might be a shock to Eunice, but I was more than happy to show off our custom-built house. Deciding to start on the lower level, so Eunice could properly appreciate the scope and grandeur of Sugar Beach, I went around the house to the rarely used front door, on the ocean side.

The door was locked. My face burning with embarrassment, I left her standing next to the porch railing and scurried back around the house to where Mommee and Mrs. Bull were still talking next to the taxi. I raced up the kitchen stairs, ran into the house and clattered back down the stairwell to the front door, opening the door for Eunice from the inside.

"You can come in now," I said, standing aside, breathless and feeling foolish.

Eunice trailed after me as I turned and walked through the paneled tunnel that led to our recreation room. She took in Daddy's bar, the playroom with our stereo set, and the toy room with all of its dollhouses, teddy bears, and games.

"Wh-wh-wha' down deah?" she asked, pointing down the hall.

"Da' de guest room," I said.

"Da' where I sleepin'?"

"No, you upstai'. Ma sister Janice duh sleep there when she come home from England," I said, adding proudly. "She's a been-to."

This new girl had better be taking note that this was no flim-flack family she was moving in with, I thought. We had a sister who went to boarding school in England!

Eunice trailed behind me as I glided up the stairs to present to her the middle level of our house, with its kitchen, dining room, music room, and sunken living room. Finally, we headed to the top level, with the bedrooms, bathrooms, and TV lounge.

I slid Eunice a sideways glance before I started "talking cullor"—Liberian slang for putting on airs by speaking with an American accent. "This is my mommee's room and my daddy's room," I said, walking Eunice by my parents' bedroom. "That's my yucky sister Marlene's room." We continued down the hall. "And this," I said with a flourish, opening the door to what would be Eunice's bedroom, "is your room. You're across from me. If you get scared at night, you can come sleep in my room."

Eunice just walked into her room and sat on the bed. She looked like she wanted to cry, so I left her alone.

For the first few months, Eunice and I circled each other warily. She was so thin and quiet, and when she did open her mouth, her stutter was pronounced. The two of us barely talked.

Eunice wasn't happy to be pulled from her home, however poor, and plopped down at Sugar Beach with strangers. She ran away twice in those early months. Each time her mother brought her back.

Then after lunch one afternoon, Mommee made a rare appearance in the laundry room downstairs. It was the domain of Galway, our washman, but that afternoon, Mommee found not Galway in the laundry room, but Eunice. Galway was outside chatting with Sammy Cooper, the yardboy, under the shade of a palm tree.

"Wha' you doing?" Mommee asked Eunice. Eunice was sitting on the chair with a bucket at her feet, washing her clothes by hand. Another bucket of cold rinse water sat next to her chair.

Eunice's stutter immediately started. "I-I-I w-w-washing my clothes, Aunt Lah," she said. She told Mommee that Galway had been separating her clothes from our pile and not washing hers.

The servants had issues with Eunice, because she sat at the table with us for dinner and slept in the air-conditioned house while they baked in the boys' house. Galway, our washman, was particularly irate about her arrival, because he belonged to the same Bassa ethnic group as Eunice.

Liberia is a country the size of Ohio, with two million people and twenty-eight different tribes, including the Kru, the Gio, the Kpelle, and the Bassa. They all have their own languages and their own customs. For Galway, washing a Bassa girl's clothes was unthinkable, and worth fighting over.

Mommee charged outside and ordered Galway to wash Eunice's clothes.

Galway refused. "No, Ma," he said. "That one, I can't do it." He looked to Sammy Cooper, who shrugged. He wasn't getting involved.

"You've got dry face," Mommee told him. Translation: You speak frankly, but without conscience. But, she added, "If you don't wash this girl's clothes, I sacking you."

That night when Daddy came home, Galway was waiting for him to hear his appeal. "How can a man like me wash a Bassa girl's clothes?" he asked my father. "You're a man, you understand. Ma doesn't understand."

Daddy was the head of the house at Sugar Beach, but he was no fool.

My father told Galway to wait. He came into the house, grabbed a beer out of the refrigerator, and then went back outside with the decision. "If you don't do what the old ma says, she will sack you," he said. "Small shame better than big shame."

Galway chose small shame and, after that, he washed Eunice's clothes.

Mommee took a shine to Eunice and lavished attention on her. She gave Eunice the key to her and Daddy's bedroom, which she often kept locked when they were out during the day to stop us from raiding her refrigerator and drinking all her Coca-Cola. Marlene routinely tried to wheedle the key from Eunice, but I wasn't about to ask some new girl for the key to my own parents' bedroom. Let her keep her key.

After three months or so, Marlene began refusing to sleep at night unless Eunice shared her room. Meanwhile, I remained in my bedroom, scared and hiding from the rogues. If Eunice at least had the decency to sleep in her own room at night, right across the hallway from mine, she'd likely hear the rogues when they came to get me, and could save me. Instead, she and Marlene disappeared into Marlene's room every night, way down the hall from me. I could hear them laughing.

When Eunice ran away the second time and her mother brought her back, I was ready to have it out.

"Why you'nt like people?" I asked.

"Who say 'I'nt like you?" she said. She had been crying, the tears had tracked her cheeks. "You de one who'dn't talk to nobody."

I was taken aback. "But you s'pose to talk to people first. You only talk to Marlene and Mommee and Vicky. And you da sleep with Marlene."

Eunice looked at me, and for the first time, she laughed at something I said. "Who able to sleep by their'self in this big scary house?" she said.

I started laughing, too. "For true. This place is terrible," I said. "Too far from anywhere."

"I know," she said. "That's why I da' keep runnin' way."

That night, I dragged my mattress down the hall to Marlene's room. Vicky was in there, too, and the three were playing "Blind Man Can't See."

I opened the door, slowly. Someone had blindfolded Marlene, and she was stumbling around the room, her arms stretched out, while Eunice and Vicky hid. Eunice had wedged herself under the vanity and Vicky was squeezed into a corner, laughing silently.

Marlene walked straight into me. "You're it!" she yelled, triumphantly.

The three of them made space on the floor for my mattress and we started jumping around, playing Corner to Corner and Blind Man Can't See.

The door opened after a few minutes and my mother came in, complaining that she could hear us yelling and screaming all the way down the hall.

"You sleeping in here, too?" she asked me. I nodded. My mother closed the door, shaking her head. The next morning I heard her muttering something to my father about why had they spent all that money to build a big house if all of us were going to sleep in the same room.

"Once upon a time," Eunice said softly one night, her voice wafting ominously from the mattress on the floor where she lay next to Vicky.

My stomach clutched in anticipation and dread. It was already full from the hot dogs and mashed potatoes we'd had for dinner that night. Hot dogs and mashed potatoes were my second favorite food, after palm butter and fufu.

"Time!" Marlene, Vicky, and I all said back to her, in the Liberian tradition of signaling a storyteller that you're willing to hear their story. I tried to yell "Time!" in an enthusiastic way to prompt Eunice to tell a happy story and not a sad one.

But Eunice hadn't yelled "Once upon a time!" the way storytellers did when they had a funny story to tell about the antics of the wily spider, outsmarting the village king into eating as much pepper soup as he wanted. She'd said it softly and eerily, her voice projecting a malevolence that could only mean one of two things.

Heartmen or neegee.

It was a toss-up which were worse: heartmen cut out your heart when you were still alive, but the truth was, with all of us in Marlene's room, I felt relatively safe from heartmen. We could tackle them and protect each other if they came.

But neegee . . . I was far more scared of neegee. I squeezed my eyes shut in the dark, and hoped Eunice wasn't going to tell a neegee story. They were bad enough in the light of day, but we were in Marlene's pitch-black room.

"Once upon a time, there was this little boy, who liked to go swimming," Eunice said.

Marlene, lying on the bed by herself, started to whimper. "Somebody plee come hold ma hand."

I scurried quickly into the bed beside her.

Eunice continued. "Anyway, this little boy used to like going swimming right here at Sugar Beach—in the lagoon."

Well, of course he went in the lagoon, I thought. Liberians hardly ever went in the ocean.

Eunice continued: "Every day, he would tell his ma 'them, 'I just going swimming lil bit, I coming right back.'

" 'But you lil boy, wha you da be doing every day, every day, in the water so?' people would ask him. But de boy wasn't doing nothing bad, he just used to like swimming. He like splashing in de water, floating 'round. He just liked to play. He wasn't hurting nobody."

Eunice was winding up. She had just marked him for death by presenting him as a good kid who never hurt anyone.

I didn't want this nice Bassa boy to die at Sugar Beach! Couldn't she just make the story end so that he lived? "His ma 'them should have just stopped him from going swimming by h'self," I muttered. What kind of parents were they, letting their kid go to the beach alone?

"So one day—it was just last month, self—de lil boy went back to go swimming again. He was splashing and playing by h'self. He could swim good, so he went to de d-d-d-d-eep part."

As the story reached its inevitable dark conclusion, Eunice's stutter became more pronounced, adding to the tension in the room. I curled into the pillow in a protective measure.

"Dat's when he heard dem calling him."

"Dey said, 'Lil boy, lil boy, you now come here now to us, you'nt going back,' " Eunice said, using the singsong voice of the neegees. " 'You'nt going back, oh.'

"You'nt going back.

"H-h-h-he didn't d-d-drown," Eunice concluded, as if that made it better. "The neegee took him."

The only good thing I could think about her awful story was that it was over. There was no way I was going to sleep after that.

I felt a chill, and made a mental note to stay away from the deep part of the Sugar Beach lagoon. But deep down inside, a thought started to flower. If I did get attacked by neegee or a heartman or a rogue, I now had someone who would protect me. Eunice, I somehow knew, would not let anything happen to me.

4

SUGAR BEACH, LIBERIA, 1974

$\mathcal{T}$he first six months after Eunice moved in with us were relatively tranquil—other than Eunice's attempted escapes—both at Sugar Beach and in the big world outside.

Everyone was still playing their assigned parts in the social structure of Liberia. The land barons and Honorables who made up the Congo People were taking vacations abroad, vis-

---

Nana, Vicky, Bridget, Helene, Mommee, Ade, Marlene, Aunt Jeanette, Daddy, and Eunice at Sugar Beach

iting their many properties and farms around Liberia, and taking their families to the beach for day trips.

The farm tenants, market women, and "gro-na" boys who made up the Country People were tapping rubber trees for $40 a month, haggling with customers outside Abijoudi Supermarket, and hanging out in front of Relda Cinema, looking for work.

My family took its role in this play very seriously. Besides our house at Sugar Beach and the farm at Kakata, we also had a house in Spain, where we vacationed in July. Daddy and Mommee had bought the house right after they got married. He called it Bassa Cove, after the place in Liberia where my great-great-great-greatuncle, Reid Cooper, 150 years before, had once sailed to rescue a bunch of settlers pinned down by angry native Africans.

The house was in Calpe, on the Costa Blanca, and we—along with Uncle Julius and my cousins, Dr. Nehemiah Cooper and Lady Cooper, who also bought houses in Calpe—were the only black people there. The highlight of our days there was when Daddy took us into the village for chocolate ice cream cones. We'd walk in the clear sun and the crisp dry air (not like that humid soup we had in Liberia). The scent of flowers from the planted street gardens was everywhere.

Eunice and Vicky didn't come to Spain. They went to Liberian schools, and their vacations were at a different time from our American school, which let us out for June, July, and August. Eunice and Vicky got their vacations during the Liberian summer, at Christmastime, from December to March.

So they stayed alone with the servants at Sugar Beach while we went to Spain. For four weeks every July we spent mornings playing in the yard with its fragrant bougainvillea and midday hours pretending to have siesta in our bedrooms with the gauzy curtains and the fresh breezes, missing nothing because the whole country was napping, too. It was peaceful, bright, and quiet. During the evening Daddy took us to the village for ice cream cones or sometimes shopping all the way to Benidorm, with its outdoor cafes and crowded beaches. The next day we did it all over again. By the time we returned to Liberia we were dying for news of Monrovia and Sugar Beach.

If Bassa Cove was a villa of tranquillity, the other Cooper property was a plantation of chaos. Kakata was a three-hundred-acre swath of bush anchored by an American plantation house that would have looked right at home in Virginia in the 1830s.

Daddy grew rubber trees, papaya (which we called paw-paw), mangoes (which we called plums), guavas, and ptanga, a greenish orange fruit that showered your mouth and cheeks with its tart-sweet juice.

The farm was Daddy's domain. Mommee usually stayed home when we visited. We'd pile into Daddy's white pickup truck for the one-hour drive to Kakata. Me, Marlene, John Bull, and Eunice squeezed into the cab with Daddy. Sammy Cooper and Jack got to ride in the back.

I wanted to ride in the back, too. But Mommee forbade it.

"Aye, Daddy," I started to whine one Saturday afternoon.

He put his hand up in a "stop" motion. "Don't even think about it," he said.

We stopped at Ma Gene's house so she and her driver could follow us in her white Toyota. Ma Gene, Daddy's mother, always wore her hair in a hairnet. She was very prim and proper and ladylike, with her 1960s librarian glasses. She wore stockings over her bandaged knee, which she kept wrapped to help with her arthritis.

We cruised along the paved road to Kakata for about forty-five minutes, passing streams of farmers walking their produce in the opposite direction, back toward Monrovia. On the hot tarmac, they stepped out of our way onto the road's dirt shoulder when we passed. Daddy blew his horn when one man didn't get out of the way fast enough. "You tryin' to get run over?" he leaned across the four of us in the cab and yelled at the man through the passenger window.

We slowed down as we entered Kakata. Market women, balancing tin buckets of oranges on their heads and babies on their backs, crowded the main road, which was filled with craters full of muddy rainwater. Daddy was talking and drove straight into a crater, splashing water on one of the market women, with a bucket of oranges on her head and her baby on her back. Her hands were free to gesticulate angrily at us.

"Na mind, na mind, my friend," Daddy said, pulling the pickup truck over to the side of the road.

"Oh, da Mr. Cooper!" the woman came smiling up to Daddy's side of the pickup. She was wearing a lapa skirt and white T-shirt, with a matching lapa cloth wrapping her baby around her back. She had on a head-tie scarf around her hair.

"Good friend, how you doin?" Daddy asked her.

"I trying, Mr. Cooper."

"Your son fine, oh."

"Aye-ya, Mr. Cooper."

The ritual went on for about five minutes. Daddy asked her about her husband; she said he was in Monrovia looking for work. She peered into the cab at each one of us, then reached over to touch Marlene's hair. "But de lil' girl fine, oh!" she exclaimed. "Look at her hair!"

Eunice and I were getting bored. We started looking for our favorite sign in Kakata.

"Here it is there!" Eunice pointed. In Liberian English, that came out as "Heah it deh." The accent is on the "deh." Her stutter didn't come out so much anymore.

The sign was on the white-washed wall behind the market. It said: "Do Not Urinate Here! By Order of City Mayor!"

We were giggling. "Hee hee."

Over on the other side of the cab, Daddy was reaching the natural close of business with the woman we splashed. "Here lil' something for your son, my friend," he said, pressing some notes into the woman's hand.

"Aye, Mr. Cooper, God will bless you," the woman said. "God will bless you too much."

Finally, we pulled away from the curb, back onto the road. This time, Daddy took his time and drove carefully around the potholes.

A left by the market, and another twenty minutes down a dirt road that only passed for a road during dry season. Daddy drove into the bush to try to avoid the craters.

And finally, there it was. The Cooper Family Farm, straight out of *Gone With the Wind* if Atlanta was deep in the African bush and Tara was overrun by vines, shrubs, and peeling paint. There were columns supporting the first-floor porch, giant Spanish moss trees in the front yard, and the ubiquitous smell of coal fires blanketing the entire place.

The farm staff trickled out of the house and from the nearby village to greet us. While at Sugar Beach we were surrounded by the Bassa people from the Bassa village of Bubba Town, the area around the farm was largely Kpelle. I couldn't tell the difference between Bassa people and Kpelle people, except that I associated Kpelle people with Daddy, because of the farm.

Daddy immediately started carping about why hadn't anyone fixed the broken window latch yet, hadn't he told them to make sure to have it fixed by the time he got back? And where was his factotum, Jacob Doboyu?

Finally, Jacob Doboyu appeared and he and Daddy headed to the house, arguing the whole time. Jacob Doboyu was

Grebo and a dead ringer for Nelson Mandela. He was another one who was raised by the Cooper family from birth. He and Daddy used to play together as children, and he usually went with us to Spain for vacation. He used to spank me when I was a baby, a point of much pride to him, since not too many Country People got to spank Congo babies.

Their voices disappeared behind the screen door and into Daddy's office. "But, John, the man was supposed to come here on Friday with the new latch," Jacob Doboyu was saying.

Eunice and I surveyed our playground for the weekend. We had one thing, and one thing only, on our minds. This was our chance to eat all the things Mommee didn't let us eat at Sugar Beach.

"Sammy Cooper," I said in a wheedling tone. "You will carry us to get some farina?" I had already picked a few ptangas from the trees in the yard and was nursing the fruit around my mouth as I contemplated my next meal.

"I na carrying you'all no where," Sammy Cooper replied, playing coy.

To get farina, we had to go to the Kpelle village on the farm. Sammy Cooper wasn't too eager to take me because he had taught me a few Kpelle cusswords and was worried that I might try to use them.

But nobody could whine like me. "I hold your foot, Sammy Cooper," I started, revving myself up even as I adjusted the pitch of my voice to its most ingratiating bleat. Finally, Sammy Cooper just started walking toward the village, without saying a word. Eunice, Marlene, and I followed him.

Along the path, I tried not to step over the lizards because that was bad luck. I could hear the Kpelle women talking in the distance. The combination of hot sun, coal fires, lizards, and voices combined into one, exotic-yet-familiar sensation. I was up-country!

I bounced over to catch up with Eunice. "I will tell them 'tene kpollu,' " I whispered with a grin. I didn't know what that meant but Sammy Cooper had told me it was something bad.

Eunice looked at me sideways.

"You do it, I telling Uncle John."

I sucked my teeth. "I wa jes' joking! You think people stupid?"

We stepped into the village clearing. There were really only about five mud huts clustered around. One young woman was giving a little girl a bath. The girl was standing naked in a small yellow plastic tub—the kind Marlene had in the toy room at Sugar Beach for her dolls. Her fat stomach jutted out over bony legs, knocked knees. She stared at us curiously.

"I want bath, too!" Marlene squawked out, running over to the little girl. That broke the ice and the village people started gathering around. They ignored me and Eunice, and clustered around Marlene, marveling over her general Cooper characteristics.

"That white girl oh!" a toothy old man announced, lifting her up to his shoulders. "Ma people, here Radio Cooper grandchild!"

We followed him into his dark hut. There were a couple of mattresses on the dirt floor, and an anteroom in front with a single green plastic chair. I started coughing right away as I always did when I went into the Country People's houses. They cooked over coal fires in the back, and the smoke scratched my throat.

The old man shuffled to the kitchen in the back and pulled a large jar of farina out from under a small wooden table. He shook the farina out into two plastic bags, tied them into neat knots on top, and handed them to Eunice. I was hopping up and down in anticipation, almost drooling. "Thank you, old man!" I yelled, tugging on Eunice's arm and hurrying her out of the hut. Back to the farm, to prepare and eat our feast in precious solitude.

Ma Gene went to bed early that night and we all hung out on the front porch with Daddy and Uncle Julius as they systematically went through a bottle of gin, washing it down with cold Club Beers, and worked on a puzzle by the light of a lantern.

"Which one of y'all gonna scratch my head?" Daddy asked.

"Eunice!" I yelled.

"Helene Cooper!" Eunice yelled at the same time. That was usually the extent of her pushing back—the safe stuff she directed at me.

"Me!" Marlene came running in from the yard, where she'd been hunting palm kernels with a flashlight. Daddy let her scratch his head for two minutes before she was fired for ineptitude. He reached around behind him and pulled her onto his lap. "Come on, Helene, your sister too young to know how to do it." He picked up the bottle of his hair tonic from the table next to him, and waved it at me.

"Okay," I said, "but not for long time co' ma stomach hurting."

It was a typically pitch-black night in the bush, with the only light coming from the lamp in the farmhouse and a couple of dying coal fires from the villagers nearby. The sounds of the bush at night wafted through the air—monkeys and crickets in a chorus of howling.

In the distance I could hear drums beating.

What were those Country People up to out there? They'd better just be dancing. I felt a chill going up my spine. We were deep in the territory of witch doctors and heartmen and neegees and country devils.

I thought about the story Mommee told me about the first time she ever went up-country. She was only about eight months old, and Grandpa and Mama Grand were living up in Zegedah, where Grandpa at the time was the commanding officer of the frontier force.

Mommee's nurse was a Loma woman named Kit, who lived with the family. One day, the country devil came to Zegedah.

There are two types of country devils: harmless ones and sinister ones. The one that came to Zegedah that day was the sinister kind.

Upon his arrival, accompanied by the usual drums, dancers, and various hangers-on, the women were immediately ordered into their houses and huts and told to stay away from the windows. It was forbidden, forbidden, forbidden for any woman to watch the country devil dance.

All the men went outside into the street. But Mommee's nurse, Kit, wanted to see, too. She crept to the window, with Mommee in her arms, and peeked out.

Within a month Kit got sick and died.

"A-ya," everyone said. "But she asked for it. She know she not supposed to look at the country devil."

Mommee peeked, too, but she was a baby so the country devil spared her. She had a lot of nightmares immediately after, my grandparents said, but she didn't get sick. Whenever she started crying during her nightmares, Mama Grand and Grandpa would look at each other and say, "She crying because she saw that country devil with Kit."

I could never get my head around what Kit saw that was so forbidden. Something unimaginably evil, I knew. Maybe the country devil had brandished a still-beating heart, or carried somebody's head under his arm.

I'd seen country devils—usually at Christmastime, when

they sang and danced for money—but the only ones I saw were the harmless kind women were allowed to see.

At the farm that night, the drums in the distance got louder.

My mind was swallowed up by stories of African magic. Voodoo. The secret societies. Medicine business.

In Liberia, you don't die of natural causes. You die because somebody witched you. You die because your father slept around with a woman who then had a witch doctor get rid of all of your father's official, "legitimate" children so her children could get his money. You die because your husband's brother was jealous of you. You die because your wife was tired of you. You die because, like my grandfather Radio Cooper, you didn't give the farm to Old Sammy Cooper after he worked there all those years.

Radio Cooper had left his farm to his children, Daddy, Uncle Julius, and Tante Ora. And now here we all were, in the middle of the night, singularly close to the lair of the Country People, and the drums were beating.

All those stories that Eunice told me from the safety of our air-conditioned bedroom at Sugar Beach . . . they were all played out here out in the bush. This was where heartmen actually performed the black magic with the body parts they collected in Monrovia. This was where the witch doctors and medicine men brewed their concoctions. This, so they said, was where the neegees brought the poor swimmers they sucked out of the Sugar Beach lagoons, who were never heard from again.

The fear surged through me. But I knew they couldn't get all of us at once. They only kill you one at a time. The closer I stuck to my family, the better.

Eunice sat on the porch swing, reading; I abandoned my post scratching Daddy's head and sidled over to her. She made space for me. I immediately felt safer.

• • •

But my fear of neegees and heartmen was getting worse.

A week later, on Saturday, Mommee's brother, Bro. Henry, showed up unexpectedly at Sugar Beach. Eunice and I were in my room reading Nancy Drew books when we heard the sound of a car at the top of the hill, heading toward the gate. Somebody was visiting! We dropped our books on the floor and ran to Marlene's bedroom window, from where we spotted Bro. Henry's brown Lincoln Town Car cruising into the yard.

"Bro. Henry here!" I yelled excitedly, skipping and jumping through the hallway, around the corner, through the kitchen, and onto the kitchen porch. Eunice was hot at my heels. Vicky had been braiding Marlene's hair, but as soon as Marlene heard me, she bolted for the porch, too, as fast as her short legs could take her. Vicky, never one to get flustered even though it was her father, trailed behind sedately.

Bro. Henry, looking like a movie star with his sunglasses on, opened the car door, got out, and struck a pose against the side of the car. He had on long walking shorts and a collarless shirt. In the backseat of his car were my cousins Bridget and Gabriel, looking smug.

"Ya'll go get your swimming suits," Bro. Henry said. "We going to Caesar's Beach."

About thirty minutes later, Eunice, Vicky, Marlene, Bridget, Gabriel, and I were all packed in Bro. Henry's car as he turned onto the dirt road to Caesar's Beach. We lived at Sugar Beach, but Caesar's Beach was a destination. As we pulled into the parking area, I noted with excitement the cars parked in the grass. There were two Mercedes-Benzes, one Peugeot, and a Lincoln Mercury Cougar: Monrovia's landed gentry were spending a day at the beach.

Climbing out of Bro. Henry's car, I felt a twinge of disquiet. Like Sugar Beach, the lagoon at Caesar's Beach was full of neegees. I had to figure out a way to look as if I was having fun, frolicking in the lagoon pretending to swim without actually getting close to that deep end where they were hanging out.

The white people—Americans from the United States embassy, a smattering of Lebanese, a few French people—were all spread out on the sand on the ocean side of the beach. The Liberians were on the lagoon side.

This was segregation based on fear. The undertow in the ocean was fierce, and we tended to stick closer to the lagoon, which—albeit filled with neegees who sucked you in and took you God-knew-where—at least didn't carry you off to be eaten by sharks. The Americans and French and Lebanese, unburdened by such knowledge, took one look at the miles of white sand along our gorgeous oceanfront and headed straight for the crashing waves.

Marlene was already running toward the lagoon, kicking her beach ball in front of her, her shovel and pail jiggling against her legs. Eunice pulled off her flip-flop sandals and took off behind her. I tried to walk sedately for a few moments, and then gave up, running behind them. "Wait for people!" I yelled. "Wait for people!"

I was torn between joy and fear. As I ran behind Marlene and Eunice, I resolved to myself that this was the day I would shed my water wings (at eight, the fact that I still needed them was a deep source of shame) and swim like a fish.

I looked behind me at Bro. Henry, who was just arriving behind us at the spot we picked next to a thatched palaver hut near the lagoon. "Bro. Henry, I will swim today!" I announced.

He looked at me and laughed. "For true? You will do it today?" He had been down this road with me before.

"For true, Bro. Henry. I can do it."

I waded into the water, gingerly, after Bro. Henry. It felt cool against my legs, but immediately my toes scrunched up as they touched foreign-feeling objects in there—rocks, sand, leaves, twigs. I stopped when the water reached my waist.

Bro. Henry was still moving. If he thought I was going in any deeper, he was nuts. I cleared my throat loudly. "Uh-hmm!"

He stopped, turned, and grinned at me. "Okay, I'm waiting."

I could hear the voices of Marlene, Eunice, and Vicky splashing and laughing in the distance. High-pitched peals of laughter, mixed in with the calls of the pepper birds—*plur-tor-tor . . . plur-tor-tor . . . plur-tor-tor.* And then they all faded away, as I took a huge, deep breath, squeezed my eyes shut, sealed my mouth full of air, and plunged in.

A mistake of monumental proportions. I had just given the underwater spirits the chance they'd been waiting for. I could hear them talking to themselves, their voices low and camouflaged by a droning sound, so the people above couldn't hear them. *"Lil girl, lil girl, we now come for you oh."*

My hair swirled around me, but that was the only part of my body that could move.

"Lil girl, lil girl, we now come for you oh."

Something slimy touched my hand. And I kicked.

I pumped my feet and stretched out my arms as far as I could trying to get to Bro. Henry. I pumped and kicked and suddenly my feet touched the sand, and I realized I could stand. I came up with a terrified surge, gulping in deep breaths of air.

I had moved a few feet. Bro. Henry was standing in exactly the same spot, looking at me resignedly.

"You using too much energy," he said. "You just splashing water and tiring yourself out. And it's too shallow here—let's go in lil bit deeper so I can teach you to float."

My cousins were already way out in the deep end, closing in on the monkey bridge that connected two makeshift lean-tos in the lagoon to each other. Eunice and Vicky were in deeper, too, though they could still stand up. They were keeping an eye on Marlene, who was paddling around with her water wings.

But I knew that the neegee wanted *me* that day, not Eunice, Vicky, or Marlene. I wanted to learn to swim, to at least get to the deeper part where Eunice and Vicky were, but they were too close to the really deep part. If the neegee came after me over there, I wouldn't get away.

"I comin', Bro. Henry," I lied. "You go, I will jes go to the bathroom first, then I will come."

"You in the water. Peepee right here."

"Aye, Bro. Henry, I'nt want peepee here."

Giving up, Bro. Henry turned and struck off toward Eunice and Vicky.

I walked out of the lagoon. When I finally left the bathroom, I went directly to the thatched palaver hut and sat with a Nancy Drew book in my lap, watching them frolic.

Eunice was apparently having a successful day. She was now floating on her back. How had she learned to do that? I wondered. Bro. Henry was working on Vicky, talking her through lying flat, putting her head back.

My cousins, Bridget and Gabriel, needed no instruction; they were already great swimmers. Probably because their mother, Aunt Jeanette, was American, and Americans all could swim, I thought.

Finally, they all came out of the water. I quickly stuck my face in my book—*The Mystery at Lilac Inn*.

Marlene and Eunice both fell asleep in the sand—on the sunny part, outside the palaver hut. I was still stinging with humiliation from my performance in the lagoon. I somehow felt betrayed by Eunice. She was the one who was always telling neegee stories and then she had the nerve to go into the deep part of the lagoon and learn to swim?

Marlene woke up and started crying. She had red splotches all over her back and down her legs. "Poke your finger in her back," I whispered to Eunice. I had seen the white children at the American school do that when they stayed in the sun too long.

Eunice poked Marlene, and the spot turned white, then red again.

Bro. Henry yelled at Eunice. "How you just sat there and let the child get burned?" he said. "You know she white."

Eunice looked at her own dark skin, free of burns, and shrugged. It was easy to see what she was thinking: How was she supposed to know Marlene was too white to be in the sun long? While Bro. Henry tended to the still crying Marlene, Eunice and I started packing up our stuff. "I can burn, too," I informed Eunice, self-importantly. "Look at my skin. I'm light, too."

"G-g-g-ood for you," Eunice said.

I felt my own anger with her burbling up. Didn't she see that I had delicate white skin, too? That's why the neegee were trying to get me. That's why they didn't want her.

"You can't burn," I told her. "You're too black."

Eunice and I remained on the outs for about a week after that. I knew I should apologize.

But apologize and say what? *"Na mind, Eunice, I was scared of de neegee."*

She wouldn't believe me. She knew the neegee waited in the deep part for you to come to them.

I kept quiet.

Since we weren't playing together, Eunice started taking Marlene to Bubba Town, the Bassa village just up the dirt road from Sugar Beach.

I didn't want to go with them anyway, because the Bassa people in Bubba Town had eaten my dog Tracks, a brown-and-white flea-ridden keke, which is what we called mutts. When the dog first came to us as a gift from my maternal grandmother, Mama Grand, I had just read a book about an American girl who got a dog that left mud tracks in the house, and named her dog Tracks. She lived on What-a-Jolly-Street, USA. Mommee wouldn't let Tracks come into our house, so he spent most of his time sleeping on the kitchen porch, or running around the yard with me when I got my roller skates. He was fast, but he had wanderlust, and was always disappearing, sometimes for days.

One day I overheard Mommee whispering something to Eunice. She said: "Don't tell Helene what happened."

"Don't tell Helene what?" I said.

"Oh, we had to give Tracks away because there was a sick little girl who needed a dog."

She just gave my dog away? I cornered Old Man Charlie. "What happened to my dog?" I demanded to know.

He shrugged. "Those Bassa people in Bubba Town ate him," he told me.

So I boycotted Bubba Town. But there wasn't much to do at Sugar Beach, and given that me and Eunice were still mad at each other, Eunice took Marlene.

The women in Bubba Town weren't immediately friendly when the two first showed up. Eunice, tall and skinny with bowlegs, a Bassa girl, holding the hand of Marlene: a short, chubby, Congo cherub. Eunice had taught Marlene a few words of Bassa, which she promptly used to try to charm palm kernels out of the women in Bubba Town.

"Moin, eh," Marlene called out to the women, standing just outside the first hut in the village.

"Eh, moin" came the reply.

"Ahwe nee buea?" She was a spoiled brat, but it was impossible not to like her when she turned on the charm.

By now the Bassa women were laughing at the fat Congo girl trying to speak Bassa. "Eh pehne eh."

Having used up her entire Bassa repertoire, Marlene switched to Liberian English. "Y'all got anything to eat?"

Years later, the irony of the cosseted youngest child of the rich family across the way going to poor villagers to beg for food would dawn on me. At the time, it seemed perfectly natural that the Bassa women would share ground nuts, farina, and the beloved palm kernels with Marlene and Eunice.

The two of them came back giggling from their trip to Bubba Town, with Marlene's new friend, Palma, in tow. Palma was the young daughter of one of the Bassa women. She lived in the nicest mud hut in Bubba Town, one with two rooms, though both were dark since Bubba Town had no electricity.

Marlene took Palma to her bedroom and locked her in her closet, allegedly playing a game called "elevator shaft." The two were supposed to be pretending to take turns in the elevator, though Palma had never seen an elevator and so couldn't have possibly understood what Marlene was up to.

On Eunice and Marlene's return from Bubba Town, I glared at them. "Did you enjoy eating my dog? What did he taste like?"

Eunice looked at me. "Don't make me shamed," she said. She went upstairs into the house. I never knew who she was ashamed of: the Bassa people for eating Tracks, or me, her new sister, for begrudging them the food.

5

SUGAR BEACH, LIBERIA, 1975

In the spring of '22, from far across the sea . . .
There came a ship of sailors, singing li-ber-ty . . .
—Congo anthem

*E*unice and I, busy thespians, were hard at work preparing
for our roles in the reenactment of the Battle of Crown Hill,

President Tubman's cabinet. Radio Cooper, third from left in back row,
stands next to Uncle Gabriel.

part of our drama group's play taking place during the annual Matilda Newport Day festivities. The play was scheduled for the upcoming weekend, a few days after the actual holiday.

Our drama teacher had told us to divide into two groups. "Who wants to be the Country People and who wants to be the Congo People?" she said.

It's always so hard to choose, because while the Congo People got to win the battle and shoot the Country People, the Country People were a better stretch for our acting ability because they got to die, and we had been practicing dying for a month now. Our inspiration was Juliet Capulet. Our stage was the yard in the back of the house at Sugar Beach.

"Oh hap-pay dagga!" Eunice said, holding a kitchen knife in front of her stomach, with her back to Mommee's hibiscus bush.

"Hap-pee, Eunice! Not hap-pay! You gotta speak cullor!"

"Look, lemme hear my ear! I thought de people s'posed to be Italian self?"

"Da' your business, then."

She started again. "Oh happeeee dagger! This is *my* sheeef! There rust, *and* let ME *die*!" With a bloodcurdling scream, Eunice plunged the back of the kitchen knife into her stomach before lurching around the grass like a drunk. She stumbled toward the dogs, who yelped and scurried out of the way. Then she flailed around and around in a circle before collapsing onto the grass. She jumped up again like someone possessed by demons, let out another scream before falling back to the ground, resting flat and spread-eagled next to a scattering of palm kernels.

"Ma people, look at trouble?" Jack muttered, shaking his head.

"That ma time now!" I yelled, running to the lawn-stage. "Watch me die!"

Clearly, our acting abilities demanded that we play the

parts of dying Country People in the Battle of Crown Hill re-enactment. When we informed Mommee, she snorted. "That's your business," she said. "You all want to go get shot up by a cannon, it's no skin off my back."

In the years since Elijah Johnson and the other colonists first arrived in what would become Liberia, tales had been told and retold of the Battle of Crown Hill. It all started with the purchase, for $300, of their new home in West Africa. Elijah Johnson and the remaining colonists who hadn't died of malaria arrived by ship to Bushrod Island, a fertile tract between the St. Paul River and Montserrado Bay, determined to build their houses before the rainy season came. It was not to be.

Members of the Dey ethnic group, angry that their king, Long Peter, had signed onto the $300 sale just a month before, gathered in front of the boat and forbade the group from landing. Brandishing swords, knives, and guns, they drove Elijah Johnson and the other colonists back across the river. There, the colonists regrouped, on Providence Island, an unhealthy, malaria-infested swampland, about two acres large.

Dr. Ayres, the white agent who negotiated the original contract at gunpoint, went back to Bushrod Island to try to talk to the Deys. He was promptly kidnapped, and hauled upcountry, to Long Peter's village. Long Peter kept him for several days, until the terrified Dr. Ayres finally agreed to take his $300 in guns and tobacco back in exchange for the land. That transaction, however, never went through.

The Deys let Dr. Ayres go, and he returned to Providence Island, where the colonists waited. Providence Island was not somewhere they wanted to stay for any length of time. The only shelter it offered were decaying thatch leaves from palm trees, woven together in a pitiful attempt at warding off the encroaching rains. There was no fresh water on the island. Dysentery joined malaria as a common malady.

Frustrated and scared, Dr. Ayres told the settlers about his three-day ordeal up-country. He suggested they abandon the whole place and head back to Sierra Leone. The malaria was slowly eating away at them. He couldn't see the small band of settlers surviving, and the native Africans seemed hell-bent against letting them build on Cape Monterrado. The choice seemed simple to Dr. Ayres: give up, go back to Sierra Leone, and look for another patch of land to buy.

Elijah Johnson said no. He, too, was frustrated and scared, but he had had it with trolling from place to place up the West African coast looking for somewhere to settle.

"Two years long have I sought a home," he said, in a stirring speech before the rest of the tattered group. "Here I have found one, here I remain."

Elijah Johnson's words moved others in the group to agree. But for all of their bravado in deciding to stay, the small band of settlers wouldn't have made it if they hadn't received aid from a crucial, although unlikely, source: the fearsome King Boatswain, king of the equally fearsome group called the Condoes.

Almost seven feet tall, handsome, and muscular, King Boatswain's name garnered respect along the West African coast. He got it from English seamen, who hired him as a youth to work on a British merchant vessel. "To a stature approaching seven feet in height, perfectly erect, muscular and finely proportioned—a countenance noble, intelligent and full of animation—he unites great comprehension and activity of mind, and, what is still more imposing, a savage loftiness and even grandeur of sentiment," described one agent of the American Colonization Society.

Boatswain was often at war with the maritime tribes; he always won. He practiced the doctrine of overwhelming force, never showing up for a meeting or palaver without bringing a large number of his warriors with him.

West African protocol dictates that the meek go to the strong to judge their palavers. So the Deys and the other groups whose chiefs had signed the agreement selling their land to the Americans called in King Boatswain to pronounce his sentence on what they should do. They met on Cape Montserrado. Boatswain, as usual, brought along enough Condo warriors to immediately carry out whatever decision he made. The chiefs of the mutinous Deys, along with chiefs of the Bassa, Mambas, and a handful of other ethnic groups assembled in the palaver hut. The agent, Dr. Ayres, was there to represent the American Colonization Society. Elijah Johnson was there to represent the settlers.

Jehudi Ashmun, yet another new agent from the American Colonization Society, would later chronicle the meeting in the palaver hut. The "savage umpire" is King Boatswain:

A desultory and noisy discussion followed, in which the savage umpire disdained to take any part whatever. But having ascertained the prominent facts of the case, he at length rose, and put an end to the assembly by laconically remarking to the Deys, "That having sold their country, and accepted the payment in part, they must take the consequences. Their refusal of the balance of the purchase money, did not annul, or affect the bargain. Let the Americans have their lands immediately. Whoever is not satisfied with my decision, let them tell me so!" Then, turning to the Agents, "I promise you protection. If these people give you further disturbance, send for me. And I swear, if they oblige me to come again to quiet them, I will do it to purpose, by taking their heads from their shoulders. . . ."

Boatswain's decision gave Elijah Johnson and the other settlers the backbone they needed to start building their houses. But no one, not the settlers, not the Deys, not the agents, actually believed this was the end of the conflict. All

Boatswain had done was buy the settlers some time to prepare for the war that was inevitable.

In June 1822, Elijah Johnson and the rest who chose to stay headed to the inland region of the Montserrado promontory. To the disgust of the native West Africans, they started cutting down trees and building houses and fortifications.

And so was born Monrovia.

Elijah Johnson remained distrustful of the native Africans. When he wasn't working on building his house, he was teaching the men, and a handful of women, how to fight. He had fought in America's War of 1812 against the British, in the colored soldiers' regiment. He put the settlers on double duty: building houses during the day, patrolling the settlement with their guns at night.

It was now the heart of the rainy season. Huge, flooding bursts of rain punctuated each day.

The Deys began sniper attacks on the colonists. Elijah Johnson responded by shooting back, killing a number of Deys. A British gunboat showed up on the coast looking for fresh water to supply the crew. The captain came ashore and offered to help the colonists fight the Deys if Elijah Johnson would cede a small piece of land to the British Empire and hoist the Union Jack flag. It was then that Elijah Johnson gave that point-blank refusal memorized by Liberian schoolchildren.

"We want no flagstaff put up here that will cost more to get it down again than it will to whip the natives," he said.

For both sides, it was clear that war was coming. It was just a question of when.

Elijah Johnson threw himself completely into preparations for war. He drilled the men daily. He drafted thirteen Kru youths into his lieutenants' corps. Then he taught them how to use the colony's cannons, which they took up the river, positioning them around the settlement.

It soon became clear that the bush circling the colony had to be cleared; as it was, an attack could be staged from as close as a hundred yards away. So settlers, along with their Kru allies, cleared as much space between the colony and the bush as possible.

Meanwhile, over on the other side of the bush, the Africans were holding a war council. They wanted the colonists gone. The time to attack was now. They were sick of Boatswain telling them what to do.

A variety of points were made at the war-council meeting. King Peter and King Bristol opposed an attack. The colonists were black people, they contended. They had a right to live in Africa.

But they were in a minority. King George contended that if the black colonists really wanted to reside in Africa, they should place themselves under the protection of the African kings. If left alone, he argued, the colonists would, in a few years, try to master the whole country.

According to the spies sent by the colonists to listen in at the war council, King George's argument was eloquent. The armed schooners were gone. The white agents had fled, were sick, or had died. Now was the time.

King Peter shrugged. King Bristol went home. Messengers were dispatched in every direction to solicit aid from the neighboring tribes. The king of Junk refused to take any active part, and sent word to the colonists telling them he was neutral. But he didn't prohibit his people from following, and a number came to the war.

King Tom of Little Bassa declined to join the war. But King Ben, Bromley, Todo, Governor, Konko, Jimmy, Gray, Long Peter, George, and Willy all joined.

Through a mediator, the new white agent with the colonists, Jehudi Ashmun, sent a message to the assembling Afri-

cans. He said he was "perfectly apprised of their hostile delib-
erations, notwithstanding their pains to conceal them, and
that, if they proceeded to bring war upon the Americans, without even asking to settle their differences in a friendly manner,
they would dearly learn what it was to fight white men." Black
men, actually. There was no reply to Ashmun's threat.

Elijah Johnson ordered picket guards of four men each to
assume posts one hundred yards apart. No male colonist was
allowed to sleep at night. During the day, the men caught a
few hours of sleep, sending their African allies on patrol in the
bush. The families in outlying houses were ordered to stay
away from the windows.

The attack came at dawn on November 11. Some eight
hundred African warriors advanced on the picket guards
posted at the outskirts of the settlement. They opened fire before the guards could get behind their cannons, which were
never fired. Several of the guards were killed, the rest ran back
to the settlement, yelling.

Quickly, the African force seized control of the western
part of the settlement. They swarmed four houses on the outskirts. There were no men in the houses, only twelve women
and children.

One woman was stabbed thirteen times and thrown aside
for dead. Another woman, running from her house with her
two infant children, was hit in the head with a cutlass; soldiers
took both of her babies. A third woman, the mother of five
children, barricaded her door, which kept the warriors at bay
for a few minutes. Eventually they forced the door open. She
then grabbed an ax, and swung it futilely around her before
the warriors were upon her, stabbing her in the heart.

But then, instead of pressing ahead with their advantage,
the African army gave the colonists a crucial break. They
began looting the four houses they had attacked.

The colonists seized the advantage, grabbing two cannons and swinging them into force. Meanwhile, five musketeers, led by Elijah Johnson, circled around to the African warriors' flank and opened fire.

The African warriors were now the victims of their own formation. Crowded together, they were easy prey for the guns of Elijah Johnson and the other musketeers.

"Eight hundred men were here pressed shoulder to shoulder, in so compact a form that a child might easily walk upon their heads from one end of the mass to the other, presenting in their rear a breadth of rank equal to twenty or thirty men, and all exposed to a gun of great power, raised on a platform, at only thirty to sixty yards distance!" Jehudi Ashmun wrote later. "Every shot literally spent its force in a solid mass of living human flesh!"

"A savage yell," he wrote, "was raised, which filled the dismal forest with a momentary horror."

The dead: one hundred African warriors; twelve American colonists. The battle was over. The colonists had won.

Not satisfied with their victory, the colonists and their descendants made up stories of a fantastical heroic colonial woman, Matilda Newport, who, they said, lit a cannon with her pipe and blew up the native soldiers. That myth became legend, and eventually Liberia would officially recognize December 1 as a day of thanksgiving, Matilda Newport Day.

The descendants of the colonists—the Congo People—would have parties and feasts to celebrate Matilda Newport Day.

The rest of Liberia's population, who descended from the Deys, the Bassas, the Kpelles, and the Krahns, would not join in those festivities.

It never occurred to me at that time that all across Liberia, native Liberians were getting more and more upset about the things I took for granted; things that, for me, were as normal as the crow of the rooster every morning. This was life in Liberia, and who questioned daily life? Who questioned the redness of the dirt, the smell of palm oil and dried fish at lunchtime, the sudden descent of the night sky that covered the country with an impenetrable blackness? Who questioned Matilda Newport Day?

6

SUGAR BEACH, LIBERIA, 1975

*M*ommee's latest set of American wheels was a two-toned green Pontiac Grand Prix. She wore leather driving gloves and big Jackie O sunglasses and she blew her horn and yelled at other drivers, passing everybody, her eight-track tape player blasting José Feliciano. Mommee always had to rev herself up before going to see Mama Grand. I was just happy to get the day off from school, even if it meant visiting Mama Grand.

Mama Grand

It was Matilda Newport Day, a national holiday.

Vicky sat in the front seat, staring out the window. Marlene, Eunice, and I sat in the backseat.

Eunice and I wore big glasses, too, but ours were not stylish sunglasses, oh no. Two weeks earlier, Mommee had come into Marlene's room one night and discovered both Eunice and I on the floor peering at our respective Nancy Drew books by the dim light of Marlene's lamp. I was reading *The Hidden Staircase* and it was so close to my face Mommee couldn't see my eyes. Eunice, her back against the wall mirror, was holding her book equally close.

Mommee just looked at us and sighed. The next day, we were hauled off to the eye doctor.

Our prescriptions were so similar we could switch and wear each other's glasses.

Marlene, who had emerged from the eye doctor beaming at his pronouncement that she had 20–10 vision, scrambled from one end of the backseat of the car to the other, climbing over Eunice and me, waving at passersby, keeping a steady monologue of rubbish going. "Car coming, oh . . . Car coming oh," she chanted, as Mommee accelerated to pass a listing Holy Holy mammy bus full of Country People. "Whoosh!"

I put my face to the window hoping the wind would drown out Marlene. I loved driving to town. How could a nine-year-old exist living light years from civilization at Sugar Beach?

We passed Catherine Mills, the crazy hospital. As if on cue, a woman wove her way into the middle of the main road. Mommee swerved to miss her. The woman's hair was loose and her dress was dokafleh, from a "Bend Down Boutique," hand-me-down clothes bought from street-sellers at the market down Waterside.

Glancing down the road to Catherine Mills, Eunice announced: "When wartime come, I will go hide at Catherine Mills."

This was a favorite game, talking about what we'd do if Liberia ever got a war. We didn't really think Liberia would get a war—that was for all those other postcolonial African countries who never could get their act together. But we loved playing our "when wartime come" game.

"Yee! You crazy? Wha' you want go hide wi' those crazy people for?"

"Who will look for me there?"

"No way. When wartime come, ma part, I will go hide in the well."

"How you will hide in the well you can't even swim?"

"I will wear my water wings."

"Old woman like you, you will still be wearing water wings?"

"Shut up."

Mommee hissed from the driver's seat. "If you two don't hush up, I putting both of your ten toes on the ground."

Marlene piped up. "Car coming oh."

"Why Marlene can talk and we can't talk?" I demanded.

Eunice whispered at me. "But you got big mouth, oh."

Mommee: "You talking back to me, Helene?"

My burst of sass disappeared immediately. "No."

I was sulking when we slowed down to pass Daddy and Uncle Julius's gas station on the left: John L. Cooper Enterprises, named after grandpa Radio Cooper. There was rarely any gas there, but Daddy and Uncle Julius also had two shops. One sold toys and the other sold chocolate milk and ground peas and beer. "I better not see John sitting under the tree drinking," Mommee muttered.

If Daddy was drinking, he wasn't doing it under the big mango tree in front of the shop today. The only person lounging under the tree, with a nice frosty bottle of Club Beer, was Jacob Doboyu, Daddy's factotum, who also ran the gas station. Jacob Doboyu waved at us cheerfully from under the tree.

We rounded the ELWA corner, home to the Christian missionaries, and then the construction zone, where Mommee slowed down to smile at the good-looking white foreman with strong tanned arms. He had crinkly eyes because he was always smiling and dimpling at us when we passed him. As usual, he was wearing khaki shorts and hiking boots, with a short-sleeved shirt tucked in. He flicked his cigarette and beamed at us as we drove by, before tipping his finger at his hat in a salute. All of us in the car, even Vicky, erupted into catcalls and shrieks, and Mommee laughed and played with her sunglasses. I forgot I was supposed to be sulking.

Then we were at Paynesville Junction, where we had to turn left at the Shell gas station to connect with the main road to Monrovia, called Tubman Boulevard. Once in Paynesville, the advertising signs started in earnest: PAY YOUR LIGHT BILL!!! (from the government). WELCOME TO MARLBORO COUNTRY (from Phillip Morris). TOTAL INVOLVEMENT FOR HIGHER HEIGHTS (government again). AFRO SHEEN FOR THE BLACK AND BEAUTIFUL (Johnson Products).

Eunice pinched me. I looked at her and grinned. We were getting closer to town!

We drove through Congo Town, the unofficial beginning of civilization, and we started paying close attention to the road, because you never knew when you'd see someone you knew. The potholes were fewer and farther between now. State-of-the-art seventies glamour homes sat side by side with squatter encampments. We started passing the houses of our various relatives. First was Uncle Waldron's rambling ranch-style bachelor pad, where he had a waterbed and a video player. Whenever we visited him, Eunice, Vickie, Marlene, and I headed straight for his bedroom and rolled around his water-bed, with its lizard-print bedspread, listening to the water slosh around. Then we collected up his videos of American TV shows to take back to the bush with us. Going to Uncle Waldron's house was like going to the store.

Next, we passed Sophie's Ice Cream Parlor. Wheee! "Mommee, can we—" I started to say before she cut me off short.

"On the way home. Not now."

I sighed, thinking that the cool kids were there *now.* I could see my classmate Richard Parker (not cool) and his older brother Philip (extremely cool) sitting at one of the booths out-side with a bunch of other boys. Two of the boys wore berets.

We passed the road to Uncle Cecil's house. He was our cousin, though I called him Uncle Cecil. He was currently the highest-ranking member of our family in the government, be-cause he was minister of foreign affairs. Uncle Julius, who was minister of action for development and progress, was the next highest, but he didn't stay in that post for very long.

We passed Bro. Henry's house in Sinkor, behind a big piece of vacant land left to Mommee by Grandpa. It was prime property. "You and Marlene will inherit that one day," Mom-mee said, nodding toward it. "Don't ever sell. Remember that."

Bro. Henry was the next highest-ranking government of-ficial in the family: deputy minister of state for presidential affairs. His office was in the Executive Mansion, Liberia's ver-sion of the White House.

When we got to the first traffic light in Monrovia, across from Sinkor Supermarket, Mommee stopped, tapping her foot impatiently. Young barefooted boys in dokafleh ran up to the car, carrying trays of hard-boiled eggs on their heads.

"Boiled egg here! Boiled egg here!" they yelled. In the car, we all dug into our pockets. Eunice handed over a dime; Mommee gave a dollar to the oldest one and told him to share.

Then we were skirting past the Executive Mansion, home to President Tolbert. When he took over after President Tubman died, he promised that the era of top hats was over among the Congo People, and drove to his inauguration in a Volkswagen Beetle to show he could be a man of the Country People, too. He insisted his ministers follow his lead and wear the open-necked, short-sleeved cotton safari jacket and pants that he wore to his swearing-in: heretofore known as "swearing-in suits" and scorned by Congo People who preferred top hats and tails for festive occasions. And ain't no way anybody in my family was going to be driving no Volkswagen, except for Mommee's father, Grandpa Henry W. Dennis, who had been a career soldier and therefore had weird common-man tendencies.

We bypassed Broad Street, Monrovia's "Main Street" and veered instead for Waterside, the marketplace at the bottom of the bridge that led to Bushrod Island, where Elijah Johnson and the settlers first built their houses in 1822. Waterside was the usual teeming stinky mass of people and vendors and shops and stray dogs and Mandingo tailors. It smelled like body odor—not body odor because people don't bathe, but body odor because people don't use deodorant and sweat all day—and palm oil and dried fish. Eunice and I loved Waterside. All those people! It was the perfect contrast to Sugar Beach, with its air-conditioning and scented soaps and marble floors.

"Wind up the windows," Mommee ordered, turning on the air-conditioning.

"Aye, Mommee! Supposed we see somebody we know, how we will say hello?" I whined.

"Don't give me none of that ashtray. Wind up the windows."

I looked at Eunice and rolled my eyes. She shrugged, pushed her gigantic glasses up against her face, and rolled up the windows.

We crossed the bridge and were on Bushrod Island, home to Lebanese merchants. Every store was selling cloth or electrical products: alarm clocks, radios, cassette decks, record players.

And then, finally, we turned right, into Mama Grand's yard. She was sitting on the back porch, and waved down at us.

My life was full of women. Besides Mommee, Vicky, Eunice, Marlene, and Janice, most of my cousins were girls. Both of my grandfathers were dead, but my grandmothers . . . "My dear! You have got it on both sides!" was a common refrain, whenever people realized who my grandmothers were.

On Mommee's side was Mama Grand: Ethel Cecilia Benedict Dunbar: formidable capitalist, onetime market woman, self-made millionaire, motorcycle-rider, member of the Liberian legislature.

Mama Grand started off as the ultimate African entrepreneur: a market woman. During the 1940s, she cobbled together enough money to buy five hundred acres of farmland up-country. She didn't have a car, but did have a motorcycle, which she rode around the streets of Monrovia. She rented trucks to drive to Firestone Rubber Plantation where she purchased high-yielding rubber stumps, which she planted on her farm, selling the produce back to Firestone. The rubber launched her, and grapefruits and cassavas also helped send her on her way. She sold her wares in Monrovia, and with the cash, went on a land-buying binge. She bought property at the

Freeport—just before development there took off. She bought property up-country. She bought property downtown. "Never sell," she instructed her children.

She called native Liberians "country" to their faces, while the rest of us just whispered it behind their backs. She bragged to others about her beautiful grandchildren, with their light skin and long hair. But to our faces, she was meaner than a Black Mamba. She could wake up cussing you out in the morning and still be cussing you out when she went to bed that night.

She was fierce and dramatic-looking and had clearly been beautiful during her youth, with slanty eyes and impossibly high cheekbones. She could act really vulnerable one minute, like a frail old lady, and then turn on you the next with a hard wallop across your cheek.

Once I made the mistake of taking an American friend to her house to visit. My cousins were there, too; we were all out in the yard, paying homage to Mama Grand while she sat under a coconut tree. In the middle of one of her diatribes about how she had just cussed out a Lebanese merchant, she got out of her chair and walked about three feet, and pulled up her dress. Then she squatted down in the yard and started peeing. She kept talking while she peed. "That damn Lebanese asshole thought he was going to cheat me out of my rent. I told him, 'You must be on a contact high. Who do you think you're messing with? Nobody cheats Ethel Dunbar . . . I am the rock from which this country was built. You Lebanese asshole. . . . You're sitting here with no country. . . . Your country is all shot up to hell. . . . You're a damn refugee. . . . That's why we're never gonna let you damn Lebanese asses own property in Liberia. . . . You'll be renting from me till the day you die . . . your children will be renting from me . . . .' "

My American friend, Alyson, just stood there, paralyzed,

as Mama Grand finished peeing, got up, and pulled up her panties. My cousin CeRue was standing next to me. Every muscle in CeRue's body was clenched as she fought the raging, physical need to laugh. Her lips were white from where her teeth were biting down on them.

Mommee stood next to her sister, Aunt Momsie (same Ma). The two of them were caught between horror, humor, and the overwhelming need to shield their mother. Finally, Mommee said: "Wow! Look at the sky! You can already see the stars coming out!" This was a fat lie. It was only about four p.m., but I guess that was the best she could come up with.

Mama Grand was the only child of an only child, Ma Galley. Ma Galley's real name was Helene Elizabeth Clark, but everyone called her Galley Clark. I was named after Ma Galley, thank God, and not Mama Grand; that dubious honor went to my cousin Ethello, the apple of Mama Grand's eye, although that didn't ever stop her from getting verbally abused like the rest of us.

Trips to visit Mama Grand were always fraught: you just never knew what mood you'd catch her in. Sometimes she would love-bomb us, showering us with money. The first time Mama Grand met Eunice, she ordered Eunice to sit down, and inspected her from head to toe. "Who' your ma?" she asked. "Who' your pa?"

Eunice, terrified, started stuttering. "M-m-m-my m-m-m-m-ma name i-i-is . . ." and I held my breath, waiting for the explosion.

But after her cross-examination, Mama Grand simply handed Eunice twenty dollars.

Eunice, who had heard the stories but still hadn't witnessed Mama Grand at full throttle, was cocky as we got out of the car that day.

The red-tiled house sat right up against the road and always smelled like mothballs. Mama Grand lived upstairs; Uncle Waldron ran his gas company out of the first floor.

"Hello Mama Grand," we all sang out dutifully, filing onto the screened porch.

"Look at my beautiful grandchildren," Mama Grand said. We each trooped over to her and kissed her on both cheeks, first Marlene, then me, then Eunice, then Vicky, finally Mommee.

We talked about various people Mama Grand had recently cussed out. We ate some fufu and soup, which her cook had prepared: a large fermented cassava dumpling, sitting in a bowl of Liberian-style pepper soup, with dried fish, chicken, and beef, and even some sweet crawfish.

I tried to make my fufu and soup last as long as possible, an elaborate ritual that involved cutting my fufu into tiny pieces, layering it with slimy okra, then mashing beneseed—a sesame-seed paste—on top of each piece before flooding the spoon with soup.

When I finished my soup, I looked at Mama Grand. Everybody was sitting with an empty bowl. She eyed Eunice. "What, you starving? Why you just sitting there like that? You think I some kind of mean bitch, where you can't get some mo food if you want? Pass from here go help y'self to some more!"

Eunice and I darted out back into the kitchen, and scarfed down two more bowls. By the time we went back onto the porch, our stomachs were swollen.

The afternoon grew stiller and quieter. Even the usually boisterous Freeport, not far from Mama Grand's house, was silent in honor of Matilda Newport. An occasional dog barked. It was so hot and after all that hot soup I could feel beads of sweat collecting on my back. Eunice sat in a rocking chair, her back upright, straining to look attentive. Marlene had crawled into Mama Grand's hammock and gone to sleep.

I was bored. "Mama Grand," I said, "tell us about Matilda Newport."

Eunice sat up even straighter, and turned and looked at me with an expression of betrayal.

I tried to mouth "I'm sorry," but it was too late. Mama Grand was off to the races.

"Oh Matilda Newport was a great woman," she said. "She whipped those country asses . . . Bam Bam—blew them all up." With that, she launched into a screed about how a single old lady had tricked the native Liberians and saved the Congo People from the hordes. Marlene, supposedly asleep in the hammock, opened one eye, cased the situation, and went back to playing possum.

"Those damn country asses . . . They got what they deserved," she said, referring to the hundred native Liberians who were killed in the long-ago battle that spawned Matilda Newport Day.

She looked at Eunice. "Those were your ancestors, girl. Stupid people . . . Now they're trying to tell us we shouldn't celebrate Matilda Newport Day. . . . Where the hell do they think this country would be without Matilda Newport? Damn Country People . . ." On and on she went, whipping herself into a fury that the native Liberians were finally starting to complain that the country should not celebrate a woman for blowing up a hundred native Liberians.

Eunice sat absolutely still in her chair, her legs crossed at the ankles in silence as Mama Grand ranted.

Finally, Mommee got up. "Mama, we have to go," she said. We all, Eunice included, kissed Mama Grand on her cheek and trooped out. In the car on the way home, I was too ashamed to look at Eunice. I wanted to say "I'm sorry," but that would be acknowledging the grave insult that had just been done her, and I didn't want to do that. The car was quiet.

Even Marlene wasn't doing her silly "car coming oh," spiel as we headed back through Sinkor, passing Sophie's Ice Cream Parlor without stopping. Through Congo Town, Paynesville, then ELWA.

Back to the bush.

It took almost forty-five minutes to reach the turnoff for Sugar Beach, and finally, Eunice broke the silence that had hung over the car all the way home.

"That woman is something else," she said.

7

MONROVIA, LIBERIA, 1976

$\mathscr{D}$ressed in crisp linen dresses, fancy straw hats encircled with ribbons, white stockings, and black patent leather shoes, Mommee, Eunice, Marlene, Vicky, and I strutted through the side door of First United Methodist Church, Ashmun Street, Monrovia, like we owned the place. Daddy stayed home, drinking beer-n-eggs and doing crossword puzzles.

Eunice and I were bubbling in anticipation. We had a surprise planned.

Aunt Momsie and the whole crew after church

Church began at ten-thirty; as usual we strolled in around eleven. I never knew how service started; even on the Sundays that Mommee was an usher, we were late.

We sat in our family pew, in the same southwest corner of the church occupied by the members of our family since Elijah Johnson helped build the church back in 1822. It sat against the side of the wall, next to the choir, so that we had an eagle-eye view of the rest of the congregation. And they had an eagle-eye view of us.

Mommee gave each of us hymn books with our names engraved in gold-plated letters on the front so we could follow the songs in church. "Helene C. Cooper" said mine, except the engraver had messed up the middle C so it wasn't capitalized. "Eunice P. Bull" said Eunice's. Her letters were perfect.

Mommee was ushering that Sunday, so she was dressed all in white, including her white hat with its blue ribbon around it. After depositing us at our pew and leaving her handbag with Vicky, she went around to the back of the church for the collection plates.

By the skin of her teeth, she made it in time for the first offertory, although she did get disapproving looks from Ma Gene and some of the other biddies who made it their business to give disapproving looks at people in church.

Marlene skipped along behind her, following her up and down the aisles as Mommee passed the collection plate around. A family friend told her to sit down and Marlene, five, loudly lectured him: "This not your church, this God's church. God said little children should come to him."

The organ pealed out a high-pitched, familiar chord. Eunice and I sat up straight, listening eagerly. Was it time to put our plan into action?

No. Not yet. We sat back in disappointment.

The Senior Choir started warbling. The choir was filled

with old Congo People who couldn't sing. This time, they were butchering "The Old Rugged Cross," one of my favorite songs.

Things started melodic enough.

"On a hill far away
Stood an Old Rugged Cross
An emblem of suffering and shame"

But then the old biddies in the Senior Choir got to the high notes in the chorus, and the whole thing started to fall apart. Not a single one of them could sing. But they each thought they were Miriam Makeba. Eunice started poking me in the side as soon as they got to my chorus.

"So I'll cher-ish the old rugged crosssssssss," they trilled.

"Rug-ged Cross!" the men, aspiring to be basses, echoed, trying to sound manly.

"Till my tro-phies, at last I lay down!" the women sang.

They were killing my chorus. I couldn't sing either, but at least I wasn't sitting up there in the choir, I thought, conveniently forgetting that I had joined the choir at school.

What came next was a high-pitched squealing not unlike the sound a crab makes when you drop it in a pot of boiling water:

"I will cliiiiiiiinggggggggg! To the oooold Rug-ged Cross!" (old women).

"Rug-ged Cross!" the old men growled.

"And Exchaaaaange it some DAY for a crown!"

By the end of the song, we had dissolved into laughter. Even Mommee, back from usher duty, had to sneak out the side door so no one could see the tears running down her cheeks.

After the song, Pastor Doe made announcements. "Sis

Marion Adigibee is abed today with an illness. Please let's pray for her speedy recovery so that she may join us in fellowship soon."

"But that woman kick the bucket last week," Eunice whispered.

"She not dead yet!" I whispered back.

"You sure? I think she dead, oh."

Bro. Henry, sitting next to us, finally intervened with a glare. "She not completely dead yet! Now hush up!"

That was our cue to go to the bathroom, where we met our friends and chatted. Then we headed to the treasurer's office in the back of the church to pay our dues to Sis. Anna E. Cooper. Her small office smelled like perfume mixed with Lysol and mothballs. She had all of our names in her very neat ledger. We each gave a dollar every week.

After procrastinating for as long as we could, we went back to our pew and sat down for the rest of the interminable sermon.

When Pastor Doe announced that it was time for communion, Marlene screeched out: "*Amen* to that!"

I looked at her, aghast. Had she lost her mind? Mommee grabbed her hand and dragged her outside and spanked her behind. We watched from our side-door perch. As soon as Marlene started crying though, Mommee started patting her on the back and telling her how much she loved her, and how it hurt Mommee more than it hurt Marlene to spank her.

"But you not supposed to yell in church like that, sweetheart, you know that," Mommee said.

"But I hungry," Marlene whined. "I jes wan' do communion."

"You too young to take communion, baby."

"Aye, Mommee, I beg you, plee lemme do communion."

"No, Marlene, you too young."

"I hold your foot, Mommee. I so hungry."

Oh for Godsakes. I rolled my eyes at Eunice.

Finally, Mommee walked Marlene up the steps and back into the church. She sat her next to Bro. Henry. When it came time for our row to go up for communion, Bro. Henry took Marlene's hand and led her up to the altar. Pastor Doe, passing the little grape juice cups, got to Marlene and hesitated. Bro. Henry said: "My niece can take communion."

Marlene beamed and guzzled the grape juice in her cup.

The girl was a pro.

After communion, Pastor Doe said: "And now, please raise your voices for Blessed Assurance."

Eunice, Vicky, and I started grinning. It was finally time.

The night before, Eunice and I had been banished to the TV lounge at Sugar Beach, and told to memorize the Apostles' Creed for the next day's church service. Mommee closed the door of the room and told us not to come out until we could say it by heart.

Instead, we worked on tooling the lyrics to Blessed Assurance, which we knew we'd have to sing the next day because *every single Sunday* at First United Methodist Church, Ashmun Street, Monrovia, we sang Blessed Assurance.

Eunice and I had exiled Marlene from our presence because she had gone on a biting spree earlier in the day. She bit Eunice on her leg and bit me on my back. Eunice didn't retaliate—she never retaliated when Marlene bit her. I smacked Marlene and bit her back, and she went crying up the stairs to Mommee's room, brandishing her stubby fat white arm where the red mark was already developing. So I got spanked. Eunice and I had both retired to my room to discuss the injustice of our lives when Mommee came in, threw the red hymnbook at us, and told us to go memorize the Apostles' Creed. She didn't see the spot on my pink wall, right behind the door, where I had just written: "I hope Marlene gets run over by a bus."

Marlene peeked around from behind Mommee's dress, where she had been cowering. "Can I come, too?"

"Yes," said Eunice.

"No way."

We went into the TV lounge and I slammed the door behind us. The door flew open. "If you slam the door in your sister's face again you'll get another beating," Mommee said. Then she slammed the door.

Eunice was laughing at me now. "You shouldn't have bitten your sister," she said. "You're older than her."

"I don't care. She's a spoilt brat."

Left unspoken was that Eunice would never ever bite Marlene, no matter what Marlene did, because she wasn't a true daughter of the house like me. A few weeks earlier, Marlene had inadvertently broken one of Vicky's Jackson 5 albums. "You damn fool, you!" Vicky yelled, snatching a broken record piece from Marlene. Marlene promptly started crying, and right at that second, guided by Satan, the door flew open and Mommee's head popped inside: "Why is my baby crying?" she asked.

I stood paralyzed against the wall, trying to will Marlene not to say anything because Vicky was already on shaky ground with Mommee because she stayed out too late at her teenage parties.

"Vicky called me a damn fool," Marlene sniveled, screwing up her cheeks.

Mommee immediately sent Vicky to Bro. Henry, where she stayed for four days, before Mommee went and got her. Since being allowed back, Vicky had been quiet and sullen, locking herself in her room most of the time.

Eunice and I worked painstakingly on our rendition of

Blessed Assurance. Before we went to bed, we slid a copy under the door to Vicky's room.

When Pastor Doe announced Blessed Assurance, everyone opened their hymnbooks except me, Vicky, and Eunice. We had no need for hymnbooks.

"Blessed Assurance, Jesus is Mine" the congregation sang.

"Breakfast this morning, with biscuits and cheese," Vicky, Eunice, and I sang.

"Oh what a foretaste, of Glory Divine," they sang.

"I had a co-old and it made me sneeze," we sang.

"This is my sto-ry, This is my song," everybody sang.

"Praising my savior, all the day long," everyone sang.

"I killed my sister, so she won't live long," Vicky, Eunice, and I sang.

"This is my sto-ry, this is my song," we all sang.

"Praising my savior, all the day long," everyone else sang.

"I killed my sister, so she won't live long!" we ended triumphantly.

We suppressed giggles and beamed in victory that no one had noticed what we'd done to Blessed Assurance.

After that, the Senior Choir marched slowly down the aisle and out of the sanctuary, singing the recessional hymn, their gray-and-blue robes swishing in opposite directions of the way they walked. The women wobbled from side to side with each step, their robes flowing behind them. We all spilled onto the sidewalk and into the street, chatting and being seen.

Then we went to check in on Mama Grand, who shared her son-in-law's aversion to churches. Then back to the bush for lunch with Daddy. Sunday lunches were always American food. A rule in the house: Liberian food with palm oil all week, fufu and soup on Saturdays, and American food on Sunday. That usually meant cabbage stew with chicken gravy and rice.

Around five p.m. that Sunday evening, we started singing the weekly preparing-for-the-Uptons song.

"De Uptons, de coming here tonight!" we sang, marching around the house, twirling imaginary batons.

Don and Ellen Upton were a British couple who came to visit my parents every Sunday night. You could set your bush-clock by them.

When the lights of the Upton's car showed up on the dirt road to Sugar Beach, we changed our lyrics:

"De Uptons, de here! De Uptons, de here!"

"Y'all shut up!" Daddy yelled from the bathroom, where he was slapping on some English Leather aftershave. "If you let them hear you singing that ridiculous song I will beat each of your butts!"

Then they were there, giving candies to Marlene, Nancy Drew books to me, Eunice, and Vicky. Eunice and I treasured our Nancy Drew collection, lovingly displayed on shelves in our bedrooms.

Mr. Upton had those red cheeks that fat white people get when they spend too much time in the tropics. Mrs. Upton was always dressed very neatly, with low-heeled pumps. Mommee and Daddy took them into the living room and served them drinks and cookies. As always, they stayed for exactly one hour, then drove away, back to the city, leaving a trail of dust behind.

And again, we were alone at Sugar Beach.

8

MONROVIA, LIBERIA, 1977

"Whaddya want," I drawled. "Yeah. Uh-huh."

Standing in my bedroom looking at myself in the mirror, I tried to relax my cheeks and drop my consonants like the American kids did, and added extra *r*'s.

"Hey thar. How ya doin? What's up, blood?"

Marlene and Eunice at Sugar Beach

Eunice appeared at the doorway, spic and span, wearing her Liberian school uniform and a smirk.

"You trying to speak cullor again?"

"I don't have to try, thank you very much. I can speak it way better than you."

Eunice was quick with the reply she always used whenever I put on my American English airs. "When wartime come and I say, Helene, get-from-daway, you m'sit down there and say 'fwenken,' " she said.

"I won't say 'fwenken.' I will say 'foot help de body.' "

I needed to practice my cullor, because Marlene and I attended Monrovia's most elite school: the American Cooperative School on Old Road in Monrovia. It was a hodgepodge of American expats, foreign nationals, Lebanese refugees, and Congo Liberians. The American kids ranged from religious Bible-study types (the children of Christian missionaries) to rebellious, pot-smoking long-haireds (the children of American embassy staff). My sixth-grade class had twelve American students, six Lebanese, six Liberian, two Spanish, two Filipino, one Swede, one Irish, one Danish, one Brit, one German, and one girl from St. Helena, an island, she informed us, that was in the middle of the Atlantic Ocean.

ACS was the most expensive school in Liberia. The only thing better than sending your children to ACS was to send them "away" to school—that is, boarding school abroad. When I first started ACS in the third grade in 1973, my tuition was $1,000 a year, a spectacular amount. By the time I got to sixth grade in 1977, it had jumped to $1,500 a year. Mommee and Daddy paid quarterly for Marlene and me to go there, and they always complained about how much it cost. But every three months they somehow managed to find the money, usually from Mommee harassing some Lebanese merchant or the other to pay her rent.

ACS was like a little America right in the middle of Monrovia. We wore jeans and T-shirts to school and we said the Pledge of Allegiance to the United States of America before class every day. It was easy to learn because it was exactly like the Pledge of Allegiance to the Republic of Liberia. We learned how to sing "My Country 'Tis of Thee" and "This Land Is Your Land."

Eunice couldn't speak cullor because she went to Haywood Mission School, right next door to ACS. If Mommee and Daddy could have afforded it, they probably would have sent both Vicky and Eunice to ACS, too. But they couldn't, so only Marlene and I went to ACS. Eunice and Vicky, the adopted daughters of Sugar Beach, went to less-expensive schools. Vicky attended B. W. Harris Episcopal School, way at the top of the hill on Broad Street in downtown Monrovia; Eunice went to Haywood.

Eunice and the other students at Haywood all wore uniforms; yellow short-sleeved shirts and black pleated skirts for the girls, pants for the boys. When you got to be a senior, you wore long-sleeved shirts. There weren't many Congo kids at Haywood. Mostly, Haywood was populated by the native Liberian kids who were being reared by Congo People. Or native Liberian kids whose parents were starting to do well.

So few people at Haywood questioned why Eunice was chauffeured to school every day. Half the school got chauffeured to school—after their Congo brothers and sisters had been dropped off at their more prestigious schools. And no one at Haywood questioned why Eunice lived in an exclusive mansion on the beach. Or why, during a school recital, she arrived in a Christian Dior dress (courtesy of Mommee) and a cloud of Chanel #5 perfume. In the Congo-Country world of Monrovia society, that's the way it was.

Our schoolyards were separated by a cement fence with

broken glass stuck onto the top to keep each school on its respective side. At the time the big joke was that the kids at Haywood all longed to be at ACS so much that when a kickball went over the fence from ACS onto the Haywood yard, they'd jostle each other to be the one to throw it back over. Eunice and I never talked about that joke.

That morning we piled into Daddy's Mercedes with Fedeles at the wheel and set off for school.

When we pulled up to ACS, Marlene screamed and hollered and had to be dragged out of the car. She had already, at the age of six, dropped out or been kicked out of three schools: Hilton Van EEE, a private school, which lasted two weeks thanks to some infraction; Paynesville Private School, where she lasted one day and was "asked to leave" after she stuck a sheet of paper in a kerosene lantern, prompting a classroom blaze. She was denied entrance at ELWA Christian School when she refused to answer the principal during her interview, because she didn't like the statue he had up of Jesus being crucified on the Cross.

"Marlene, show Mr. Wilson how smart you are," Mommee whispered to Marlene as the two sat before the ELWA principal during Marlene's "interview." Marlene zipped her mouth shut. She just stared at the statue in awkward silence until the principal suggested that perhaps she wasn't ready to be integrated into the population of ELWA just yet. Mommee was furious when they got home that day.

ACS was billed as Marlene's last chance at education and she seemed determined to squander it. Fedeles and Vicky dropped us off with evil waves then pulled away, leaving Marlene sitting, screaming on the ground in front of the school. "Nooo! Noooo! Don't leave me here like this," she wailed. "I beg you oh! My people, please please no no no no no."

"I say, you juke with rusty nail, Marlene," I said impatiently.

"No I hold your foot oh! Don't make me go inside!"

"Marlene, plee don't make people weak today." I stood over her, trying desperately to shut her up before my friends saw us. The last thing I needed was one of my friends like Richard Parker showing up and witnessing this latest Cooper family disgrace; I would never hear the end of it. I looked at Eunice imploringly. Before I could open my mouth to beg her to try to deal with Marlene, she was backing away. "Try hard ya. She's *your* sister!" she replied.

Then she skipped off next door to Haywood, grinning as she escaped. As she disappeared around the fence, she had one last taunt for me. "Remember what Bro. Henry said?" she yelled, holding up two fingers side by side. "You and Marlene are like this! Hee hee!"

Marlene's tantrum lasted about five minutes. Finally I dragged her to her class, dumping her on Miss Hill, her first-grade teacher. It was a relief to finally get to my sixth-grade class, even though I had what seemed like the universe's meanest teacher in Miss Grimes.

I didn't have piano lessons that day so Mommee came to pick us up after school. As soon as we all got in the car I started lobbying to go to Aunt Momsie's house. What, after all, was the point of heading back to the bush since we were already in town?

Aunt Momsie's house was the center of my social universe. First of all, it was in Sinkor, near the airfield, the best residential district in Monrovia. It was split-level, like the house that the Brady Bunch lived in. They had a telephone! Their number was 26597. Their house was nowhere near as big as Sugar Beach, but it was the epitome of 1970s cool: wood-paneled walls, shag carpeting, and a big den in the basement for the kids to hang out. One whole wall was lined with vinyl albums.

Aunt Momsie was seven years younger than Mommee and the two of them looked just alike, except that Aunt Momsie had slinky eyes that made her always look like she was about to fall asleep. She was named after Mama Grand, except her full name was Ethello Greaves McCritty, not Ethel. She and Uncle Waldron came from Mama Grand's second marriage, after Mama Grand and Grand-Pa divorced.

Uncle Mac was even shorter than Daddy, but very handsome, with dark chocolate skin and dimples whenever he smiled. Aunt Momsie and Uncle Mac were always having parties. Their house was always packed with people being ultracool, sipping Martini & Rossi, and smoking cigarettes.

Their daughters—my cousins CeRue, Michelle, and Ethello—were everything Eunice and I wanted to be: popular, sophisticated, and smooth.

All three were pretty. CeRue Izetta Louise McCritty took all of Aunt Momsie's best physical qualities and then multiplied them by ten. She was funny and smart. She ran around with the born-again crowd for a while, then dumped them and started going to the movies and dance parties again.

Michelle Magauwa Juanita McCritty was the more studious middle sister. She was Mommee's favorite, probably because she was the quiet one. Mommee called her her "special god-child." She was the first one in Liberia to get a perm and she looked like Donna Summer.

Ethello Cecilia Benedict McCritty, aka Tello, my favorite cousin in the world, was exactly what you would expect from the youngest of three girls: a know-it-all brat. She bossed me around because she got bossed around at home and I was four months younger. She had a mouth on her that rivaled Mama Grand. Still, everything I learned about how to conduct my social life, I learned from Tello.

Eunice and I tried to go to Aunt Momsie's house whenever we could. CeRue, Michelle, and Ethello were so popular that they always had lots of friends visiting. So their house was always full of people, and by hanging out with them, we could bask in their reflective gorgeousness and be gorgeous, too.

Their house was just up the road from where Eunice's mother lived in Sinkor, so sometimes Eunice visited her mother when we were visiting Tello 'them. Mrs. Bull's house was cement but it had a zinc roof and an outhouse. I only went with Eunice to see her mother once, and I was taken aback by how dark it was in the house. She had a single lightbulb in her bedroom, where there was a mattress on the floor. There was a lightbulb screwed into the wall in the living area. The kitchen was outside on the back porch—a coal pot actually. The smoke blew into the house, giving it that familiar smell that clings to Liberia like a second skin.

"Mommee, we going to Aunt Momsie 'them house today?" I asked after I slid into the backseat of the car, noting with alarm that Mommee was already turning left toward the road leading in the opposite direction, toward Sugar Beach.

"Does it look like we're going to Momsie's house?" Mommee replied sarcastically.

She honked her horn at the security guard at the gate of Uncle Cecil's house as we drove past, and then turned onto Tubman Boulevard.

Sighing, I looked out the window as civilization receded. It was back to the bush for us.

Life's big events took place at the Saturday afternoon matinees at Relda Cinema. It cost seventy-five cents to get in, plus twenty-five cents for popcorn with extra butter. There were always two movies: an American movie and a kung fu movie. Eunice and I wore short shorts and white go-go boots that Daddy bought us from America, and strutted down the aisles, pretending we were looking for somewhere to sit. Really we were just scoping the place out to see who was there.

The American movies were always raucous, because Relda showed big action Hollywood blockbusters that proved how much white men can lie. The phrase "white man can lie" was well known in Liberia; it dated back to 1969 because no one in Liberia believed Neil Armstrong really walked on the moon.

"One giant step for mankind," said Neil Armstrong.

"Oh, white man can lie, oh!" said Liberians.

That was the litany for us at Relda whenever we watched the American movies, especially the ones that showed robots and space travel.

After the first American movie of the matinee, there was intermission, and the lights came on and we could see who all were there. By the time the kung fu movies came on, everybody at Relda had regrouped to sit with different friends.

One Saturday near Christmastime in 1977, a boy approached me at Relda to ask for my hand in girfriendhood. His name was Lawrence Lincoln, and he was the native Liberian adopted son of a wealthy Congo family. I wasn't much interested in boys yet beyond my crush on Fedeles, but I wanted to seem cool, and Tello and Eunice both advised me to accept this rare proposal. So I gave Lawrence what I thought was a husky "yes," as instructed by Eunice and Tello. "Let's give it a try."

That night back at Sugar Beach, Eunice and I sat on my bed plotting for hours how I would leverage this new relationship to make the two of us more popular. "Now that you have a boyfriend, other boys will come running," she said. "You'nt mind they will come to Sugar Beach, self."

For three Saturdays straight, Lawrence and I went to Relda and sat apart during the first movie of the afternoon, giggling with our cousins. Then, when the kung fu movie came on, I left Eunice and Tello and went and sat by myself, making sure there was an empty seat beside me. Lawrence slipped into the empty seat and put his arm around the back of my chair. We never spoke, just sat there in the dark, watching Bruce Lee wreak havoc for the usual killing of his teacher by gangs in Hong Kong.

Two weeks into our relationship came Christmas season. I didn't know what to get Lawrence for a Christmas gift. Tello, who also had a boyfriend, Ronnie Weeks, was way ahead of me. The Liberian radio airwaves were full of an ad for a cologne from America called Trouble. Sultry ads said: "Give your man Trouble this Christmas."

A few days before Christmas, Mommee took us Christmas shopping on Broad Street. "I say, Eunice," I whispered, as we walked into Evans Drugstore. "Plee help me sneak and buy Lawrence Trouble."

"Yee! You crazy? So Aunt Lah can cuss me! I beg you, yah."

"Aye you girl, why be wicked?"

Ignoring me, Eunice went over to the bath gel section and started playing with the bottles of Badidas. With a surreptitious look at Mommee, I headed for the men's cologne section. Mommee spotted me immediately.

"Do not let Helene buy any men's cologne!" she yelled at Helen Gibson, one of the clerks at Evans Drugstore. "She's too young for that nonsense."

"A-ya, namesake, you want buy cologne for your boyfriend?" Helen Gibson said, pinching my cheek like I was some baby.

Mommee trooped us over to the bookstore across the street and made me buy a copy of *Huckleberry Finn* for Lawrence.

I was mortified, but I gave him the book the next day at

Relda. "Merry Christmas," I muttered. He gave me a dollar and a silver-plated ring.

Tello came walking up to us. We were standing at the side door of Relda. "Wha' Helene gave you f' Christmas?" she asked, smirking.

"She gimme one book," Lawrence said. "Wha' you gave Ronnie?"

Tello had clearly been practicing, waiting for this moment. "I gave my man Trouble this Christmas," she breathed, sultrily.

The next Saturday we were watching Bruce Lee's *Enter the Dragon,* sitting next to each other at Relda, when suddenly Lawrence leaned over and kissed me on the corner of my mouth. It was wet. I jumped out of my chair and bolted to the girls' bathroom. I stayed in there for about fifteen minutes, before going back to Lawrence and breaking up with him. "I don't think it's working out," I said.

He looked at me. "I hear you've been going around telling people you were going to break up with me," he said.

"No I haven't!" I denied, even though that's exactly what I had been doing. A few days before, Nyemale, a schoolmate, had asked me if Lawrence was my boyfriend. Acting on Eunice's instructions for leveraging our newfound popularity, I told Nyemale "yes," but added "not for long." I was trying to make myself seem like a player.

I should have known that Nyemale would spread it around and now Lawrence had heard and his feelings were hurt. Confronted, I lied. "I'nt say nothing like that! Nyemale is a big fat liar!"

Now I'd impugned Nyemale's honor. And she had friends who had already beaten me up once before, two years ago.

In the days that followed, the accusations flew. The next Saturday at Relda was clearly going to be a showdown between

Nyemale and me. And her friends. The last time they had beaten me up was, at least, in the privacy of the girls' bathroom at ACS. Now this would be in front of all of Monrovia society, at Relda.

"Eunice, wha' I will do?" I wailed to Eunice the Friday night before the big fight day.

I was shuffling around the TV lounge while Eunice watched *Mission Impossible*. I loved that show but this was no time to be thinking about exploding tape recorders. My butt was about to get beat in public.

"But wha' made you go lie, so?"

"I'nt know!"

Eunice looked at me. I was puny. "They wi' beat you, for true."

Eunice took me outside, to the ocean side of the house, to teach me how to fight. The waves from the ocean were pounding the shore, so loud we had to shout to hear each other. The lesson was coming a little late, since the showdown was scheduled for the next day, but I was desperate.

"Okay, here' wha' you must do if she kick you," Eunice said, kicking me in the stomach.

"Ow!" I toppled over backward into the grass.

"But you girl, you lazy oh!"

"Wha' you kick people like that for?"

"How you will learn how to fight if people can't kick you?"

I got up, wiping the back of my jean shorts, where wet grass clung to my backside and scratched my leg. "Mosquito now bite me."

I knew I was acting like a spoiled princess who deserved to get her butt beat. Tears were starting to rise. "Eunice, wha' I will do?"

She was shaking her head, completely disgusted. "The girl ain't touch you yet you already crying?" Turning, she walked around to the front and went inside the house, and I trailed behind her. As we crept down the hallway toward the bedrooms, the house was still except for the rattle of the various air-conditioning window units; Daddy's central air-conditioning had long conked out. Eunice quietly opened the door of Marlene's bedroom, and we crept in, sliding onto our respective mattresses on the floor.

The silence extended for ten minutes. I could hear Marlene's deep breathing; she was fast asleep. I couldn't hear anything from Eunice though, which meant she was awake.

"Eunice," I whispered.

"S-s-stop wh-whining. You think I will let anybody beat you?" Her stutter was back, she was fed up with me.

The next day, we went to Relda at two p.m. as usual. My heart was in my mouth. I knew our fight was unofficially scheduled for after the show—that's when all fights happened. It would be in the parking lot in front of Relda, just as the parents and drivers were picking up their kids. That's where everyone congregated, to draw out the long good-byes before going home.

I trailed out of the cinema after the show, clenching and unclenching my fists. The group was assembled outside, waiting for me. I saw Lawrence sitting on the fence, slightly apart, watching the whole thing. Nyemale, flanked by her awful friends, stood to one side. In front of them was an empty space, where I was supposed to be. I hovered in the doorway.

"Come on, Helene Cooper!" somebody yelled.

Then I saw them. Surrounding my side of the fight space were Eunice, Vicky, Ethello, CeRue, Michelle, even Marlene. They were clapping for me. They were all primed and ready to jump in.

I had backup.

I swaggered over to Nyemale, hands on my hips. I paused

dramatically, waiting for the place to quiet down. Then I spat out: "What is lying going to get you Nyemale? Silver and Gold?"

I never gave her a chance to open her mouth. All of the strength of my sisters and cousins was flowing through me. The blood I got from Mama Grand pounded through my veins. I cussed her out. Then, flanked by my sisters and cousins, I flounced away, into the waiting Mercedes-Benz with Fedeles at the wheel. We peeled off in a righteous cloud of dust. It was going to be a Merry Christmas after all.

9

SUGAR BEACH, LIBERIA, 1977

"They are spoken of as orderly and decent people; many of them, except for the color of their skins, would have been valued members of society in the United States."
—*Niles Weekly Register*, **February 7, 1829,**
Norfolk, Virginia

*E*unice and I were in my bedroom working on our Christmas lists when we heard the drums sounding in the distance,

Uncle Julius, Mommee, Bro. Henry, and Daddy

from the top of the Sugar Beach road. Eunice looked at me, her eyes widening behind her glasses. At exactly the same time, we realized who it was.

"Santa Claus!" we yelled, running through the house to the kitchen porch. Marlene followed us, almost tripping down the stairs. Mommee, Vicky, Daddy, John Bull, all crowded behind me and Eunice. The entire household squeezed onto the porch and spilled onto the lawn. Santa Claus had come to Sugar Beach! All the way up to our house!

Santa Claus, on stilts and wearing a grass skirt, a wooden mask with eyeholes, and a long blond wig, loped into the yard. He was surrounded by three drummers. The Bassa people from Bubba Town crowded behind him, clapping their hands to the beat of the drum. Palma darted from behind her mother and scampered up the stairs to Marlene. The two of them were bouncing up and down, grinning.

When Santa Claus stepped onto the grass, the yard got quiet. The humid nighttime air clung to my face, filled with the scent of Santa Claus and his outfit; the ripeness of the bone hanging from a necklace around Santa Claus's neck, the pungent odor of his skirt. It was a raw scent, musky animal-like and oh-so-familiar. He smelled like home.

The drummers sounded a beat.

Boomp. Then another boomp.

The hair on my arms stood up straight. Eunice grabbed my hand and squeezed it tight.

Boomp. Boomp.

Then the Bubba Town people behind the drummers started singing.

"We-ah we-ah, Santa Claus we-ah, aye. . . .
We-ah we-ah, Santa Claus we-ah, aye."

The drummers were going faster now, and we were all singing the same phrase.

"We-ah we-ah, Santa Claus we-ah, aye"
"We-ah we-ah, Santa Claus we-ah, aye."

Faster on the drums. Santa Claus jumped from one stilt to the other, stomping on the grass to the beat. Marlene ran behind him trying to imitate him, and he whirled around and picked her up. She was laughing, her eyes wild with excitement. Palma bounced behind him, and he bent and picked her up, too. Now he had two little girls, one in each arm, balancing, and still he kept whirling and dancing. On cue, the rest of us all poured into the yard to dance with Santa Claus.

We formed a circle, with Santa Claus, Marlene, and Palma in the middle.

"We-ah we-ah, Santa Claus we-ah, aye,
We-ah we-ah, Santa Claus we-ah, aye."

Round and round we went, singing and dancing and laughing into the night air. I felt free and happy and burbling over with joy. Christmas was coming and I was dancing and singing on my front lawn, with my family and Santa Claus.

"We-ah we-ah, Santa Claus we-ah, aye,
We-ah we-ah, Santa Claus we-ah, aye."

And finally, it was over and the drums quieted and we stopped dancing and Santa Claus bent down and gently put down Marlene and Palma, who both clung to his stilts, not wanting to let go. And Santa Claus turned to Daddy.

"Where' ma Christmas?" he demanded.

Daddy reached into his pocket and gave him a five-dollar bill.

Daddy was often at work, or hanging out with Uncle Julius next door, or drinking Club Beer at the gas station, or up on the farm.

So I was very excited the day his friends came to visit him at Sugar Beach. I knew that the group would head downstairs to the recreation room to discuss world events, so I grabbed Daddy's *Newsweek* magazine and sprinted down the stairs before they got there.

I was just checking my favorite purple velvet chair for lizards when they entered the hallway tunnel that connected the stairs to the recreation room. I jumped into the chair quickly and crossed my legs, opening my *Newsweek*. I didn't bother to read anything, but pursed my mouth self-importantly as if I were studying the magazine.

Daddy entered with Uncle Julius, Mr. Upton, and Lomax. The men sat in the leather chairs around the coffee table while Daddy mixed them drinks at the bar: gin and tonics for Uncle Julius and Mr. Upton, a brandy for Daddy. He and Uncle Julius had already been drinking beer that morning, and I frowned. They seldom seemed really drunk and didn't usually stumble around. But they were always drinking beers like they were Cokes.

A roach crawled out of the folds of my chair and up my leg. I smacked it to the floor, continuing to study my *Newsweek*.

The men started talking about the Sino-Soviet pact. I knew what Sino was, it was one of Liberia's nine counties—way up-country somewhere. Soviet, I had just learned at school, was a different word for Russia. I scooted out of my chair and perched myself on Daddy's armchair, adopting what I hoped was an intellectual look.

"President Tolbert had better watch out," Uncle Julius was saying. "This Sino-Soviet pact is going to make the Americans even more paranoid about Africa."

Daddy said: "Tolbert doesn't care. And to tell you the truth, I don't blame him. The Americans have been taking Liberia for granted for too long."

Aware that the conversation was about to take a familiar turn, into the usual rantings about how America treated Liberia like a stepchild, and I was about to lose my ability to show off, I jumped in: "I've been worried myself about the Sino-Soviet pact," I said. "There are too many Russians in Sino County anyway."

There was silence in the room for about ten seconds. Then the laughter that broke out lasted for what seemed like hours. Daddy had tears running down his cheek he was laughing so hard. He hugged me to him. By now I'd realized I'd made a complete fool of myself, but I almost didn't care, because I had made Daddy laugh. "That's my daughter," he kept saying, shaking his head.

Mommee was a skinny girl with big sad brown eyes. Daddy was a wise-aleck and too smart for his own good. He was the jokester in the family, while his brother, Julius, who followed him around from pillar to pole, was the serious, studious one, thus earning the nickname "Prof."

When Daddy and Uncle Julius were little, Ma Gene, Daddy's mother, used to braid Uncle Julius's hair into three plaits. One day, a woman saw the two brothers and stopped to coo over the pretty little girl—Uncle Julius. Daddy was incensed. "Ju-ju!" he said, "Let me take down your diaper and show her your John-Thomas! You not no lil girl!"

Mommee and Daddy both went to college in America during the 1950s. Mommee traveled to Washington, D.C., for a wedding, and came down with the chicken pox. She hid at her friend's house until her face cleared up. It was springtime, a beautiful Sunday afternoon, when her brother, Bro. Henry, drove up to the house with two people in the car. Sitting in the backseat was his latest girlfriend. Sitting in the front seat was a grinning Daddy. Bro. Henry blew the horn, and Mommee came out.

"Come on, Lah," he yelled from the convertible. "We're going to Haines Point."

Haines Point, in Potomac Park, had long been the Washington, D.C., park most welcoming to blacks. Bro. Henry wanted Daddy to occupy his sister while he smooched with his new girlfriend: both men had blankets that they spread on the grass.

So there they were, my parents-to-be, two Congo Liberians, both born with the proverbial silver spoons in their mouths. Mommee was still reed-thin, a ninety-nine-pound, five-foot-seven-inch beauty with a complexion the color of milk-coffee. Daddy was exactly the same height, but with the fat cheeks that identify all members of the Cooper family. Like many others in his family, he loved his wine as much as he loved his women and song.

With the other couple a few feet away, Mommee and Daddy settled on a blanket. Mommee immediately decided to show Daddy she was cultured and smart, and recited for him her favorite poem.

Serene, I fold my hands and wait
No care for wind nor tide nor sea
I rave no more 'gainst time or fate
For lo, my own shall come to me.

When she was done, she looked at Daddy. "What's your favorite poem?" she asked.

His response couldn't have been more different. Daddy recited "Invictus."

Out of the night that covers me,
Black as the Pit from pole to pole,
I thank whatever gods may be
For my unconquerable soul

It matters not how strait the gate,
How charged with punishments the scroll,
I am the master of my fate
I am the captain of my soul.

Mommee promptly took umbrage with Daddy's choice. "What do you mean 'whatever gods may be'? There's only one God."

Ignoring that early warning sign of incompatibility, the two blundered on, reciting poetry to each other in the Sunday-afternoon sun.

But Daddy was just being a Cooper. They were hard-nosed from the start, more about business than romance.

The Coopers arrived in Liberia on March 18, 1829. My great-great-great-granddaddy Randolph Cooper was thirty-three when he and three of his brothers—Reid, Garret, and Thomas—sauntered off the good ship *Harriet* bearing the trademark Cooper looks, a penchant for making deals, and an abiding love of their own wit. The ship manifest listed the occupations of two of the four Cooper brothers: Reid and Garret, both seamen.

The four Cooper brothers had boarded the ship *Harriet* in

Norfolk, Virginia, on February 7, 1829. The back-to-Africa movement was at a fever pitch in America, and there was a strong belief among many prominent Americans that getting rid of freed blacks was in the long-term interests of the country. The dominant thinking, particularly among those that wanted to keep the institution of slavery going in America, was that having freed blacks running around was a bad example to set for the blacks who were still slaves.

The ship *Harriet* was full of freed blacks from Virginia, including Joseph Jenkins Roberts, who would become Liberia's first president; James Spriggs Payne, who would become Liberia's fourth president; and a fellow by the name of Abdul Rahman Ibrahima, a West African prince who was sold into slavery forty years before. Ibrahima had been captured by warring tribesmen in Timbo, West Africa—now Guinea—and sold to slave traders before eventually ending up in a Natchez, Mississippi, cotton and tobacco plantation.

In Natchez, Ibrahima married another slave, fathered nine children, and eventually became the overseer of the plantation. His story would have ended in a grave in Mississippi, as did the lives of countless other Africans, were it not for a freak meeting in 1807 at a nearby market with a white doctor whose life had been saved by Ibrahima's father years before in Africa. Ibrahima, in town to sell potatoes, spotted the doctor and, recognizing him, approached him, his basket of potatoes balanced on his head.

The doctor immediately recognized Ibrahima as the prince who's family he had stayed with in Africa. "Do you know me?" he asked Ibrahima.

"Yes," Ibrahima replied. "I know you very well."

The doctor tried to purchase Ibrahima's freedom from his owner, who refused to sell him. Years later, a southern journalist told the story to President Adams's secretary of state,

Henry Clay—a founding member of the American Colonization Society—and he personally persuaded Ibrahima's master to set him free and put him on the ship *Harriet* to Liberia.

Unfortunately for Ibrahima, that was where he ran into the Coopers.

Many of the settlers on board the *Harriet* came with prefabricated frames to build houses for themselves when they arrived in Liberia. Besides the wooden planks and joints of the house frames, the settlers also brought kegs of nails and other tools.

Ibrahima didn't have a house frame, but an American Colonization Society agent told him that they had purchased a frame on board the ship from one of the Cooper brothers. Ibrahima approached the Coopers on the ship; they refused to give him the house frame. "I am sorry to say that McPhail disappointed me," Ibrahima later wrote to the American Colonization Society, referring to the agent who said he purchased the house frame from the Coopers. "He told me that he had purchased a house fraim [*sic*] for me and it was on board, but when I arrived here, I found that he had not paid for it." A colonist named Cooper, to whom it belonged, "would not let me have it." A keg of nails, also promised, was not delivered. "I have no house nor can not build one for there is not one nail in the Colony for sale, nor can I get one for love of money."

So the Cooper brothers kept their house frame. They walked off the *Harriet* and viewed Monrovia, their new home. Elijah Johnson had been busy in the past seven years. He had built two forts, with twenty guns each, guarded by two companies of uniformed armed forces, reporting to him. There were now about one hundred houses in Monrovia, along with the church that would evermore be my family's standby—the First United Methodist Church, on Ashmun Street. There was a school and a library. There was even a jail.

Ibrahima wrote to the American Colonization Society that "I shall be in the colony all the rains without a house."

The rainy season started in May, as it always does in Liberia. The Cooper brothers built their house and took cover within its sturdy walls, protected from the rains. The bamboo walls of Ibrahima's makeshift new home were hardly enough to keep him dry. As June progressed, and the new streets of Monrovia became flooded, Ibrahima got sick

On July 6, 1829, just four months after his return home to Africa, Ibrahima died. He was sixty-seven.

Had the American Colonization Society paid the Cooper brothers for the wood frame and the brothers reneged on the deal?

I hope not, but it's doubtful I will ever know the truth of what happened.

All I know is that my great-great-great-grandfather Randolph Cooper and his brothers remained healthy, in the house they erected with their wood frame from Virginia. They started trading the goods they brought with them from Norfolk. Reid and Garret took to the sea, and by the time Reid Cooper turned forty-five, he was commander of the Liberian government schooner *Lark,* and responsible for the safety of the Liberian coast.

The Coopers were coming into their own just as Elijah Johnson's time was coming to an end. Elijah Johnson led numerous army sorties up-country to fight the native Africans, including a foray, with 170 militia and 120 liberated African slaves, into the heart of Liberia to fight the native chief Brumley, who had just sold the slaves to traders. In 1847, Elijah Johnson was a delegate to Liberia's Constitutional Convention, and he was one of the signers of the Declaration of Independence.

Elijah Johnson lived to see the country he ostensibly

founded become the first black Republic in Africa. By the time he died in 1849, Liberia had declared its independence from the United States, expanded its territory all the way to the British-owned Gold Coast and the French-owned Ivory Coast, and, with the help of the British, exterminated the slave trade in that tiny patch of land.

The obituary that ran in the *Liberia Herald* after Elijah Johnson died, of natural causes, reads like a paean:

"His services in the conflicts in which the Colony has been engaged with the natives—in most of which he bore a conspicuous part—were invaluable. His bosom was the seat of a spirit that never quailed. The energies of his mind rose with the exigencies of the occasion; and the furious shock of conflicting hosts, like the collision of flint and steel, only struck out the fire which had laid concealed within."

The Coopers took up the reins of fighting to keep the colony, now a country, alive. In 1851, Reid Cooper commanded the *Lark* when it took Liberia's new president, Joseph Jenkins Roberts, and seventy-five of Elijah Johnson's former militia men, up the coast to Bassa Cove to rescue a group of settlers who were pinned down. In 1854, he turned his ire on the British when a British captain seized a Liberian boat, the *Anna Maria*, which had come to his aid when the British boat *Wellington* sank. The *Wellington*'s commander tried to sail the *Anna Maria* to Freetown. Randolph Cooper, by now a commodore in the Liberian navy, recaptured the *Anna Maria*.

Randolph Cooper eventually married and had a son whom he named after his brother, Reid. And Reid fathered Randolph Cassius Cooper, who fathered John Lewis Cooper Sr., known throughout Liberia as Radio Cooper. And Radio Cooper fathered John Lewis Cooper Jr.

My daddy.

As for Elijah Johnson, before he died in 1849, he fathered

several children, too. One of them, Hillary R. Johnson, became the country's first Liberian-born president. More significantly for me, though, was Elijah Johnson's oldest daughter, Ellen Ray. She was born in Monrovia in 1825. She married Gabriel Moore, a freed black from Mississippi. They had five children, including a daughter, Rachel. And Rachel had a daughter, Johnette Louise, who married Wilmot E. Dennis. Johnette Louise had a short life, dying when she was twenty-eight years old. But before she died, she had three children: my great-uncle Gabriel, my great-aunt Louise, and my grandfather Henry, known throughout Liberia as Captain Dennis. And Captain Dennis fathered Calista Esmeralda Dennis. Mommee.

The poetry was not enough to bring Mommee and Daddy together. Daddy went back to Liberia and married Toulia Dennis, the daughter of another branch of the Dennis family. After Daddy and Toulia divorced five years later, Mommee and Daddy picked up their story again.

By now, Mommee was thirty years old, a veritable old maid by Liberian standards. She was back in Liberia as well, and living at home with Mama Grand after ten years in the United States. She was sick of listening to Mama Grand yelling at the servants. She wanted her own servants to yell at.

One morning a messenger came to the house to inform the two that Ma Galley, Mommee's beloved grandmother and Mama Grand's mother, had died at home. They rushed to Ma Galley's house.

Mommee was sobbing, holding the cold hand of her grandmother. Mama Grand was bustling around the house. She needed some time in the house alone, so she conjured up an errand for her daughter.

"Lah," she said, "go find a doctor."

"What do we need a doctor for? She's dead."

Mama Grand erupted. "We have to have a pronouncement that she's dead! We have to prove she's dead! Go find a
doctor!"

Mommee took her car, a Ford Galaxy, from Ma Galley's
house on Randall Street. It was still early on that Sunday
morning, and Broad Street was still empty, when she saw
Daddy coming out of a local bar. She blew the horn, and he
walked to her window. He smelled like beer. "Where the hell
do you think you're going at this hour?" he said.

"Ma Galley is dead. I have to find a doctor."

"Why do you have to find a doctor if she's dead?"

"Because Mama says we have to pronounce her dead."

Daddy told her to go back to the house. "I'll find a doctor
for you."

Later, when Mama Grand dispatched Mommee to find
someone willing to preach at Ma Galley's funeral, Daddy
stepped in to help, too. The first preacher she had asked had
declined the request. "I can't do it," he told Mommee. "Ma
Galley didn't like me, and to tell you the truth, I didn't care
too much for her either." Daddy steered Mommee toward
Reverend Falkner, who agreed. On the way home, Mommee
ran into a friend of Daddy's, who invited her to a bar to help
console her. She declined, but the friend told Daddy he
thought Mommee was beautiful. Daddy told him to back off.

Mommee decided she would woo Daddy. She was tired of
living at home with Mama Grand. Her friends were all married. People were calling her an old maid. She knew that
Daddy was always drinking with his friends at Max's Corner, a
local bar downtown. She parked her car three blocks away,
prettied up her hair, and walked into the bar. There was an explosion of surprise.

"Lah's in a bar! Who died?" Daddy was there, but so were

all of his friends: Lomax, Clarence Parker, Cecil Dennis. Even Mommee's little brother Waldron (same Ma).

She said: "Something happened to my car. I came here to get a ride home." She looked pointedly at Daddy.

He seemed about to get up when Uncle Waldron jumped up. "I'll take you home!"

She was yelling at him as soon as they got outside. Standing on the dirt sidewalk in front of Max's Corner. "Who asked you to carry me home? I wanted John to carry me home!"

Uncle Waldron was laughing now. "Na mind . . . let's go back inside and I'll say I couldn't find my car keys."

It was an obvious lie, but she didn't care, and went back in the bar. This time Daddy took his cue, but so did everyone else. Lomax was chortling as the two left. "You know Lah just wanted John to carry her home."

He drove her all over Monrovia, past Mama Grand's house on Bushrod Island, heading to the St. Paul riverbank, where they parked. She tried to tell him she wanted to marry him, but instead ended up just telling him she was sick of Mama Grand bugging her all day.

"Is that what you see me as?" he said. "A ticket out of home?" He laughed at first, but then stopped. "This isn't a joke to me."

Ma Gene, Daddy's mother, didn't like Mommee one bit; she felt competitive with Mama Grand, going back to the time Mama Grand took care of her youngest son, Uncle Julius. Back when he was just a baby, Ma Gene and Radio Cooper were up on the farm, and Uncle Julius took ill with malaria. Ma Gene fluttered around with no idea what to do with him. Mama Grand swooped in, moving into the farmhouse and sleeping in the baby's room. She brewed him fever tea—a vile concoction of African tea leaves mixed with basil. She bathed him in cold water to get his fever down and swathed him in blankets when he got chills. She sang to him. She stayed with him for six days, and eventually the baby got better.

Ma Gene thanked her, but nursed a grudge forever. She was not going to react too well to Mama Grand's daughter marrying her precious son.

Mommee knew all that. But nonetheless she told Daddy: "I'm not joking either."

They were married on July 15, 1964.

At the wedding reception, Ma Gene said to one and all: "For decades, that woman has held it over me that she saved Julius's life when he was a baby."

She concluded: "Well, there goes the debt of gratitude."

MONROVIA, LIBERIA, 1978

I always dreaded that my parents would divorce. It was my third biggest fear, right next to the fear that one of them would get abducted by heartmen on the road to Sugar Beach, or my first fear, that I would get sucked into the lagoon by neegee. From the time I turned five years old, I had a coda for the end of my prayers at night: Please don't let Mommee and Daddy get divorced.

Cyrus Vance, Jimmy Carter, William Tolbert, and Cousin Cecil at the state lunch for Carter at the Executive Mansion

They fought all the time, usually over the fact that Daddy, like most Liberian men, had girlfriends. Mommee didn't like that. She would start crying and confront him with questions, and Daddy would get quiet and not answer. And she'd keep asking, and he still wouldn't answer, until finally he'd blow up and yell at her. I could hear them, because my bedroom was right next to their's.

When they weren't fighting, though, they laughed a lot. I loved it when they teased each other, Daddy's deadpan ability to wind Mommee up, the sly smile that spread across his face, Mommee's exasperated eye-rolling when she realized she'd been had again. Daddy was always teasing Mommee for being a worrywart. One Saturday morning, Daddy woke up sneezing. He sneezed every minute or so for what seemed like an hour. He walked around the house, sneezing. Each time he sneezed, he yelled at himself, as if he was Mommee yelling at him.

Sneeze.

"John, go put on your bathrobe!"

Sneeze.

"John, put some slippers on! The floor's cold!"

Sneeze.

"John, get out of that cold pantry!"

Sneeze.

"John, go blow your nose!"

Sneeze.

For almost an hour, he sneezed and received different orders from Mommee to supposedly address why he was sneezing. Jack; Old Man Charlie; and Sammy Cooper were all doubled over in stitches: a rare opportunity to laugh at Mommee. Eunice, Marlene, and I all followed Daddy around the house, giggling.

In retaliation, Mommee put on some opera music, blasting *La Traviata* as loud as the stereo could go. That only made us laugh harder. *La Traviata,* punctuated by Daddy sneezing and yelling at himself as if he was Mommee.

That night they were going to a black-tie ball at the Executive Pavilion in Monrovia. Eunice and I sat on the bed in their room, watching Mommee put on her makeup in the bathroom, while Daddy put on his cuff links in front of the mirror. Mommee wore a strappy black Japanese-looking Oscar de la Renta dress that Daddy bought her in Tokyo. She put dark green eyeshadow on her eyes. Then she ever-so-carefully applied her mascara—black, always black. She bit her tongue between her front teeth to concentrate.

When she went to put on her high-heeled strappy shoes, Eunice and I looked at each other and rolled our eyes.

Sure enough, the argument erupted like clockwork.

Daddy: "I don't like those sandals."

Mommee: "These sandals are Charles Jourdain!"

Daddy: "They make your feet look big."

Mommee: "I am wearing heels, John, like it or not. If you wanted to be taller than your wife you shouldn't have married a Dennis."

Muttering, Daddy dug out his two-inch shoes and they swept out at about the same height.

A month later, Daddy got sick with hepatitis. Mommee said it was because of his drinking. He was in Cooper Clinic for two weeks. We went and visited him every day, marveling at how yellow his eyes were. He had been diagnosed a diabetic about a year earlier and his insulin syringes sat on the bedside table. Every time we visited him and I saw the insulin syringes, I shuddered, imagining him poking himself in the arm or leg.

The whole family, including Ma Gene and Uncle Julius, accompanied him home to Sugar Beach after he got released, under strict doctor's orders to lay off the alcohol. All the way home, Mommee lectured him on his drinking, and told him she would be watching him.

After he got home from the hospital, I took to following Daddy around surreptitiously. I was hiding in the pantry watching him when he came into the kitchen, opened the freezer, and filled one of the ice cube trays with vodka.

A couple of days after Daddy got out of the hospital, Ma Gene showed up and ordered the household to gather in the dining room for prayers. We all stood around the dining table while she droned on. Her eyes were closed, but Eunice and I, standing next to each other, kept our eyes wide open. How else could we see who closed their eyes during prayers?

Eunice looked at me across the table and crossed her eyes. I stifled a giggle and tried to cross my eyes back. Eunice rolled her eyes and shook her head. I tried again, straining until I felt one eyeball shifting. Slowly Eunice became two Eunices. I quickly uncrossed my eyes because Vickie always told us that if our eyes are crossed and the wind changes they stay that way.

Eunice grinned and gave me a surreptitious thumbs-up.

"Someone in this house has a black heart," Ma Gene announced.

Mommee's eyes flew open. She looked like she wanted to pitch Ma Gene out of the window. A horrified gasp escaped Eunice's throat. We all knew Ma Gene meant Mommee. I looked around. Daddy was rolling his eyes. Vicky looked like she wanted to laugh.

Mommee snatched her hand from Ma Gene and walked out of the dining room.

"I guess prayers are over," I said.

Later that night, I heard Daddy consoling a still angry Mommee. "Don't pay any attention to that old lady," he said, soothingly. I fell asleep to the sound of their voices.

But the girlfriend thing wasn't going away. Daddy still had them. Mommee told us that if they got divorced and a judge asked us which one we wanted to stay with, we better pick her. We all promised that we would. She had me cornered in the TV lounge promising one afternoon when I looked up and saw Daddy standing at the doorway.

He turned and walked away, leaving me feeling like Judas.

Mommee and Daddy were barely speaking to each other when President Jimmy Carter, of the United States of America, came to Liberia. It made the all-consuming excitement we were experiencing harder to take: here was the American president, the head of the free world, coming to visit our little country and my parents kept snapping at us, and not talking to each other. Mommee was sulking around the house, locking herself in their room all day playing opera music, while Daddy started coming home later and later at night, sometimes long after we had gone to bed. He started going to the farm every weekend, and stopped taking us with him.

Every time I ran to one of them with a question about Carter, they would refer me to the other one.

The build-up to the Carter trip had Monrovia incoherent with excitement. The government declared it a national holiday. President Tolbert ordered spanking new American limousines to take his entourage to the airport to meet President Carter.

We lined the road from Robertsfield airport all the way to Monrovia, squinting to catch a glimpse of President Carter. At least, that's what most people wanted; Eunice and I were straining to see Amy Carter. We had worked with other Liberian kids on a gigantic mural that had a picture of a blond girl with braces surrounded by a bunch of African kids.

Under the picture, we wrote: THE YOUTH OF LIBERIA WEL-COME YOU, AMY.

The entire Tolbert cabinet went to Robertsfield. Since Bro. Henry was deputy minister of state for presidential affairs, he was right by Tolbert's side when President Carter showed up. On the other side of Tolbert was Uncle Cecil, minister of foreign affairs. No traffic was allowed and the roads, freshly washed, gleamed in the afternoon sun.

From our perch at the side of the road to Sugar Beach, Eunice and I waited and waited and waited for the motorcade to go by. We were sick with anticipation. Would we see Amy?

"Wha' you will tell Amy when you see her?" Eunice asked me. We were sitting side by side on buckets we'd brought from Sugar Beach. There wasn't a stick of shade on the side of the road. We could see the three-headed palm tree that always gave us the marker that we were near Sugar Beach just across the road, but we knew that if we sat under it not only would we have bad luck for the rest of our lives, but we also wouldn't be able to see the motorcade properly.

"I'nt know." The vast universe of things I needed to tell Amy Carter stretched before me, too infinite for me to corral into one straightforward statement. What would I tell her?

"I will ask her if we can move to Sinkor," I finally decided.

"How Amy will move us to Sinkor?"

Good point. "Then I will ask her not to let Mommee divorce Daddy."

"Don't worry," Eunice said. "Aunt Lah will not leave Uncle John."

"How you know?"

"She will not leave him, Helene. You will see." Eunice said it with so much authority I believed her.

"Okay, wha' bout you? Wha' you will ask Amy for?"

Eunice had been thinking about this for some time. "I will ask her to carry me to America w' her."

Now I felt guilty. I knew it wasn't fair, that me and Marlene got to go to America and Spain and Switzerland for vacation every year and Eunice didn't. I didn't know what to say, and the silence just stretched. Then Eunice laughed. "I just joking! Who want go to America?"

We went back to peering down the asphalt in the direction of Robertsfield. Where was the motorcade? All along the road, people were starting to show up from the bush, milling around. We were the only ones who had brought buckets to sit on. A bunch of boys sat on the asphalt, with their backs to the road, facing the bush.

The sweat was rolling down my back as the hour stretched into two, then three. Sammy Cooper arrived with oranges, sent by Tommy, our other cook. "Y'all still waiting here?" he smirked, handing them over.

Tommy had already peeled the oranges for us, slicing off the tops so we could suck the juice out. Greedily I grabbed the biggest orange.

"Here them coming!" Eunice yelled, jumping up. Way in the distance, we could hear the sirens. Peering down the road, finally, finally, I saw the first lights.

I grabbed Eunice's arm. "Wha' you think she will be like?"

Oh, how we wanted to meet Amy! She was the daughter of the American president and she had yellow hair!

The lights grew larger, the wail of the sirens louder. And then it was there, right there, right in front of us going by so fast. The motorcycles in the motorcade passed us first. The police officers riding them glared at us self-importantly.

Then limousine after limousine was upon us. Which one was Amy in?

The motorcade stretched almost a quarter of a mile. Everybody who was anybody had just attached their car to the back and were following the sirens.

Before we knew it, the motorcade had passed. Which one was Amy in? We hadn't even seen Amy!

Eunice and I went running down the dirt road, back to Sugar Beach, skipping, jumping, and yelling. "We saw Amy!" we yelled. "We saw her!"

President Carter stayed in Liberia for exactly four hours. Then he left and went to Nigeria, where he stayed three days.

A few months later, the American news show *60 Minutes* came to Liberia to do one of their famous exposés. Morley Safer heard that Liberia was a country founded by freed American slaves who were now the ruling elite. The Congo People were quick to correct him; our ancestors were *freed American blacks,* not slaves. "But weren't the ancestors of the freed American blacks slaves?" I asked Mommee.

She ignored me.

On the show, A. B. Tolbert, President Tolbert's son, talked at length about his plans for one day ruling all of Africa. Then, when asked by Safer why it was that he, a practicing Baptist minister and president of Liberia, had so many children by women who weren't his wife, he replied that Liberia's system of men constantly committing adultery worked "very well."

The Bernard brothers (same pa) then showed up. Morley Safer asked them how many kids their father had by women other than his wife, and Archie Bernard said, grinning: "Thirteen."

The best thing on the *60 Minutes* show was a full one-minute spiel by Mama Grand blasting out President Carter to the Liberian legislature. Her gold-capped tooth glinted in the glare of the camera lights, as she voiced her ire.

"You see? The president passed through here, and went to

Nigeria and stayed there for days, and came here for few hours. That's your daughter?" she said.

Gathering steam, she continued, her entire demeanor one of affront over America's constant neglect of the country it colonized. "You pass by your daughter and go to somebody else's place and stay two, three days, and you don't even lay your head on one pillow in her house? Tell her! We don't like it. And she must change her ways. Thank you."

Instead of traveling to Spain the summer after I turned twelve, Mommee, Marlene, and I went to Knoxville, Tennessee, to visit Aunt Jeanette and my cousins Bridget and Gabriel, who had just moved to America. We were about one week into the visit, which entailed furious shopping trips to K-Mart and the shopping mall, when the letter arrived from Daddy, postmarked Monrovia. He must have mailed it the same day we left. It was addressed to Mommee. She sat on the back deck outside Aunt Jeanette's house, staring at the pages.

"Your father wants to divorce me," she said. Her voice was devoid of emotion.

My stomach dropped.

Whenever I'd imagined Mommee and Daddy getting divorced, I thought Mommee would leave Daddy, not the other way around. That's why I had taken Eunice's assurance that Mommee wouldn't leave Daddy as gospel; if Mommee didn't leave Daddy, they wouldn't get divorced. It was Mommee who was always talking about how she planned to leave Daddy if he didn't stop having girlfriends. And if Mommee left Daddy, I figured Daddy would beg her and we'd all beg her and talk her into coming back. I had a lot of faith in my ability to talk Mommee into coming back to Daddy if she left him.

Never, not once, had I thought it would be Daddy who would leave. I hadn't practiced talking him out of leaving.

My mouth opened but no sound came out. I turned away and left Mommee on the back deck.

The whole extended family was at the airport to meet us on our return to Liberia. They were all gathered in the VIP lounge, in what was supposed to be a show of support for Mommee, but what, in retrospect, was an awful intrusion on a painful, private family moment. On one side of the lounge was Mama Grand, Bro. Henry, Aunt Momsie, CeRue, Michelle, Ethello, and Uncle Waldron. Eunice and Vicky were there, too, kind of in the middle, not sure where to ally themselves. On the other side, sitting alone at the bar nursing a gin and tonic, was Daddy.

Up until the moment when I saw him sitting by himself, I had hated him. I couldn't believe he was leaving us, most likely for some floozy he would dump in two minutes. Didn't he love us?

But Daddy looked so alone sitting there by himself, waiting for us to arrive. Mommee was immediately surrounded by her family, who had been shooting nasty looks at Daddy. Daddy got up and walked over to me and Marlene, like he wasn't sure what to say or do. Marlene turned her back on Daddy and ran over to Mommee. I offered him my cheek, and he walked behind me to baggage claim, his arm awkwardly around my shoulder. I could smell his English Leather after-shave and his hair tonic.

Daddy drove back to Sugar Beach that night by himself, while the rest of us piled into cars with the family. I was anxious to get rid of the extended family, because I was sure that once we got together alone at Sugar Beach, Daddy would say he had made a mistake and that he wasn't leaving after all. And if he didn't I planned to talk him out of it.

At Sugar Beach, I ran upstairs first, heading straight to Mommee and Daddy's room, where I looked in the closet.

All of Daddy's suits were gone. His shirts were gone. In the bathroom, only Mommee's toiletries remained. Daddy's hair tonic was gone. So was his English Leather cologne.

I stood alone staring into the closet for several minutes. In the distance, I could hear the rest of the extended family bringing in our suitcases and trooping around the house.

Finally, Mama Grand and the family left. Mommee and Daddy went into the living room, while I sat with Marlene, Eunice, and Vicky in Marlene's room, staring at one another quietly. After about thirty minutes, Daddy came into the room and asked Marlene and me to join them in the living room. The separation, between the two sets of Sugar Beach daughters, took none of us by surprise. Marlene and I left Vicky and Eunice and trailed after Daddy.

Marlene and I sat on one side of the living room, across the table from Mommee and Daddy. They were supposed to be presenting a united front, but really it was only Daddy talking. Mommee wouldn't look at any of us, just looked into the corner, her back rigid.

"Please don't leave." Finally, I'd said it. I just knew that if I begged, he would stay.

He said, "Sometimes things don't work out."

He said he loved Mommee, but that they couldn't live together. He said he loved us, that nothing would change. He said we'd spend weekends with him. He said he'd be staying with Ma Gene.

I wanted to tell him, "No way! If you're not going to live with us then I'm not going to come spend no weekend with you." But what was the point. I was angry. Did he think he would find something better than us? We wanted to be with him; why didn't he want to be with us?

Marlene just sat on the couch and cried. Mommee seemed to be in a trance.

Finally, Daddy got up. I followed him into the kitchen and out the back door.

Daddy, I hold your foot, don't leave us.

He turned to me, cocking his head to one side in that familiar motion I knew so well.

"Daddy, please, I beg you."

He said nothing, just pressed his lips together. His eyes were filmy with tears. He put his hand on my shoulder and started to say something. But then he stopped, turned, and ran down the back porch steps and got in his car.

I stood on the back porch steps watching him drive out of the yard. It seemed like it took the taillights forever to disappear.

The next day, Mommee drove into town. When she came back, she had new license plates with her. No longer were they CDC-1 and CDC-2. Now they said CD-1 and CD-2.

From then on, except for the servants, it was only women at Sugar Beach.

11

SUGAR BEACH, LIBERIA, 1979

$\mathcal{T}$he first battle of our war was on April 14, 1979. It was a little skirmish, only the first shot, really. But at the time, we thought the sky had fallen.

Native Liberians were still angry at the Congo People. The two sides had never settled the land issue that pitted them against each other when they first met in 1822. For 150 years, the Congo People had engaged in one of the most extensive land grabs anywhere. Some families had acquired es-

---

Eunice, Helene, Marlene, Michelle, Jim, and Gabriel at Caesar's Beach

tates of up to twenty thousand acres for as little as fifty cents an acre. Increasingly, native Liberians were waking up and discovering that they had sold off what little land they had to Congo People, spent the money, and were left to farm as tenants on their own ancestral land. By 1979, four percent of the population owned sixty percent of the wealth.

The perfect example of this was Bentol, the recently renamed town that President Tolbert's family had gobbled up. Before the freed blacks came to Liberia, the area was owned by the Deys. In the 1860s, it was renamed Bensonville, after then-president Stephen Allen Benson. Tolbert ancestors settled there upon their arrival from South Carolina. When Tolbert became president, Bensonville was renamed Bentol, in his honor, and the place was transformed into a Versailles, Liberian-style. Each family member had their own opulent estate with high walls and security systems to keep out rogues. While bare-footed Country children begged on the side of the road for food and money, the Tolberts built a private zoo and an artificial lake for motorboat racing and waterskiing, that not-so-famous Liberian pastime. They made Bentol the new county seat for Montserrado.

Monrovia had a growing middle class, but that growing middle class was experiencing growing inflation. Enrollment of children in primary schools had doubled to sixty-six percent from thirty-one percent in 1960, but Liberia's adult illiteracy rate was still about seventy-five percent. New paved roads into the countryside provided better collection opportunities for collectors of an odious government "hut tax."

The Country People were finally agitating for change. After 150 years of one-party rule—the True Whig Party of old-guard Congos—people started to ask why there were no opposition parties? The dissent started at the University of Liberia, where Amos Sawyer, a political science professor from

Greenville, Sinoe County, began making noises about running for mayor of Monrovia against the True Whig Party's candidate, Edward Davis, President Tolbert's nephew. The hard-line Congo establishment promptly labeled Amos Sawyer an agitant, but other agitants were sprouting up like anthills on the savannah.

President Tolbert was torn. Unlike his predecessor, he didn't have the native Liberian political base because he hadn't bought off the village chiefs. The previous president, William V. S. Tubman, kept a lid on Congo-Country tensions by making sure powerful chiefs up-country were kept healthy and happy through routine government payments. The money seldom filtered down to the local people, but President Tubman nonetheless depended on the chiefs to keep their people in order.

When Tolbert came to power, he ended that under-the-table system under the guise of modernizing the government and cracking down on corruption and embezzlement.

Meanwhile, Tolbert wasn't strong enough to stand up to the hard-liners in his own administration who urged him to clamp down on political dissent. The True Whig Party had split into two camps: the reformers and the hard-liners. At first, the progressive wing seemed to have the edge. The progressive reformers, including Uncle Cecil Dennis, the minister of foreign affairs; Clarence Parker, the treasurer of the True Whig Party; and James T. Phillips, the minister of finance, argued for getting rid of the ridiculous property clause in the Liberian constitution that required voters to own land. They argued in favor of legal opposition parties. They said dissent should be encouraged.

The progressive wing was in favor of a slow reform—too slow to satisfy the increasingly restless population. Uncle Cecil, tall, mustached, with a deep mahogany complexion, looking like a black Omar Sharif, always cut an imposing figure in his white two-piece swearing-in suit, the self-consciously casual attire that President Tolbert made his ministers wear. My parents always derided the swearing-in suits. "You'll never catch me wearing that nonsense," Daddy said once, decked out in his usual western-style suit and tie. "That is just common," Mommee agreed.

Uncle Cecil never paid Mommee much mind when she ribbed him about wearing the suit. "Laugh all you want," he said. "I'm just doing my job."

Uncle Cecil invited lead agitant Amos Sawyer to his house in Sinkor to chastise him for pushing too hard in his drive to run for mayor of Monrovia. The two sat in the living room of Uncle Cecil's house, with the security guard at the gate.

"You're being too pushy," Uncle Cecil told Amos Sawyer. "Slow down." He told Amos Sawyer the reformers in the True Whig Party were having a hard time pushing back hard-liners like Joseph Chesson and Richard Henries, the powerful minister of justice and the speaker of the house. If it were up to those two, he said, all political agitants would be locked up in jail.

The meeting between the two didn't go well. "We've been waiting for 150 years," Amos Sawyer argued. He left Uncle Cecil's house angry, and promptly fired off a letter to him telling him so.

Three days later, Amos Sawyer received a reply from Uncle Cecil. He opened the letter, and looked at it, astonished.

It was in legalese. He could barely make out anything beyond the "Dear Mr. Sawyer." Uncle Cecil had written page after page of legal gibberish, peppering his phrases with words no one but a trained lawyer could understand, like *sua sponte* (Latin for "of one's own will").

"What the hell is this man trying to say?" Amos Sawyer

thought. It took him a good day to finally boil down the letter
to one message: "Don't blame me for doing my job."

Amos Sawyer eventually saw the humor in Uncle Cecil's
letter. But that didn't stop him from pushing for change. The
time was now, he thought.

Ignoring the political simmering, Liberia's Congo threw
themselves into preparing for the big parties they had planned
around the upcoming OAU meeting. In 1979, Liberia had the
presidency of the Organization of African Unity, the umbrella
organization of African countries. (Except South Africa,
whose apartheid white government was not welcome.) Liberia
was hosting the OAU meeting in July, and feverishly trying to
apply cosmetic repairs to its social holes. Rich Congo busi-
nessmen, aided by equally rich Lebanese merchants, were
building beachfront resorts. The Hotel Africa opened up, with
its disco and dance hall, Bacardi's, and its outdoor cabanas
and villas. It was the talk of the town: Liberians had a new
place to party. Hotel Africa soon became the spot for wedding
receptions and cool seventies themed parties. All the disco
dances from the States made their way to Bacardi's, from the
Bus Stop to the Robot to the Hustle.

New American cars started showing up at the port, all des-
tined for proud Congo or Lebanese owners. Uncle Waldron,
fresh from Las Vegas where he'd won more than $100,000,
showed up with a new car for each one of his siblings: Aunt
Momsie got an orange Thunderbird, Bro. Henry got a brown
Lincoln Town Car, and Mommee got a tan Chevrolet Caprice
Classic, four-doors, just like she liked them, to supplement her
two-year-old two-toned green Pontiac Grand Prix: Mommee's
old Lincoln Continental Mark IV (CDC-1) promptly got
kicked to the curb.

Uncle Waldron, a forty-year-old bachelor, bought himself
a black Corvette and parked it right in front of Hotel Africa.

All the looking-for-a-good-catch Liberian women made eyes at him when he walked into Bacardi's sporting his aviator sunglasses. The women never talked much, but posed, solo, on the bar stools, legs crossed, feet clad in stilettos, or languidly on the arms of the Congo and Lebanese men who strutted about, smoking cigarettes and drinking Club Beer.

Giant posters of each OAU member head-of-state lined Tubman Boulevard, although six of the posters were blank because those countries were in the middle of various coups and revolutions and no one was sure who the head of state would be when the conference started. The government purchased forty motorcycles to escort the motorcades of the visiting African heads of state. Within three days, half of them had been wrecked by their drivers. But so what? Liberia was preparing for the biggest show on the African stage.

Into all of this frenzied preparation, President Tolbert announced a fifty percent increase in the price of rice, the Liberian staple. The rationale he presented was that if he increased the price of imported rice, consumed by ninety-nine percent of the population, Liberians would be forced to grow their own rice and would stop being dependent on foreign rice, and become self-sufficient.

For weeks, the radio airwaves were full of government-sponsored advertisements pushing President Tolbert's new plan raising the price of rice.

"I'm proud to be a farmer's daughter!" (Country woman's voice in radio commercial)
"I'm proud to be a farmer's son!" (Country man)
"No more pussava rice after 1980!" (Congo man)
"If you don't work, you won't eat!" (Congo woman)
"And if you cannot feed yourself, we cannot feed the nation!" (Congo man)

But the average monthly income of Liberians living in the city was about eighty dollars. Tolbert's new price increase would raise the price of a bag of rice to thirty dollars. For all of his talk about economic self-sufficiency and the need for Liberians to grow their own rice, Tolbert hadn't bothered to include rice as one of the "export crops" that the government subsidized. So most growers and farmers did not produce rice and had, as anyone would, focused instead on growing the crops that were subsidized and for which they could get more money.

Tolbert said that he was trying to make Liberia more independent, but it's hard to see how making rice, the staple of every Liberian's diet, too costly for most Liberians would make the country independent. The rice affair was seen in the Congo community as business as usual; after all, we could afford to pay thirty dollars for a bag of rice, even if we didn't like doing so. But in native Liberian circles, it was the last straw. Egged on by the burgeoning political movement of students and professors at the University of Liberia, thousands of native Liberians showed up for a protest march on Saturday morning, April 14.

Tolbert deployed police and soldiers along the main route of the march, and placed army tanks at the intersections in a not-so-subtle display of power. The soldiers didn't fire on the unarmed protestors. But the Monrovia police weren't quite so restrained, and quickly forsook the tear gas they were supposed to be using and started firing indiscriminately into the crowd. The planned demonstrations quickly degenerated into a full-fledged riot. By the end of the day, more than fifty protestors were dead, and hundreds more were injured. Uncontrolled looting continued over the next two days.

A hysterical Tolbert sent for Amos Sawyer and a number of other political dissenters and religious leaders that Saturday afternoon as the riots continued in Monrovia. The men reported to the Executive Mansion, where President Tolbert and his justice minister, Joseph Chesson, were waiting for them. "You see what you all have done?" an enraged Tolbert said. "You all happy now?"

"Mr. President, the police opened fire on unarmed demonstrators," Amos Sawyer said. "Let's not give up on reform now."

President Tolbert snorted. "Reform? We've got an uprising outside and you're talking about reform?" He turned to Joseph Chesson, and told him to suppress the uprising by any means available.

Reaching into his pocket, Chesson took out a sheet of paper. On it was a list of names of wanted ringleaders of the demonstration. They were mostly students, but included Gabriel Baccus Matthews, Teepoteh, and Chea Cheapoo, who, incidentally, had been a ward of Joseph Chesson.

"There are warrants out for their arrest," Chesson told Amos Sawyer. "Tell them that if they don't turn themselves in, they will be hunted down." Amos Sawyer hurried out of the room to deliver the message.

President Tolbert called for reinforcements from neighboring Guinea. The Guinean president, Sekou Toure, sent MiG fighter planes to make low passes over Monrovia. That, in itself, was enough to terrify most Liberians. A protest that began with some two thousand students demonstrating peacefully had degenerated into riots with foreign fighter jets roaring over the capital.

On the Saturday morning of the planned rice protest, Fedeles and Eunice picked me up after my morning ballet class, near the American embassy in Mamba Point. I wheedled Fedeles into letting me drive. I was just about to turn thirteen, and had been sneaking drives with Fedeles for a month. Daddy had let me drive his pickup truck on the dirt road up at the farm, but had banned me from trying to drive in the city, so I was left to sneak my city driving when it was just me and Fedeles. Mommee was completely in the dark.

"I telling Aunt Lah!" Eunice yelled from the backseat as soon as I got behind the wheel.

"Then I telling her you went to that party with Vicky when you were supposed to be at Aunt Momsie's!" I was a strong believer in nuclear retaliation against conventional weapons.

Unfortunately, so was Eunice. "Then I will tell her you've been reading Vicky's books!" Vicky had stashed dirty books and *Playgirl* magazines under her bed, and I'd found them and been devouring them, muffling my laughter at the pictures of naked white men posing on the sides of their boats. Eunice caught me locked in Vicky's room one afternoon while Vicky was away, and had been holding this over my head.

The two of us were still bickering when we rounded the corner by the Capital Bypass and ran smack into the rice riot. Within seconds, hundreds of young men surrounded the car.

"Get from behind the wheel!" Fedeles yelled at me. I scrambled to the backseat with Eunice, knocking my knee against the emergency brake. Fedeles contorted himself from the passenger seat to the driver's seat and took the wheel, slamming the car into reverse. Outside, a swarm of young boys were pushing against the car. One banged his hand on the window. Fedeles quickly wound the windows down, so they couldn't break the glass. Immediately, the car filled with the scent of unwashed bodies, and the sounds of staccato gunfire. For a few seconds, all I could see were the ragged T-shirts worn by the boys. An arm shoved its way into the back window at me, and I cowered closer to Eunice. She had her arm around me, and was yelling at Fedeles to reverse the car. "B-b-b-back

up! Back up!" she yelled, her stutter immediately more pronounced.

Ignoring the crush of people now behind the car, Fedeles
backed up. He was intent on running anybody over who didn't
get out of the way. I heard someone yelling: "Move from the
way oh! Move from the way oh!" Turning the wheel furiously,
Fedeles spun the car around as the crowd behind us cleared,
and we peeled off in the direction from which we had come.
We would be taking the long way home, across the bridge, via
Bushrod Island.

Eunice and I were incoherent with excitement when we
finally got back to Sugar Beach that day. I had never used the
word *riot* in a sentence before in my life, and didn't know that
that was what we had just seen. Instead, I kept talking about
the crowd of angry Country People.

"They surrounded the car! They were gonna kill us!" I
said.

"Aunt Lah, you should have seen all those people oh!" Eunice said. "You should have seen them! You should have seen
them!"

We spent the whole day at Sugar Beach, with no phone,
listening to the radio. Government officials spoke over and
over about "agitants" at the University of Liberia who had
stirred the Country People into rioting about rice. Late that
afternoon, a car came up the driveway with the news that my
second cousin Gabriel Scott—not to be confused with my first
cousin Gabriel Dennis—had been killed in a gunfight near the
university. Gabriel was a policeman in the Monrovia force.

"This is ashtray," Mommee kept saying.

April 14, for me, became about the shooting death of my
second cousin. We had not been that close—he was ten years
older than me and always seemed so sophisticated, worlds
away from my silly adolescent life. But he was one of our own.

One of our own had been killed. How could that have happened? I threw myself into preparations for the funeral.

But there were other dead. Estimates of the number of demonstrators killed on April 14 range from 40 to 140. Two days later government workers used shovels to dig a huge hole next to the cemetery that would become the home to those put to death by Liberia's government. The bodies were thrown into the mass grave, directly next to Palm Grove Cemetery on Center Street, where Congo society was buried. Dead Coopers are buried in the Cooper plot, which, as it happens, is right next to where dead Dennises are buried in the Dennis plot.

Following the rice riots, President Tolbert rounded up every political opponent he could find. He suspended the writ of habeas corpus, and charged thirty-three protest organizers and political dissidents, including Gabriel Baccus Matthews, a Congo Liberian educated in the United States and agitator supreme, with "treason and attempting to overthrow the government," charges that carried the death penalty. He ordered the University of Liberia, that hotbed of political discontent, closed. Tolbert had decided that the best way to restore calm was to suspend what little civil liberties existed in Liberia.

Tolbert also quietly rescinded his order raising the price of rice, but few took notice of that, what with the seven hundred Guinean soldiers trooping about Monrovia. Nor did many take notice of the growing alienation of Liberia's own military, whose dignity had been affronted by the call-up of the Guineans.

Liberia was like a pot of water that had been put on the stove at a slow boil and forgotten about. For years, I had thought Liberia was one of the few peaceful countries where disasters did not occur. We didn't get earthquakes or tidal waves or monsoons, and we certainly didn't have wars. That was for places like Lebanon. As the forgotton pot of water got hotter and hotter, I took no notice.

With the much anticipated OAU meeting coming up and all those African heads of state coming to town, it would look unseemly for Tolbert to have all those protestors locked up at the barracks at Barclay Training Center. So he struck a deal with Matthews, who, as head of new political dissident party PAL (Progressive Alliance of Liberians), was representing the rice protestors. The deal was truly Liberian—style over substance. From his prison cell, Matthews wrote a groveling letter of apology to Tolbert, and promised to refrain from public acts against the government.

Tolbert responded in the same quaint style and "extended the hand of forgiveness" by declaring a general amnesty. Then he released the rice riot detainees.

Monrovia could get back to the parties and celebrations around the OAU meeting. Both native and Congo Liberians who didn't have squat to do with the OAU showed up at Hotel Africa every day, decked in their finest attire, to strut their stuff. R&B and West African highlife music blared through the nights and into the mornings. The government brought in a forty-year-old cruise ship that docked in the port and turned it into a hotel for reporters and delegates. The ship had a casino and a bar, and Liberians went nuts at the idea of high-rolling, Vegas-style. In fact, so many people showed up on the summit's last night that the ship's captain ordered everyone to leave, fearing the cruise ship would sink. The partying Liberians refused to leave. It took Monrovia's police force, outfitted in riot gear, helmets, and billy clubs, to finally clear out the casino.

We started the new school year at ACS in September 1979. For the third time in a row, I ran for student government—this time to represent my ninth-grade class in the Student Council. During my campaign I ended my speech with a dire warning to the class: "Life," I said, "is what you make it. Make it good and it will be good. Make it bad and you will be sorry."

I told them that those were the immortal words of Paul Lang, an America poet. I made it all up, including Paul Lang. I had heard a similar saying somewhere, but couldn't remember where. I figured no one else at ACS would know either. It worked. I won the race for one of the two class senator seats, along with Michelle Veakins, an Irish girl who had lived in Liberia all her life and spoke Liberian English like a Bassa.

We beat Aloysius, a new student in our class, and a native Liberian. Can you imagine? I whispered to Michelle. Here he is, just new to the school, and Country to boot, and he has the nerve to run for student council already?

The first day of school, Aloysius showed up wearing a "Sawyer for Mayor" T-shirt! He walked into home room, and my friend, Veda Nyoth, pointed to his shirt and busted out laughing. "Sawyer for Mayor!" she said. "Are you crazy?"

Aloysius sat in his chair, folded his arms, leaned back, and sneered at us. His clothes weren't as up-to-date as the rest of the class: besides his T-shirt, he wore gray slacks that he had clearly grown out of.

He seemed to have a permanent snarl on his face. Whenever he looked at me, with my new American jeans and trendy T-shirts, I felt like he was judging me and finding me wanting. He didn't seem to care one whit that he didn't have friends; in fact, he seemed to not want to be friends with us. "He acts like he despises us," I whispered to Veda. She nodded. "He's got a chip on his shoulder, that's for sure," she said.

Veda was one of the many Liberians whose ancestors had helped make Liberia a melting pot of the African diaspora: her father was Cameroonian and her mother was born to a Grebo woman, Alma Quadayou Carter (whose real name was changed from Cala to Carter because the missionaries wanted the converts westernized), and a naturalized Togolese man, Adolf Ajavon.

The reality of Liberia, in some ways, transcended Congo and Country. In the years since Elijah Johnson and Randolph Cooper had arrived, Liberia had become a destination point for black people from all over the world. Africans had come to Liberia, fleeing colonialism in other African countries. A huge group came from Sierra Leone (including the Bright family), Guinea (some wealthy Muslim families), Ivory Coast, Ghana, Togo, and Nigeria.

Blacks emigrated to Liberia from the West Indies too—including the former president Edwin Barclay. Ever so slowly, during the hundred and fifty years since the arrival of Elijah Johnson, all of these groups had started to coalesce into something more than just Congo People and Country People.

But the change wasn't happening fast enough to cool down that pot of water, which had now reached a slow boil.

At the Ministry of Foreign Affairs, which my uncle Cecil Dennis headed, a young native Liberian named Joseph Guannu was hired. Uncle Cecil gave him a big title: director of training and development. Mr. Guannu, a graduate of the University of Montana, held two Ph.Ds.

At first, Mr. Guannu was excited about his new job. But frustration crept in quickly. Uncle Cecil wouldn't let him train anyone; the jobs actually training future diplomats went to the old Congo guard, while Mr. Guannu, with his two Ph.Ds., was relegated to writing speeches for Uncle Cecil.

At about the same time that Mr. Guannu was getting more and more frustrated at work, Mommee took Eunice to see Uncle Cecil at the Ministry of Foreign Affairs.

The two of them swept in on a rainy morning in August.

The ministry was next to the Executive Mansion, across from the University of Liberia and City Hall. Eunice wore a pantsuit that Mommee had just had made for her by Gay, her Mandingo tailor.

"Cecil, you know Eunice, my foster daughter," Mommee said, making a formal introduction. "She'll be graduating from high school next year." Eunice sat in the leather guest chair, stuttering up a storm, so great was her terror. Uncle Cecil was one of the most powerful men in Liberia.

He smiled at Eunice, and she calmed down. Thirty minutes later, she and Mommee walked out of the Ministry of Foreign Affairs with a promise from Uncle Cecil that Eunice would get a government scholarship to go to college in the United States.

Eunice was giddy all the way home. She, Eunice Patrice Bull, who had never been out of Liberia and barely out of Monrovia even, was going to go to America for college. The possibilities were huge. The first thing she said when she saw me was: "I going to America."

"A-ya, Eunice," I said, my mouth open in admiration. I knew I wasn't going anywhere until I graduated from high school—four years away.

"When I come back from America," she bragged, "I'm gonna be a 'been-to.'"

My admiration quickly turned to jealousy. I had been to America and Spain and Switzerland, but only for vacation, so I couldn't claim "been-to" status.

And now Eunice was going to be a "been-to" before me.

Still, in 1979, the possibilities for me seemed huge as well. I was finally in the ninth grade—a full-fledged high schooler. I was finally popular, the result of simply outlasting most of the transient students at ACS. Life had settled down since my parents' divorce; Mommee and Daddy seemed to spend more time together now than they did when they were married, and Daddy sometimes spent weekends at our house.

I was suddenly tall. I, at long last, had acquired breasts. People were suddenly telling me how much I looked like Mommee.

And during this year, the last tragic year of the Congo regime in Liberia, I finally discovered boys.

12

SUGAR BEACH, LIBERIA, 1979

*A*ugust 1979 to May 1980, my ninth-grade year at the American Cooperative School, Old Road, Monrovia, Liberia, West Africa, encapsulated everything that would be Part One of my life.

It's all there: the taste of the Tuc biscuits—a more buttery, salty version of Ritz crackers—that I ate for lunch every

---

Earl, Tello, Philip Parker, and Helene at wedding reception

day when I walked to the shop across the street from school; the smell of the bleachers in the ACS gymnasium—turpentine mixed with rubber; the feel of my green linen blouse that I always seemed to be wearing during the big events of that year, from the Sadie Hawkins dance to the Miss ACS beauty pageant to the night of May 16 when we went to Robertsfield.

All I have to do is close my eyes and I'm thirteen years old again. I have one best friend, Eunice, and lots of other friends, a place in the school choir, a permanent seat on the "in-crowd" trips to the beach on Saturdays, and a crush on Philip Clarence Parker IV.

He was simpatico, a word Mommee used when she wanted to show that she knew a little Italian, usually referring to good-looking foreign men who had tried to get her to marry them. ("Bertil Solander was simpatico! I don't know why Papa wouldn't let me marry him! He wanted to take me to Hong Kong!")

Philip was definitely simpatico. He was from an old Congo family, the son of Philip Clarence Parker III, a banker who was the treasurer of the True Whig Party and founder of Parker Paint. His mother, a pharmacist, was from the Bright family, which boasted a couple of government ministers.

Philip was athletic. He was a starting forward on the ACS boys varsity basketball team.

He was smart. A senior at ACS, he was planning to major in chemical engineering when he graduated and went to college in America. Philip and his brother, Richard, had basically been around all my life. Philip was three years older than Richard, and Richard and I were born one month apart. Richard had been in my class at ACS since fourth grade.

Everyone called Philip PCP, from the cool guys who hung out in front of the shop across the street to the cool teenage girls who all seemed to have crushes on him. I had heard that

PCP was some kind of drug, so I always laughed in what I hoped was a sophisticated manner when people said "There's PCP," and Philip walked into a room.

He was always smiling. He had one of those shy smiles that crinkled his eyes and made him look as if he wasn't sure you really wanted to talk to him, but if you did, why, then, he'd be overjoyed to talk back to you.

He was fierce, Liberian English for good-looking: five-foot-eleven, with a chocolate complexion and a really cute, tight butt and a washboard stomach and one dimple.

"Yes, Helene," Eunice said one night as I regaled her with Philip's virtues. "You now talk 'bout his smiling eyes. You now talk 'bout his tight butt. You now talk 'bout his dimple. Please, please, please leave people alone about PC." PC was another of Philip's nicknames, in case PCP was too long to say.

We were hanging out in my room listening to my new record player. Eunice and I were both enthralled with the latest disco songs.

The song we both loved the most was "I Don't Love You Anymore" by Teddy Pendergrass. It was dramatic, filled with declarative sentences. In front of the mirror in my bedroom Eunice and I practiced how we planned to get boyfriends and then sack them. (I had no intention of sacking Philip in the unlikely event that I ever even got him to notice me, but I played along with Eunice anyway.) "I'm sorry," we practiced saying, tossing our heads. "It's like Teddy Pendergrass said. I just don't love you anymore."

Eunice actually got to carry out our plan. She chose the perfect moment: after school, as the Haywood kids were milling around with the ACS kids on Old Road. Her boyfriend, James Sirleaf, a fellow classmate at Haywood, was innocently buying orange Fanta and kola nuts at the shop across the street from the schools.

Eunice had been "going out" with James for a whole month, so it was long past time to sack him anyway. He was nice enough, but boring, never having anything much to say beyond how beautiful he thought Eunice was. Any guy worth his salt should have known that was a recipe for being sent to the shed. Adding to James's disfavor, Eunice, like me, had identified a new love. At the same time I'd decided Philip Parker was for me, Eunice decided she was in love with Cherif Abdullah, a wealthy Congo-Mandingo boy. Cherif was tall and lanky with chocolate skin and an Afro, and he talked in a really low voice, as if he was too cool to have vocal chords.

He winked at Eunice occasionally when we were at the movies on Saturdays, and he asked her to dance at Philip's party a couple of weeks before. They danced one fast record, but that was enough for Eunice. After much practicing at home with me at night, she was ready for the dramatic encounter with poor James.

Still wearing her school uniform—yellow shirt and black skirt—she strode across that street to the shop, trailed by me, Marlene, Vicky, and a few ACS friends. "James! Come here! I need to talk to you!"

James never knew what hit him. Before he could open his mouth, Eunice was off and running: "It's over," she said. "I've found true love."

"Hehhn?" James said.

"You and me are finished. Please don't be too sad. It wasn't meant to be."

James started to talk. Eunice and I had practiced the night before for when he tried to talk. She was spectacular.

"Stop!" she interrupted, holding up her palm in a dramatic "stop" gesture. "In the name of love, I can't listen anymore! It's too painful."

With that, she turned in a glorious flounce and strode out

to Fedeles in the waiting Mercedes. We followed, poking each other in the ribs. How fantastic.

The next week Cherif showed up at school "all-hugged-up" with an eleventh-grade girl. Rounding the hall from English class, I stared at the couple, aghast. When had this happened? Why had he been running around winking at Eunice?

On the Philip Parker front, I was having my own problems.

I started my campaign for him in the tried-and-true way: I ignored him whenever I saw him. Seeing him walk down the hallway toward me, I looked everywhere but at him. Finally he passed me, which gave me the green light to turn and stare at his butt until he was out of sight.

Several weeks of this yielded no results. Then one afternoon, after school, Michelle Veakins and I were hanging around on the triangle-columns out front, waiting for Fedeles. We'd just finished a student council meeting. "I'm not telling you who I like," I announced to Michelle. "You'll tell everybody." That was a vain invitation to get Michelle to try to guess, and hopefully come up with Philip on her own, by realizing that I was cool enough to maybe land a senior. Michelle immediately got busy guessing the boys in our class, like Lennart van den Ende, the cute Dutch boy.

"No, not Lennart!" I snapped. "My true love is a *man,* not no ninth-grader!"

"Emmett Dennis?"

"Michelle, I will hurt you oh."

Suddenly, the door of the school gymnasium opened, and a sweaty Philip walked out, wearing his ACS Sundevils basketball uniform—tank top and shorts—with a ball tucked under one arm. I was immediately frozen.

He walked over to us and stopped. "How you doing, Cooper?" he said.

I just nodded, grinning foolishly.

Philip smiled, and walked to his blue Honda. I was standing there, heart pounding, staring at his butt, having completely forgotten about Michelle, when I heard her yell, "Eh-Henh!!!!!"

"Eh-Henh" is one of those expressions that any Liberian, or white Irish girl who grew up in Liberia and therefore thinks she's Liberian, knows. It means: "Aha! I've caught you!"

"Shut up!" I whispered, furious. "He'll hear you!"

"Eh-Henh, eh-henh, eh-henh!" Michelle was bouncing up and down, making that "caught-you" motion that Liberians do with our fingers, taking one finger and swatting through the air until it hits the thumb.

"Michelle, I swear, you don't shut up, I will hurt you."

But the damage was done.

Michelle wasted no time. The next day, she walked into Algebra 1, took one look at me, and then announced to Richard Parker: "Helene wants your brother." I felt the blood heating up my face, as Richard pounced. At first, I tried to deny it. "I don't know what Michelle's talking about!"

I soon realized that it was hopeless, so I changed tactics. "Richard, I beg you, don't tell him."

But that, too, was a lost cause. I had just spent the last few weeks torturing Richard about his girlfriend, Patience Jabba. I'd written notes on the blackboard, made up songs making fun of her name. There was no way Richard was going to ignore the fat juicy plum Michelle had just placed in his lap.

After class, I followed Richard to the front of the school, still begging. "Richard, I hold your foot. Please." He just kept laughing. "Don't worry, Helene Cooper. I won't tell a soul." Then he looked over at where his brother was walking toward us, and said, "Philip! Guess what!"

I was at the Haywood gate in under five seconds, looking for Eunice. All the way home she tried to comfort me, but I was inconsolable. In the ninth grade, there seemed nothing worse in the world than for the boy you liked to know you liked him.

Outside my little bubble, Congo-Country tensions were heating up. More and more now, people seemed to be staking out what side they were on. All of a sudden, some Congo People were claiming that they were Country, declaring tribal affiliations like a badge of honor. "Don't call me Congo, my grandma da Vai woman," my cousin CeRue actually had the gall to say to me.

"Oh, gimme a break, CeRue!" I said. But I muttered, "I got Country blood, too!"

"I beg you ya!" she hooted. "I say, Eunice! Guess who say she Country! This red Cooper girl!"

Eunice just laughed.

Richard told Philip—and everyone else at school, Relda, and greater Monrovia. I was furious. But Richard got his own comeuppance soon after.

At twilight one evening, Richard took a shortcut home via the beach, trying to avoid the German shepherds that lived on the street nearby. He knew better than to walk on the beach at night, but thought he could make it home before it got really dark. The moon was already out, and the sky was pretty clear. Richard strolled along the top half of the beach, the sandy part. The strong surf of the Atlantic Ocean beat the shore. That's probably why Richard didn't hear the silent approach of the heartman behind him.

Finally, Richard felt someone approaching, and turned and looked. About a hundred yards away, but running toward him at a flat-out speed, was a man with a machete. He also had two knives dangling onto his pants. He had no shirt.

Richard wasted no time, and started running like a demon was chasing him. At first, he put space between him and the heartman, but his first burst of energy quickly drained him, and the heartman started to catch up.

Richard realized that one reason the heartman was catching up with him was because he was running on the wet part of the sand, while Richard was clinging to the soft part. So Richard veered closer to the water. It allowed him to run faster, but also had the disadvantage of placing him farther from the houses.

The heartman steadily gained on Richard, until Richard, looking back, could see the carvings on his face. He was now only about eight feet away, and gaining. Digging deep, Richard accelerated one more time, and cut sharply to the left, plowing back into the soft sand. He was close enough to see the lights of his own house.

The heartman followed Richard up the incline and onto the road leading to Richard's house. He swung his machete back, preparing to fling it. Richard started yelling: "Mom! Philip!" He swerved one more time, flinging himself toward the gate of his yard, praying it wasn't locked.

Philip and Mrs. Parker were standing in front of the house, along with the watchman, when Richard came barreling into the yard. He could barely talk. He collapsed on the ground, pointing and gasping: "Heartman! Heartman!"

Philip and the watchman ran outside, and saw the foiled heartman as he ran by the house. The watchman followed the heartman, and saw two others join him just down the road. They had machetes, too. And garbage bags, presumably to carry away Richard's carcass.

The next day at school, all Richard could talk about was his escape. Listening to him, a chill went down my spine. So they were real, I thought. In Liberia, we put on civilized airs, but the truth was that we always seemed to be teetering one step away from something dark and savage.

I thought about the many terrified nights I spent in my own pink bedroom at Sugar Beach when we first moved there; the dark uncontrollable thoughts that filled my head until Mommee and Daddy brought Eunice to live with us. Even now, at age thirteen, we were all still sleeping in Marlene's room, on mattresses on the floor, protecting one another from witch doctors, rogues, and heartmen.

And now I had proof that they were real. I didn't want to think about it. "It's too bad that heartman didn't cut out Richard's tongue," I muttered to one of my friends. The entire school now knew about my crush on Philip. "What are you going to do if he ever says, 'Okay, let's go out?' " one senior boy asked me.

I was waiting for that day to come. I had my answer prepared in my head. "Relationships can be so difficult," I would say, lowering my voice in sexy sophistication, "but I'm willing to give this a try." Not too eager, hinting at past romantic entanglements without actually lying and saying I'd had a real boyfriend before.

ACS held a Sadie Hawkins dance in October, at the end of Hick Day, the annual festival we had when we all were supposed to dress like country hicks and do sponge throws and pie-eating contests. During the Hick Day talent show, I did a tap dance I'd learned at ballet class. It was a jazzy number to "King of the Road," danced by three of us in identical black leotards, black top hats, white tights, and black tap shoes. And batons.

Calling our school dance following Hick Day a Sadie Hawkins dance was really a misnomer because none of the girls asked the boys to dance. The girls all hung out at one end of the gym and waited for the boys to come and ask us to dance. I went with my friend Veda. I wore a knee-length skirt and high-heeled sandals. My skirt was fuchsia linen, with my favorite dark green linen top and a fuchsia belt.

Veda, tiny and exotic with slinky eyes, wore a wine-colored pantsuit.

The gym was dark, decorated with crepe lanterns. Someone brought in chairs and tables, though most people still sat on the bleachers. Mommee had told me we could only stay out until ten p.m., even though the dance let out at eleven. I wasn't pleased, but determined to make the best of it.

Philip had on tight white trousers, like John Travolta in *Saturday Night Fever*. He prowled around the gym all night, not dancing much. He talked to his basketball buddies. I made a determined and quite good effort at not talking to him.

When Michael Jackson's "Don't Stop 'Til You Get Enough" came on, everyone swarmed the dance floor. My classmate Lennart asked me to dance and a tenth-grade boy asked Veda. I tried my hardest to move to the beat, my eyes darting around to make sure no one was looking at me as if I couldn't dance. Everyone was concentrating on their own moves.

I spotted Philip across the floor dancing with Olga Madiou, one of the members of the ACS Dancers group. She was Haitian and really cute and athletic and she danced like she was on fire, with a lot of furious arm waving and upper body twists. The ACS Dancers were the best dancers in the school—Olga and Karen Mygil and Lisa Cooper and Veena Kaul and Zinnah Holmes, the most beautiful girl in Liberia. I whispered a quick prayer of thanks that Philip at least wasn't dancing with Zinnah, followed with a small addendum that Olga trip and fall.

Olga didn't fall, she just kept changing moves and doing

stuff no one else could do. Now she was moving her neck like an Egyptian. I knew that I couldn't do that, so I shook my booty harder. I'd show her.

Finally the song ended and Veda and I hurried to our spot at the bleachers. "Did you see . . ." I began, furiously.

Veda interrupted me. "Olga does not want Philip. You know she think 'that small boy.' "

I sighed. It was ten p.m. and time for us to leave and I hadn't exchanged a single word with the love of my life. I collected my baton from the corner where I'd put it, and Veda and I headed for the door.

The strands of the Barry White version of "Just the Way You Are," the Billy Joel single, sounded throughout the gymnasium, blanketing it in 1970s Soul coolness. I was concentrating so hard not to look at Philip that I almost missed him as he scanned the gym and found me lurking by the door, standing next to Veda.

"He's coming over here," Veda said.

He walked up to us, and took my hand. I was going to slow dance with Philip Parker! Halfway onto the dance floor, I realized my other hand held my baton. Shit. I tapped him on the shoulder. "Uh, I gotta put my baton down," I said, then ran across the dance floor, practically throwing the baton at Veda before turning and dashing back.

Philip put his hands on my waist and I put my hands on his shoulders. Barry White was crooning. "I just want . . . someone to talk to . . . I want you just the way you are."

Obviously Philip had chosen this song because the words expressed what he felt about me, I thought gleefully. I was lost in the moment, and wrapped myself around him. My heart felt like it was going to jump out of my chest.

Far too soon, the song ended. My eyes were still closed and I didn't notice until I heard him say, "thanks." I jumped back. "Oh, um, you're welcome!" I said, and strutted across the gym to Veda, beaming.

I swooned all the way home. "How did we look?" I kept asking Veda.

Veda was a true friend, and knew her answer was extremely important. She got it right. "Like lovers," she said.

"Like lovers," I sighed.

Back in the real world, President Tolbert and the Liberian ruling group were getting ready for the trial of Gabriel Baccus Matthews. The post-OAU truce between Tolbert and Matthews had ended after Matthews's PAL registered as a political opposition party. PAL renamed itself the Progressive People's Party (PPP) and held a rally one night calling for the ouster of Tolbert.

"I am tired of being Mr. Nice Guy," Tolbert announced. "I will be tough and mean and rough from now on. I want to show you that this is the time to carry out the law of this country to its fullest. If in the past I have been lenient, I want the people to forgive. I am not going to be lenient with them anymore . . . and I know I am steady on the rock because I have the support of the Liberian people."

Tolbert tapped his "constituents," and delegations from various branches of his True Whig Party trooped from up-country to pledge their allegiance and show their support for Tolbert. They "demanded" that Matthews and others be tried for treason. They "demanded" that Liberia declare itself a one-party state under True Whig Party leadership. Tolbert "responded" by banning the PPP, and rounded up thirty-eight political dissidents, including Matthews, who he charged with sedition.

Also arrested was Chea Cheapoo, a native Liberian ingrate if ever there was one, as far as the Congo People were concerned. Chea Cheapoo was the foster son of the hard-line minister of justice Joseph Chesson. Cheapoo had been raised in Chesson's house, until he decided to join PAL.

So Chesson had his son arrested.

Tolbert set the treason trials of Matthews, Cheapoo, and the rest of the agitants for April 14, 1980, the one-year anniversary of the rice riots.

I was experimenting with a different way to wear my hair on the day that Philip carried my books to the car after school. We hadn't said a word to each other since the memorable slow-dance at the Sadie Hawkins dance weeks earlier, and I was getting increasingly frustrated with the slow pace of my love affair.

I had parted my hair in the middle with a pigtail on the top quarter, with the remaining three-quarters hanging around my face. It was a hairstyle I had seen Kelly on *Charlie's Angels* wear.

Mommee had been picking me up after school every day that week because she didn't trust me and Eunice to come straight home with Fedeles. I was in the doghouse because my entire ninth-grade class except Janine Padmore and, freakishly, Richard Parker had received "Ds" in Algebra 1. Mommee went nuts and told me I was grounded for a year. Then she started picking us up after school herself, as if that would somehow translate into an A in algebra.

I was walking away from my locker after school when I saw Philip coming out of Ms. Ross's music class. I quickly darted my eyes away, as I usually did around him, but this time he walked right up to me and put his arm around me.

"You look cute today, Cooper," he told me, smiling.

I was tongue-tied.

As we got near the gate, he reached over and took my schoolbooks. "Those look heavy," he said. That same smile.

I finally found my voice and started blabbering something about how good he had been in the basketball game the other day, and how I loved watching him play, and what an avid basketball fan I was. We were getting closer to the car now, and I realized, with dismay, that Mommee, Eunice, and Marlene were already sitting there watching us approach, slackjawed. Eunice beamed.

"I was playing for you," Philip said. He opened the car door, kissed my mother hello, smiled at Marlene and Eunice, and handed me my books. He closed the door and leaned through the window and kissed me on my cheek. I tried to turn my mouth toward him but, alas, wasn't quick enough. Then he jogged away, back toward the school.

The whole car was quiet, for about ten seconds. And then, I scrunched up my face and let out a war whoop.

13

SUGAR BEACH, LIBERIA, APRIL 12, 1980

𝒟uring the early-morning hours of Saturday, April 12, 1980, native Liberian enlisted soldiers, led by twenty-eight-year-old Master Sgt. Samuel Kanyon Doe, stormed the Executive Mansion.

Tolbert had just returned from a speech in downtown Monrovia to his private quarters on the top floor of the Israeli-built mansion overlooking the Atlantic. His room had a security elevator chute that was capable of squiring him deep into the basement, where a tunnel could shoot him out to the nearby beach, and, presumably, to safety, if ever that was needed. But Tolbert hadn't maintained the upkeep on the elevator, so it was not in working order.

He put on his pajamas and went to bed. Around two a.m., nineteen soldiers, led by Doe, a member of the Krahn tribe, and aided by a few rebels in the presidential guard, scaled the mansion's iron gate. They quickly killed the president's security detail. During the firefight, a stray bullet severed the telephone line between the mansion and Barclay Training Center, the army barracks known as BTC, the "million-to-one shot that prevented Tolbert from summoning his army," one journalist would later note.

It took them less than an hour to get to the top floor. President Tolbert, in his dressing gown, had come out of his secured bedroom, and was trying to cross the hall to get to his wife and children's quarters. The soldiers bayoneted him in the hallway, gouged out his right eye, and disemboweled him. They put Mrs. Tolbert and the children under house arrest. Then they went on the radio to announce that Liberia was now under new management. They asked that all government ministers and their deputies report to the army barracks.

Uncle Cecil Dennis went to the American embassy and asked for political asylum. The ambassador turned him down. Uncle Cecil then drove himself to BTC and turned himself in. Philip and Richard's father, Clarence Parker, treasurer of the True Whig Party, was arrested, as were the fathers of a number of my schoolmates at ACS who were in government.

Eleven miles away at Sugar Beach, I woke up that Saturday morning to a bright sky. I had ballet class that morning. Then a wedding, in which I was to be a bridesmaid, in the afternoon. I walked out of my bedroom and heard Mommee saying to Eunice: "Don't say anything to Helene yet. You know how excitable she is."

"Don't tell Helene what?" I said.

"There's been a coup."

"What's a coup?"

A coup d'état, I learned that day, was a French phrase meaning "overthrow of the government," or literally, "cutting off the head." On the radio, the broadcaster was saying that people should remain calm, and that all government ministers should report to BTC.

"Wha' will happen to Daddy?" I asked. The highest government position Daddy ever held was deputy postmaster general—and he had resigned from that in 1974. After spending years bemoaning the fact that Daddy's private practice meant we were more dependent on the capricious whims of capitalism than the security of high-ranking government employment, I was suddenly hugely relieved. "Let him stay right up there at the farm in Kakata and don't come down to Monrovia," Mommee said.

Walking into the kitchen, I overheard Tommy, our other cook, whispering to Eunice that the soldiers had a list of Congo People they were going to kill, and Daddy was on the list. With no phone at Sugar Beach, we couldn't call to check on him.

Never before had our isolation at that house felt so acute. Eunice and I were sitting on the floor in the TV lounge trying to concentrate on our crazy 8 card game when Mommee walked in, turned on the radio, and sat in her armchair.

The radio broadcast was midway through playing the Liberian National Anthem, "All Hail, Liberia, Hail." Then a Country man came on the air. He didn't have the usual Liberian broadcaster's accent: a creolish mix of cullor, the Queen's

English, and Liberian English. This one didn't even aspire to Liberian English, it was pure Country.

"The People's Redemption Council now take over the government to end all this corruption," the man announced. "Master Sgt. Samuel Kanyan Doe is in charge. All government ministers are to report to BTC."

Mommee rolled her eyes. "Oh great, you know that's trouble whenever they say 'People's,' " she said.

"Why?" I asked.

"That's shorthand for communism."

"What's communism?" I'd heard that word over and over again.

"It means the government will take your land and say it belongs to everybody."

"What!" That was crazy.

"Yup. It's when they say, 'everything belongs to everybody.' "

Over and over again, the radio kept repeating that programming. First, the national anthem, the muzak all-horn version. Then that announcement. "The People's Redemption Council now take over the government to end all this corruption. Master Sgt. Samuel Kanyan Doe is in charge. All government ministers are to report to BTC."

Eunice and I huddled in the TV lounge. Vicky had left four months earlier to go to college in America, in Toledo, Ohio. Janice was in England at Essex University, and John Bull no longer lived with us now that Mommee and Daddy were divorced; he lived in town with his mother, Toulia Dennis, and was preparing to go to college in the United States. So it was just Eunice, Marlene, Mommee, and me at the house.

"At least we far from town," Eunice said. "Nobody will be able to find us up here."

The day felt so heavy, with that awful radio broadcast

going on and on, interspersed only by patriotic music. The state had taken over our house, so all we could do was sit around and listen to the radio and think about Liberia. I'd never really thought about Liberia as a "state" before. I didn't want to ponder the state. I wanted to go to ballet class and the wedding I had scheduled.

The day passed slowly. That night we went to bed early, around nine o'clock, if for no other reason than to just bring a close to the day.

Sunday dawned as bright and sticky as the day before. Eunice and I were sitting at the kitchen table drinking Ovaltine when Mommee walked in and announced that we were going to church.

"Henh?" I said.

"We are going to church, and then we're going to find Mama. I am not going to stay here cowering all day."

Left unsaid was that Mama Grand was the last person you wanted surrounded by soldiers with guns. I could imagine her cussing them out, and getting killed for her trouble. I understood why we were going to check on her. What I didn't understand was why we were going to church first.

We piled into Mommee's Caprice Classic—me, Mommee, Eunice, and Marlene—and drove into town. The streets were deserted of Congo People . . . they largely seemed deserted of native Liberians as well, though there were plenty of marauding bands of soldiers drunk on retribution and cane juice. Nobody seemed to pay too much attention to us, and we made it to church fine. There was hardly anyone there. The Senior Choir, on tap to perform that Sunday, consisted of two old men. The pastor mumbled something about forgiveness and reconciliation, and that was the service.

After church we drove across the bridge to Mama Grand's

house. Driving into her yard, the place looked deserted. We got out of the car and went upstairs to her back door. Mommee banged on it a couple of minutes. Silence. She was about to open the door when an old man who lived nearby walked into the yard. "They took the old lady to BTC," he said.

Mommee ordered all of us back in the car, but before we could get in, two soldiers, with machine guns came into the driveway. "You're the old lady's daughter?" one said. Mommee nodded. "Come on, you're all going to BTC."

They pushed us into Mommee's car. I sat in the back with Eunice and one of the soldiers. The other soldier got into the driver's seat. Mommee sat in the front with Marlene on her lap.

The car filled with the scent of the soldiers—alcohol mixed with pungent sweat.

The soldier at the wheel couldn't drive. He kept lurching and swinging wildly. Marlene started to cry. "Don't cry, Marlene," my mom said. "Yeah, don't cry Marine," the soldier said, laughing.

Mommee started yelling at him. "Look, you're going to kill us!" The soldier sitting in the backseat looked uneasy. "I say, ma man, take time oh," he said.

The same people who had seemed all docile on the way to church now suddenly were showing signs of life—and celebration. A group of women were singing and dancing, clapping their hands to the beat. Some ran up to our car, throwing rocks and yelling "Congo People!" "Congo People!" We were dressed in our church finery—dresses, stockings, and hats.

Eunice and I sat in the backseat, pressed side to side. She took my hand, silently, and squeezed.

Finally, we arrived at the compound at BTC, and got out of the car. The place was its usual dusty frenzy of activity. Except that instead of soldiers milling around, there were Congo men being pushed behind squat buildings. Scanning quickly, I looked for Daddy but didn't see him.

It smelled like a combination of urine and dust and dried fish. I couldn't imagine that Mama Grand was in there somewhere. And Bro. Henry, too? We stood by the car, unsure of what was coming next.

Then: "Hey! That's Captain Dennis's daughter!" A staff sergeant came running over to us, his eyes on Mommee.

We were freed within five minutes. My grandfather, dead for nine years, had been a career army captain, promoted to general before his death, but known and loved by the enlisted men always as Captain Dennis. The staff sergeant who recognized Mommee got in the car with us, and rode with us all the way back to Sugar Beach. He refused Mommee's offer of money. "Your father was a good man" was all he said, before leaving us. "Stay home this time. "

The next day, April 14, the one-year anniversary of the rice riots, we stayed home.

The sun was already hot by ten-thirty in the morning. It was going to be another dense stifling day, courtesy of the approaching rainy season. From the kitchen, the radio was still playing; it had been going strong for more than forty-eight hours straight now. The people who worked for ELBC, the government-controlled radio station, had gone back to work and were busily broadcasting the plans of the new People's Redemption Council. Those plans mostly revolved around trying to round up former government ministers at the army barracks.

I was sitting in the kitchen, again drinking my morning Ovaltine, when I realized the servants had all disappeared. Where was Tommy, our cook? Or Jack?

Slurping up the last of my Ovaltine, I wandered out onto

the kitchen porch. The yard was empty; the boys' house deserted.

"Eunice!" I hollered.

"Wha' you want?" she yelled back from somewhere deep in the house.

I didn't answer, knowing that curiosity was the surest way to get her out there. Sure enough, she showed up about a minute later, barefoot. As soon as she walked out of the air-conditioned house, her glasses fogged up.

"Where everybody?" I asked her.

"Henh?"

"Tommy 'them gone."

The two of us stood on the second-floor kitchen steps, looking out into the yard and the Sugar Beach Road and beyond. Even Bolabo's door was wide open and we could see he wasn't on the bed having his usual all-day nap.

Like me, Eunice immediately became uneasy. "How everybody gone so?"

Then we saw the truck flash briefly through the trees up the road as it approached the house, a cloud of dust trailing it.

My stomach clenched. It wasn't rogues coming to Sugar Beach this time. These intruders weren't bothering to cloak themselves under cover of darkness. They were brazen. They had nothing to hide from and nothing to fear, and they could come into our yard and into our house and take whatever they wanted and do whatever they wanted to us.

Eunice and I bolted into the house, yelling: "Aunt Lah! Mommee! Soldiers!"

Marlene's dogs, all four of them, were barking furiously, running up to the approaching truck and then back to the house, as if they wanted to make sure the truckload of soldiers were properly escorted to us. Mommee, dressed in a black T-shirt and green shorts, went to the kitchen porch, then yelled back at us. "Y'all stay inside."

But we were, all three—Marlene and Eunice and I—peering from the kitchen window, in full view of the truckload of soldiers who were now pouring out of the truck and into the yard in front of the house.

There were eight of them. Some wore green fatigues, some wore tank tops that showed off their shoulders and arms, with scars and markings on them.

One wore a uniform that looked to be that of some kind of noncommissioned officer. He pulled up his belt and strutted to the front of the house. He looked at Mommee, standing above him on the porch, and grinned. Then he looked at us, peering from the kitchen window, and grinned some more.

"Everybody out of the house," he said, waving his arm toward us.

Marlene, Eunice, and I followed Mommee down the steps into the yard. The dogs—Christopher, Christopher Junior, Savage Sam, and Happy—continued their excited barking and scampering. Like Mommee, I had on my bedroom slippers, shorts, and a T-shirt. Marlene and Eunice were dressed similarly, except Eunice was still barefoot.

"What do you all want?" Mommee said, articulating carefully.

"Where John Cooper at?" the lead soldier asked. Mommee told him Daddy was not home. She said that he didn't live here anymore. She made it sound like we never saw him.

Shifting from one foot to another, I was torn between rage at my father for not being there and relief that he wasn't. The rage came out of nowhere, as I watched Mommee answering the soldiers' questions, getting clearly more agitated. Daddy was supposed to be there taking care of us! He was more level-headed than Mommee, who had Mama Grand's quick temper and was apt to yell at the soldiers at any moment. What kind of father was he?

But if he were there would they hurt him?

"My father isn't in the government," I said.

The soldiers ignored me. They walked around the yard for a while, conferring among themselves. Then they ordered us to stand against the wall of the house.

All four of us moved to the wall. One soldier grabbed Eunice's arm. "Not you," he said. He pulled her aside.

Mommee, Marlene, and I lined up against the house, next to the laundry room. Three soldiers pointed their guns at us. "We're going to splatter your blood against this wall like paint," one said. Then they fired into the air above our heads.

"Stop, stop, please stop," Eunice said. She kept repeating that: "Stop, stop, please stop."

The soldiers were all laughing and grinning now. Marlene's dog, Christopher Jr., ran to one soldier, barking furiously. One of them pointed his gun at the dog and made as if to shoot him. Marlene bolted from the wall, running to the soldier and jumping on his gun arm. He flung her to the side. Mommee ran and grabbed Marlene.

Mommee started yelling at the soldiers. "What the hell is wrong with you! You want to shoot women? Then shoot! We're going inside. We're not putting up with this shit anymore."

Mommee grabbed my arm and motioned us to go back into the house. "Speak for yourself," I muttered. I didn't think her Congo Lady of the Manor act was a good idea.

We went into the house and the soldiers followed us inside. One turned to Eunice. "Where you da sleep?" he asked her. "On the floor?"

Eunice was calm. "Come," she said. "I'll show you my bedroom."

She took the soldiers to her bedroom. When they challenged her that it wasn't her bedroom, she showed them her clothes and shoes in the closets. "There's my school uniform," she said.

One soldier turned to me and grabbed my arm. He dragged me into the TV lounge and closed the door behind him.

I didn't know what he wanted, even when he sidled up close to me and put his mouth near my cheek. "Are you married?" he asked me, running his hand against my arm. He was standing too close, way too close, and started to push up against me. He smelled like alcohol.

"No, I'm only thirteen!" I said. "How can I be married?"

"You're fine, oh," he said, taking my other arm.

Before I could respond, the door flew open. It was Mommee, with two soldiers beside her. "Get that man away from my child," she said. She walked in and grabbed me, dragging me with her into the kitchen.

Suddenly, the soldiers left. Just like that, they were gone. The four of us sat at the kitchen table. Mommee's chest was heaving and she was still shaking. "You think they're gone for Daddy?" Marlene asked.

Mommee didn't bother to try to phrase her response. "Yes," she said.

Marlene started to tear up promptly. I glared at Mommee. The least she could do was sanitize things for us.

"I wonder if we should leave," Mommee said.

"Wha' we leaving for? Ehn that soldier yesterday told us to stay home?" I asked.

Mommee and Eunice exchanged a pointed look, then left the kitchen. Marlene went outside to check on her dogs, while I made for the living room and curled into a ball into the folds of my favorite chair in the corner, the one where you couldn't tell I was there even when you walked into the room, unless you looked diagonally behind you.

An hour later, the soldiers came back, walking straight through the kitchen door and into the foyer by the piano, like they owned the place. Marlene, Eunice, and I stood in front of the TV lounge while they took Mommee aside. I couldn't hear what they said to her. She looked fixedly at the lead one, then kept turning and looking at the one who had taken me into the TV lounge and asked me if I was married. He looked at me and smiled, then said something to her. She was shaking her head violently. He kept talking, she kept shaking her head furiously. The lead one started talking again, smiling, too. I couldn't hear them.

Then Mommee pointed at the one who had taken me into the TV lounge, and said something to the lead one. He looked at the other soldiers. They all started grinning.

Mommee walked over to Eunice, and pressed a key into Eunice's palm. "The three of you go into my bedroom, and lock the door from the inside," she said. "Whatever you do, do not let anyone in."

By now, I was crying. "Where y'all taking Mommee?" I said. The soldiers were herding her down the stairs to the basement. She yelled over her shoulder: "Just get in the room."

Their boots were clomping down the stairs. They laughed and jostled each other before they disappeared from view.

We locked the door of Mommee's room and sat on the floor, looking at each other.

We heard three gunshots from downstairs.

My heart convulsed.

It was unthinkable for me to even consider that they had just shot my mother. No way, no way.

"Eunice . . . they shooting her?"

"Don't cry, don't cry," Eunice was saying to Marlene. Marlene had crawled onto Eunice's lap, and Eunice was cradling her like a baby, rocking her back and forth.

Eunice looked at me. "They not shooting her," she said quietly. "They jes' tryin to scare her."

There were three more shots.

"I going downstairs," I said, starting to get up.

"No!" Eunice yelled at me, her voice sharp, her stutter uncharacteristically absent. "Sit back down. For once in your life, do wha' Aunt Lah told you to do."

I slowly sat back down. Finally, somewhere inside, I started to understand what was happening.

I was rocking back and forth now, too, sitting on the floor, with my back to the mirror. Eunice got up and turned the air conditioner on. It started to rattle, as it usually did when it first came on, before smoothing out to coat the air with its bland hum. I looked at Eunice in confusion; at a time like this she was thinking about air-conditioning? Plus, now I couldn't hear anything. We wouldn't be able to hear what was happening downstairs.

I wanted to hear.

I got up and turned the air-conditioning back off.

Eunice said: "Stop it."

I looked at her.

She spoke again. "Stop it. It no' your fault."

I shook my head at her.

Even with the air-conditioning off, I couldn't hear anything except Marlene's soft sobbing. Beyond that there was silence. I couldn't even hear the ocean. Usually in Mommee and Daddy's room, facing the ocean, you could hear the sound of the breaking waves against the shore. How could they be so quiet downstairs? What were they doing to her that they were so quiet?

Oh God, please, I hold your foot, don't let them hurt my ma.

No one was going to come to save us. This was no movie

when, at the last moment, a hero rushes in to save you. It was just the three of us, locked in the bedroom, and Mommee, downstairs with the soldiers. The only person between the three of us and the soldiers was Mommee. The only person who was going to save us was Mommee.

Finally, we heard the truck leaving the yard. We were terrified to unlock the door.

Then came a loud knock. "Open the door, that me," Mommee said.

She walked into the room, eyes flashing with anger. She was unkempt, her T-shirt loose on her, as if it had been yanked or stretched. Her hair was undone, one hairpin hanging from a clump at the back of her head.

She stripped off her clothes and headed straight into the bathroom to the shower.

"Those damn soldiers gang-raped me," she said.

She wasn't crying. She seemed angry. She left the bathroom door open while she showered, and Eunice, Marlene, and I hovered at the door. I wanted to climb into the shower and hug her but I was afraid to. So we just stood at the bathroom door, listening to the water run, watching her behind the glass, as she soaped herself. Again and again, she washed. She stayed in the shower for almost an hour.

I was filled with an anger so intense it boiled through me. I wanted to hurt those soldiers who had hurt my mother. I wanted to watch them bleed, I wanted to sit back and watch them die, slowly, aware that they were dying. I wanted to be there to laugh while they died. Standing in the doorway, my muscles were tense, my fists clenched.

Finally she turned the water off, and the three of us moved away from the bathroom door.

When she came out of the bathroom, she was holding a gun. "If they try to come back here, I am shooting them," she said.

That night, they came back.

The servants had returned to the house. I heard Tommy and Galway in the kitchen talking, but the four of us didn't leave Mommee's room. The rage inside me was directed at the soldiers but not our servants. I knew that they had run away because they had been scared of the soldiers. What could they have done if they had stayed? They didn't have guns. Now that they had come back to the house, and were still there even though the truckload of soldiers had returned, I felt almost a strange sense of gratitude, that they had not given up on us, had somehow decided, maybe, that they shouldn't have left us, and were trying to make up for it.

The truck of soldiers parked in the yard again. We listened, silent, as they banged on the kitchen door. "Get behind the bed," Mommee told us.

She put herself between the bedroom door and us, and stood, her gun in her hand, cocked and ready.

Then, I heard Galway, the washman, saying to the soldiers: "De people gone."

There was a long silence, as I waited to hear the soldiers coming toward us. But they didn't. They talked to Galway a little more. I couldn't hear what they were saying, but I heard one of them laughing. And then they left.

We never left the bedroom that night. Eunice and I lay on the floor and Marlene lay Mommee's bed. Mommee sat in her white leather loveseat, her gun in her hand on her lap. She gave each of us a Valium tranquilizer. I lay awake wondering why people said tranquilizers were strong medicine. The one Mommee gave me wasn't strong at all.

I stared at the shadows on the ceiling until dawn broke. And when it did, we left Sugar Beach.

14

MONROVIA, LIBERIA, APRIL 22, 1980

The morning after the rape, Mommee moved on autopilot. She walked stiffly, almost like a robot. Eunice, Marlene, and I tiptoed around her, not knowing what to say.

There was a bruise under her eye, which she tried to cover with makeup. When that didn't work, she resorted to her trademark Christian Dior sunglasses, which she kept on in the house, as well as in the car on the drive to town. She

---

Samuel Doe and his bodyguards

was silent in the car, her hands gripping the wheel each time we came to newly set up military checkpoints, where soldiers stopped the car and waved their guns into the windows.

I had finally gotten my wish: my family was moving from Sugar Beach to Aunt Momsie's house in Sinkor.

When we got to Aunt Momsie's house, Mommee immediately told Uncle Mac and Mama Grand, who had been released from the army barracks and was also ensconsed at Aunt Momsie's, what had happened. Aunt Momsie was out of the country at the time, and Mommee, Mama Grand, and Uncle Mac went out onto the front porch to talk. Captain Stevens, a U.S. embassy attaché who was a friend of the family, was there, too. The four of them sat outside.

Eunice, my cousin CeRue, Marlene, and I monitored them from the living room window. In the distance we could hear the Country People singing and celebrating.

"The soldiers told me that if I didn't go downstairs with them, they would rape my daughters," Mommee told Captain Stevens. "There were three of them. At first, one soldier tried to stop the others, but he gave up soon. The last thing he said to me before he raped me was 'You think the Americans are going to come and help you? Well, they back us.'"

When she said that part, she looked straight at Captain Stevens. He looked back at her for a moment, and then he looked away.

That night, Eunice, Marlene, CeRue, and I watched *The Exorcist* on TV. We were all sleeping on the floor of the same bedroom as Mama Grand, who snored all night. Her snoring sounded just like the girl in *The Exorcist* right before her head started spinning around.

The next day, we all went to school. ACS seemed shockingly normal, except some of the Liberian kids had bruises and several of the girls had been raped, according to murmurs in the classrooms. But even the ones who had been raped still went to school.

Students whispered in the hallways:

"Soldiers came to Ronnie's house and messed with them."

"I heard they beat Joseph's pa with the butt of their guns, then they used the same guns to rape his ma."

"They took Jackie on the beach behind their house and seven of them raped her."

"They took John's whole family to BTC."

I wasn't sure how much to tell. I didn't want any of my friends knowing soldiers had raped my mother, but at the same time, it seemed pointless to pretend nothing had happened to us when so many students suddenly had their fathers locked up at BTC, waiting for military trials. War scars proved your family had been important.

"They came to our house, too," I finally reported to Veda. "They wanted to rape us but Mommee wouldn't let them."

We still hadn't heard from Daddy, although rumors were floating around that he had been arrested and was at BTC. The ELTV broadcast the military trials every night, and every night we watched, alternatively terrified that Daddy would show up on trial, and hoping that he would, because at least that would mean he was alive.

"You think they will kill Uncle Cecil?"

Eunice shook her head. It wasn't an answer, we both knew, just an acknowledgment that the world had upended. The top members of Tolbert's cabinet were on trial. The accused were all familiar names and faces: Uncle Cecil; Clarence Parker; J. T. Phillips, the finance minister and father of my classmate Elbert Phillips; Joseph Chesson; Frank Tolbert; Frank Stewart; and seven more. There were thirteen in all.

Besides the Liberian press, American journalists, including Leon Dash of *The Washington Post* and David Lamb of the *Los Angeles Times,* were on hand to record the proceedings.

The trials were in a second-floor conference room with bare cement walls. The accused men, most wearing only their underpants, sat before the five-member military tribunal. On the beach outside, four telephone poles had been erected.

The public crowded into the trial room to watch the proceedings, while outside, hundreds of native Liberians danced and celebrated as the former government officials were brought in. Former minister of finance J. T. Phillips was pistol-whipped by soldiers on his way into the trial room. The crowd around him chanted: "Who born soldier? Country woman! Who born minister? Congo woman!"

Uncle Cecil, wearing jeans but no shirt, told the tribunal he saw a lot of problems with the old-guard system, and that he had urged the right wing of the True Whig Party to liberalize. Clarence Parker said the same thing, as did J. T. Phillips. Indeed, most of the thirteen ministers said that the system they had set up was unfair. Budget director Frank Stewart, his hair flaked with sawdust, pleaded not guilty to the tribunal's charges of corruption.

David Lamb, the *LA Times* writer, recorded this exchange between Stewart and the tribunal.

Officer: Mr. Stewart, for the benefit of this tribunal, please state how many houses, lots, and farms do you own?

Stewart: I will answer that by telling a story about how I happened to get—

Officer: We are not interested in stories. How many houses you got?

Stewart: Well, houses, there are, let's see, four.

Officer, holding up four fingers, looking at typist: Four. You got that down?

Typist: Got what down?

Officer: Four houses. Mr. Stewart got four houses.

Typist: Four houses, yeah, I got it.

Stewart: Yes, but in 1957 the price of cement was very cheap, so my wife, who was earning one hundred and twenty-five dollars a month at the Justice Department, and I—my salary was two hundred and fifty dollars—we used small loans from the bank, and for seven years we worked building the blocks we needed to construct—

Another officer: Holy Christ, cut this short or we goin to be sittin here right through lunch.

Another officer: No, le' him finish. Mr. Stewart, is it right for a government official to build a house, like you did, and then lease it back to the government? That's a question.

Typist: Wha' de last part?

Officer: I said, 'that's a question.' You don't have to write that down.

Typist: None of it?

Officer: No, just the last part, the part about the question.

On Tuesday, April 22, I turned fourteen.

Mommee woke me up that morning, still at my cousins' house, where we were staying. She always made a big deal about our birthdays, and today was to be no exception, coup or no. "Happy birthday, sweetheart," she said, and presented me with a diamond pendant on a delicate gold chain.

"A diamond necklace," I breathed, excitedly. "You got me a diamond necklace!"

I went to school, where we were all becoming increasingly convinced that somehow our world would soon right itself. I was in a weird euphoric mood; not only because it was my birthday, but also because someone had come by my cousins' house that morning with word that someone had seen someone who said my father was alive. But they didn't know where he was.

Five miles away from my Algebra 1 class, the new minister of information, Gabriel Nimely, called a press conference at the Executive Mansion. "Gentlemen of the press," he announced. "You are all invited to some executions at Barclay Beach."

Asked who would be executed, he replied: "Enemies of the people."

The American journalists hopped into their hired taxis and raced to BTC. It was about two-thirty, and the equatorial sun had the Western reporters all beading over in sweat, with rivulets dripping down their faces.

Hundreds of native Liberians crowded and danced on the beach near where the four execution poles had been placed by the Atlantic Ocean. Then two large mechanical hole cutters and five additional poles were brought to the site, and quickly erected.

Now there were nine execution poles standing. Inside a white Volkswagen bus, thirteen men, including Uncle Cecil, Clarence Parker, Frank Stewart, and J. T. Phillips, sat huddled, watching the poles go up.

Close to one hundred drunk soldiers strutted around, clapping each other on the back and waving their machine guns toward the white Volkswagen bus. A crowd jostled around the bus, yelling at the thirteen men inside. They pounded on the windows and kicked at the doors.

The chant was familiar. "Who born soldier? Country woman! Who born minister? Congo woman!"

Leon Dash, *The Washington Post* reporter, got out of his taxi, incredulous, and looked at a fellow reporter from *Time* magazine. "They are serious," he said.

Up until that point, Dash had believed that the killing of Tolbert the night of the coup had been done in the heat of the moment. He'd thought there was a good chance that Liberia's new leaders might eschew revenge killings, and that practical matters like running the country and establishing diplomatic relations with the rest of the world would seem more important than killing more Congo People.

The soldiers opened the door of the VW bus and pulled out nine men. Frank Tolbert, President Tolbert's brother, the former president of the Senate, J. T. Phillips. Uncle Cecil.

They marched the nine men to the poles and tied each to one. Frank Tolbert had a heart attack, and slowly sank to the ground, unable to stand on his own feet. Fluid poured out of his mouth.

The American journalists started protesting to the soldiers that international law says you can't execute an unconscious man. The soldiers ignored them, and shot Frank Tolbert.

The soldier assigned to shoot Uncle Cecil was drunk and a poor shot. Uncle Cecil, wearing only his jeans, stared him straight in the face, making eye contact. The bullets kept missing him. Then he closed his eyes and mouthed a prayer. One soldier screamed at him: "You lie! You don't know God!"

The bullets continued to miss Uncle Cecil, who continued to stand up straight, now with his eyes closed, as the other eight men fell, one by one. A brief fight broke out as one of the other soldiers tried to take the position of the soldier assigned to shoot Uncle Cecil.

Finally, the soldier who kept missing Uncle Cecil ceded to the new soldier, who positioned his Uzi, walked up to Uncle Cecil, and opened up the gun into his face.

The crowd cheered, and the soldiers dragged the bodies from the pole. Leon Dash walked back to the VW bus, where four men remained, including Clarence Parker, Philip and Richard's father.

He looked in the window at Clarence Parker, who looked

back at him, smiled softly, and waved. Leon Dash waved back. Clarence Parker then shrugged. Leon Dash remembered something he had heard earlier in the day: that during the past week at BTC, Clarence Parker has been the one telling others imprisoned with him that trial or no trial, he thought they'd all be executed.

"You don't seem to understand," he had told the others. "These boys are going to kill us."

The soldiers came to the VW bus for the remaining four. Clarence Parker walked quickly to a pole, turned and faced the firing squad, and smiled slightly. A single shot later, he was dead.

The soldiers then sprayed all thirteen bodies with automatic fire, emptying, and then replacing, their ammunition clips.

The American journalists got back in their taxis, rode back to their hotels, and filed their stories.

That night, we watched the executions on TV. In particular, we watched Uncle Cecil die, noting how he kept his head up until the end; how he didn't look scared, but proud; how he didn't beg, how the soldier kept missing him, and what that meant. CeRue had one hand on her throat all evening. Eunice's stutter became more pronounced, making her almost impossible to understand. "T-t-t-they k-k-killed those people," she kept saying.

Finally, Mommee and Uncle Mac sent us to bed, but I couldn't sleep. In the middle of the night, I crept to the kitchen to get water, and saw Mommee, sitting in the dark in the living room. She wasn't crying, she was just rocking back and forth.

The next day, we went back to school.

In Algebra, the whole class talked about who was leaving Liberia and how soon.

"I heard Richard and Philip already left," one student said.

"Their ma took them to America last night right after they killed their pa. That's why they're not in school today."

Suddenly the class door opened with a huge sweep, and Richard made one of his trademark entrances, throwing open the door and kicking his leg out like he always did when he's walking into a room. There was a moment of stunned shock, then I yelled "Richard!" and leaped from my desk and ran to hug him.

Then the whole class was crowded around Richard.

"Na mind, ya, Richard."

"Aye man Richard, I so sorry."

"I sorry ya."

"Na mind, na mind."

"Aye ya Richard, na mind."

Richard was smiling and shaking his head. It flashed through my mind: *How are you supposed to act at school the day after your father is executed by a firing squad?* Mrs. Boyce gave up on quadratic equations. She walked over to Richard and put her hand on his shoulder, before walking out of the class.

"I say, Helene Cooper!" Richard suddenly called at me.

Before he even opened his mouth, I knew what was coming. Sure enough: "This is not going to help your chances with my brother," Richard said. "Yesterday was your birthday."

I sucked my teeth at Richard. But I knew he was right.

I was so overcome with shame about my birthday connection to the execution that I said nothing to Philip when I saw him in the hallway after class. I remained tongue-tied, locked in adolescent misery. I felt like I was partly to blame, because they killed his father on my birthday.

It was the same thing I would do for the rest of my life when something bad happens: I focus on something else. I concentrate on minutiae. It's the only way to keep going when the world has ended.

• • •

My own father surfaced the next day—in the hospital.

Soldiers had gone up to the farm looking for him, wanting money, since he wasn't on the primary list. They took him outside and started taking potshots at him, mainly to scare him. He said: "You damn soldiers are so drunk you can't even shoot straight." So they shot him near the groin.

But then they drove him to Catholic Hospital in Monrovia. We raced to see him—Mommee, Eunice, Marlene, and I. "What possessed you to say that to those people?" Mommee kept asking him. I looked at Mommee and snorted. She was a fine one to criticize anyone for saying stupid things to soldiers with guns.

That day in the hospital, Mommee and Daddy decided that we would leave Liberia. Mommee would take us to the States, and Daddy would come after his wound healed.

John Bull, who had gone through hell himself when he was stalked by soldiers and hidden by friends in the days after coup, would also be leaving for the United States, where he would attend Cedarville College in Ohio.

And Eunice?

Because she was on the Liberian school system, Eunice was in the middle of her senior year in high school. She told Mommee that she wanted to stay and finish. She would go back home to live with her mom, with whom we all kept in regular touch. Mommee didn't push the issue.

Eunice would not be coming with us.

For six years, Eunice had been my sister, a Bassa girl living in the same house with me, sleeping in the same room, sharing the same secrets. We were the same, yet we were different; had always been different. In my sheltered existence, I had never dug deep enough to wonder how much native Liberians resented us. I had been shocked at the level of hatred expressed when those people started chanting, as Cousin Cecil was killed, "Who born soldier? Country woman. Who born minister? Congo woman."

Did Eunice feel that way too?

And as soon as the thought entered my mind, I rejected it. There are some things you can't let yourself even think, or you will fall apart. So I cast the thought out. Those damn soldiers had taken my childhood away. They were not taking my sister from me too.

We went back to the house at Sugar Beach one last time to pack. We could each take two suitcases. But how do you pack up your life into two suitcases?

My choices were the choices of a fourteen-year-old girl too naïve to realize that things wouldn't be the same ever again.

So I packed Michael Jackson's *Off the Wall* record album, along with the Commodores, and my oft-played single of Barry White's "Just the Way You Are." I did not pack any of the piano lesson books that Daddy made me stumble through in my eight-year quest to learn to play. In the years to come, I would remain familiar with every song on that *Off the Wall* album, but I would not play the piano again.

I packed my teddy bear, Gentle Ben, and my Bible, which I never read, but didn't pack my First United Methodist Church hymnbook, even though I had used that hymnbook so often every week that I knew which page to find Blessed Assurance by heart.

I packed the purple pants I had on when Philip walked me to the car, and the green linen shirt I wore to the Sadie Hawkins dance, and my ACS yearbooks. I did not pack the three miniature Japanese dolls—one grinning, one frowning, and one bawling—that Daddy brought me back from Tokyo when I was seven and that I'd kept on my bedside table.

I went to the music room to get two of our family photo

albums. But I forgot the photo on my bedroom desk of Mommee, Daddy, me, Eunice, Marlene, Vicky, John Bull, and Janice standing in front of our plastic Christmas tree in December 1975, our hair wild from the previous night's sleep, our eyes even wilder with excitement over the coming opening of presents. It was the only photo I had of my whole entire family at Sugar Beach, and I forgot to pack it.

Clutching the two photo albums, I walked to the French doors behind the piano in the music room and looked out onto the porch, across the yard, and onto the ocean. Fierce-looking clouds were gathering; there was a storm coming. White caps were taking over the water.

"You girl, wha' you will do wi' these books?"

Eunice was standing behind me. In her hand she held *The Secret of the Old Clock,* the first Nancy Drew book in our collection.

"I can't carry 'dem," I said.

"You want me take 'dem?"

I nodded, and followed her back up the steps, past the TV lounge and into the sleeping quarters. We parted at our rarely-slept-in bedrooms, across the hallway from each other.

I put the two photo albums into the suitcase. The tears were starting now. All my life I had wanted to leave Sugar Beach and now I didn't want to go. My pink room seemed to be chiding me. *See? You didn't like me when you had me.*

Fighting back tears, I went to my bookshelf and started pulling down books, which I shuttled to Eunice. I made three trips, before she stopped me.

"Aye, tha' enough. Wha' you think people wi' do wi' all these books?"

"But wha' bout the Barbara Cartlands?" We had both started reading paperback historical romances, and imagining we were English roses. Our favorite author was Barbara Cartland, who wrote *The Disgraceful Duke* and *The Lady and the High-wayman.*

"I na taking that stupidness."

I looked at her. Then she started laughing. "Okay, gimme *The Bored Bridegroom.*"

Mommee appeared at the doorway. "Y'all ready?"

Outside, the servants were lined up. Fedeles, tall and thin in his trademark blue jeans and orange shirt. Tommy, who had taken Old Man Charlie's place full time after Mommee and Daddy divorced. Galway, looking grim as always. And Bolabo, standing slightly to the left, legs apart.

Marlene ran to Fedeles and hugged him. He passed her to Tommy, Galway, and Bolabo. I followed her in the opposite direction, shaking each of their hands, until I got to Fedeles, who I kissed on the cheek. A silent wave, and I got into the car.

As we pulled out of the driveway, the house at Sugar Beach was absorbing the first fat raindrops of a thunderstorm.

On May 16, 1980, one month after the coup, we left Liberia. "Don't cry," I told Eunice, as we left her and Bro. Henry at Robertsfield airport. "You'll get to come to the States soon." I needed to hold on to that belief even though I had no way to know whether it was true.

Eunice shook her head. "I na crying."

"Yeah you crying."

"Wha' bou you?"

"I gwen to America. Wha' I will be crying for?" I said through my tears.

Eunice laughed. "A-ya you foolish Cooper girl. You gwen to America."

At the passport control line the officious soldier asked for our exit passes—a new bureaucratic hoop that Doe had come up with to get some quick revenue from fleeing Congo people. While Mommee showed him the passes, purchased with a quick forty-dollar bribe from somebody at the Ministry of Foreign Affairs who knew Mommee was related to Uncle Cecil, Eunice and I said good-bye.

"Eunice you wi'mind ma Nancy Drew books?"

"Look, you girl, don't mae' me laugh tonite."

"Maybe you wi' come w' Daddy when he come."

She said nothing, just hugged me, then grabbed Marlene, who was bawling. Mommee turned to Eunice, whispering something into her ear and pressing something into her hand.

Then we were walking out to the tarmac at Robertsfield, up the steps and into the Pan Am DC-10. The cabin engulfed us in its foreignness; it was like we were already in America, with its carpets and air-conditioning and air fresheners.

I hadn't seen Mommee break down during the whole month since the coup. But when the plane's engines raised and it accelerated down the runway, her chest started to heave with big racking sobs.

Part Two

15

KNOXVILLE, TENNESSEE, 1980

an Am's Flight 150 from Monrovia to New York's JFK Airport was one of the airline's legendary routes, billed by advertisers as the gateway to sub-Saharan Africa, the only American flight that directly connected people in the United States with the Dark Continent.

Of more import to me, it connected fleeing, newly poor, tired, huddled masses of Congo people in the Dark Continent with the U.S.A.

CeRue, Bridget, Tello, and Helene in Knoxville

After we took off, it seemed like Mommee would never stop heaving.

I tried to touch her arm and comfort her, but I didn't know how. Marlene unbuckled her seat belt, climbed into Mommee's lap, and hugged her. They rocked back and forth, for what seemed like hours. Looking at them, I felt a hole in my stomach that would never fill back up.

We changed planes at JFK and got on Delta Air Lines.

Destination: Knoxville, Tennessee.

In my fantasizing about attaining "been-to" status among Liberians by living in America or Europe, I had imagined myself in Minneapolis like Mary Tyler Moore. Mommee had rented the show on video for us to watch at Sugar Beach. I dreamed I would become a career girl and stride down the streets of Minneapolis turning the world on with my smile. Or maybe I'd end up in Los Angeles, like Kelly in *Charlie's Angels,* running around the beaches in my bikini and jumping into my convertible when Bosley called.

Not Knoxville. Never Knoxville, Tennessee.

When we climbed aboard Pan Am 150, we were privileged, elite Congo People. When we arrived in Knoxville, we were African refugees.

Aunt Jeanette and Bridget and Gabriel met us at the airport and took us to their ranch-style house at 5921 Meadowland Drive, the same house where we'd been two years earlier when Mommee got the letter from Daddy that he was divorcing her.

Mommee shared Aunt Jeanette's bedroom; I shared Bridget's; Marlene shared Gabriel's.

As resident refugees, Knoxville took on a different personality. It was no longer an exotic vacation spot where we spent two weeks running around buying hair perms and shampoos to take back to Eunice and Vicky in Liberia. Instead, it now seemed like a place where I was trapped, a prison far from home.

The sheer number of fast-food restaurants was mind-boggling. In Liberia, we had heard of McDonald's and Burger King, which seemed far more exotic than the single joint in Monrovia that served burgers, Diana's Restaurant on Broad Street. In Knoxville, there was Biscuitville, Bojangles, Sizzlin Steakhouse; there was Cracker Barrel and Shoney's. There was International House of Pancakes and Arby's and Hardee's and Kentucky Fried Chicken. There was Wendy's, PoFolks, Taco Bell, Long John Silver's, Dairy Queen, Arthur Treacher's, Chick-fil-A, Pizza Hut, Godfather's, and Piccadilly.

Knoxville's I-40 ran east about twenty miles to the turnoff for Gatlinburg and Pigeon Forge. Bridget and Gabriel loved going to Gatlinburg and Pigeon Forge, so Marlene and I got in the car and went with them. The radio played country music by the Oak Ridge Boys. By the time we got to Pigeon Forge, a fake town with fake buildings and country music stages, Marlene and I were singing:

My heart's on fire for Elvira.

Knoxville's biggest sin was that it did not have a beach. There was no ocean to lull you to sleep at night, no sand to walk on looking for crabs, no horizon to connect you with the outside world.

Though I never swam in the ocean at Sugar Beach, its presence assured me that there were other people out there, living other lives on the other side. The ocean connected us to the world, giving me a sense of security. Then the world failed to respond after the coup, demonstrating that security was false. Still, being near the ocean made me feel that there was something out there for me should my own circumstances suddenly become untenable.

Sitting on the floor in Aunt Jeanette's living room, I studied her road atlas, the big page at the beginning that has the whole United States on it. We were landlocked between North Carolina and Arkansas. Lakes didn't count, and rivers didn't really either, except maybe the Mississippi, since it seemed to connect you to the Gulf of Mexico. But I wanted a connection to the Atlantic.

To get to the Atlantic from Knoxville we would have to travel east for more than five hundred miles, through Morristown and Johnson City and Roanoke and Newport News all the way to Virginia Beach.

"Bridget, y'all da ever go to the beach?" I said.

"We da go to de lake."

"But wha' bout de ocean?"

She shook her head. "It would take too long. Days."

That summer passed in a mist. I tried to track down my Liberian friends who had all fled to the States, too. Philip and Richard were in Massachusetts, Tello 'them were in Washington, D.C., Veda was in Cameroon with her father.

My Sugar Beach family had scattered. John Bull was at college in Cedarville, Ohio, a tiny Christian college. Vicki was in Ohio, too, at the University of Toledo. Janice was in England at Essex University. Two months after we arrived in Knoxville, Daddy left Liberia. He was now in North Carolina, some place called Durham, which was near where he'd gone to college. He'd followed us out of Liberia as soon as he got out of the hospital.

And Eunice was still in Liberia.

Mommee seemed to be healing. I overheard her talking to Aunt Jeanette a couple of times about what happened at Sugar Beach, but as soon as they caught me eavesdropping, they stopped talking. In August 1980, just days before the start of the new school year, Mommee found an apartment nearby for us to move into, and we left Aunt Jeanette's house.

Our new home was as different from Sugar Beach as a squat shrub is from a tall cypress. It was one of the legions of apartments throughout the South that was put up in the 1960s and 1970s with all the character of an air-conditioning vent (there was one in each room). It had beige carpeting and all the windows, as well as the sliding doors that led to a rectangular cookie-cutter balcony, came with their own beige curtains. It had two bedrooms—one for Mommee and one that Marlene and I shared. A small, dark galley kitchen. Wood paneling on the wall in the living room and the dining alcove.

Sharing a room with Marlene should have felt familiar because we often slept in the same room at Sugar Beach. But in Knoxville, at night when we both retired to our twin beds on each side of the wall, there was a cavernous emptiness in the room. No Eunice.

Mommee tried to make it homey. On the first day of school, she turned up the heat in the apartment, even though it was only September and still hot. She went to Kroger supermarket. When I came home that afternoon, the very warm apartment smelled like Jiffy corn muffins and vegetable barley soup, American-style. I immediately yearned for Old Man Charlie's Liberian pepper soup.

Marlene was already home. Mommy had been called to pick her up from school early after she had gotten into a fight with another girl in her fifth-grade class at Chilhowee Elementary School. The girl had walked up to Marlene and said, "You're from Africa so you must steal."

Marlene had replied to the girl, who was black: "You're from Africa, too."

"No, I'm not, I'm from Detroit!" With that, the girl punched Marlene, who started crying.

When I got home, Mommee looked tired. "How did it go?" she asked me.

I went into our room and closed the door behind me, quietly.

I had stood against my locker in the cavernous hallway, shaking. I wasn't just the new girl, I was the new girl from Africa. It was my first time in a public school, and all the kids seemed rough. ACS in Liberia had only three hundred students in the whole K-twelve school, Holston High School had three hundred students in my tenth-grade class. I clutched my schedule of classes in my hand. My first class was homeroom, and I was the last one there because I hadn't realized there were two floors to the school, and wasted ten minutes walking around the first floor looking for Room 207.

When I finally walked into my class, everyone stopped and looked at me. Unlike the desks and chairs we had at ACS in Liberia, Holston's desks were actually chairs with desks built onto them. They were all made for right-handed students; I was left-handed.

I tried to slide into my desk-chair but kept bumping into the front desk part. For some reason I couldn't figure out how to just sit in the desk-chair. A couple of students giggled. Finally, twisting my body, I sat down and peered intently at my schedule sheet in my hand, trying to look as if I was focusing on something other than how stupid I felt.

"And who is this?" asked the homeroom teacher, walking over to me.

"My name is Helene Calista Cooper."

"Where are you from, Helene?"

"Monrovia."

"Where's that?"

"Liberia."

"Where's that?"

"West Africa."

"You're from Africa?"

"Yes."

"You sound like you're from Boston. Why don't you have an African accent?"

Because I can speak cullor, you dingbat.

What did she think I'd been doing for fourteen years living in Liberia if not learning how to talk American? That was the whole point of watching all those American TV shows. I spoke raw Liberian English in my head and at home, but put me around an American and I immediately started talking like I had okra in my mouth.

I ventured into the cafeteria at lunchtime. It was crammed with kids talking and laughing. A long line snaked past some vile-looking refried potato balls they called tater tots. And re-fried meat cutlets they called chicken-fried steak. I glanced at the rows of tables. Kids were starting to look back at me. I turned and ran out, down the hall and into the girls' bathroom, where I locked myself in a stall and sat on a toilet with my feet up on the bowl so no one could tell I was in there.

That night, I stayed in my room and started a letter to Eunice.

"Dear Eunice," I wrote.

"Today was the first day of school, and it was so great. There are all these cute boys in my class, but I don't like them because I've got bigger fish to fry: Junior Lowry, this GORGEOUS guy in the 12th grade. He's tall and handsome and has pretty eyes and he asked me out on a date. We're going to the movies on Friday. He's almost as cute as Philip! (smile)"

Sitting on her bed across the room from me, Marlene worked on her own letter. Eunice, stuck in her mother's house in Sinkor while she finished out her last year of high school at Haywood, was about to get bombarded by two glowing reports from America. The Cooper girls had arrived! No problems for us! Those Country People thought they had gotten us by rap-

ing our mother and killing our relatives? Well, we were showing them, weren't we?

The next day at school, I spent lunch in the stall in the girls'
bathroom on the second floor again. After about twenty minutes I finally emerged, to find a girl from my homeroom leaning against the sink looking at me. Her name was Norma and
she was wearing a pair of Jordache jeans and a blue sweatshirt.

I stared back at her. I couldn't tell if she was waiting for
me, and if she was, why? Was she friend or foe? Deciding to
chance friendly, I smiled. "Hi," I said.

"How come you're not dark-skinned?"

I rolled my eyes and walked out of the bathroom.

Why oh why couldn't we have moved to Washington or
Boston, with Tello 'them and all the other Congo kids who'd
run away? Knoxville was just another version of Sugar Beach,
and this time I didn't even have Eunice. My whole family, in
one swoop, had disintegrated.

In time, I hit upon a way to get through lunch. I smuggled
the sandwich and V-8 juice Mommee packed for me into the
library, behind the book stalls. I headed for the farthest
reaches—the biology section in the back. There, I settled in
with the romance novels that Eunice and I had taken up that
last year at Sugar Beach.

They didn't have Barbara Cartland, but they had Harlequins, which were basically the same thing. Among the many
constants in Harlequins was that the hero was tall, handsome,
and rich. The heroine could be rich, too, but more often was
poor and plucky. They were never black—always white—which
is why on that day in the Holston High library when I started
working on writing my own Harlequin I faced a huge dilemma.
What color would my heroine be? As a black teen, I couldn't
really write about a white girl, right? But all the Harlequin
women were white!

I finally settled on a mulatto. She was half-black and half-French, and her name was Reina. His name was Tristan, a masculine, Harlequin-man name if ever there was one. It was fine for him to be white.

From my perch in the corner of the Holston library, I either worked on my romance novel or continued my letters to Eunice. My letters were as imaginative as the Harlequin I was working on: glowingly describing my new life and my make-believe friends. I painted a story of a life that echoed the American dream as we had imagined it to be from Liberia. My imaginary relationship with Junior Lowry progressed to his escorting me to Homecoming. Junior was on the basketball team and I had made the cheerleading squad. He was always taking me for ice cream after practice. We had started making out, but he had only gotten to second base so far. I was always turning down dates from other guys, who found me "exotic." I was trying to stay faithful to Junior, but it was hard because so many of the boys at Holston were chasing after me.

In the real world, Junior was on the basketball team. He was in my geometry class, and had smiled at me once.

Each week, I left my letters on the dining room table and Mommee mailed them during the day.

Eunice could read me like the cheap novels we both loved. "Aye, Helene, you know you're not no cheerleader," she wrote back.

Eunice's letters were written in red ink. She was sleeping at night with a wet towel on her chest because her mother's house had no air-conditioning.

Bro. Henry had driven her back to Monrovia the night after our Pan Am flight departed Robertsfield airport. It was almost two a.m. when they stopped at Sugar Beach.

There were no servants there when Eunice and Bro. Henry

stopped by—they had collected their paychecks, said their good-byes, and struck off to try to figure out for themselves how to traverse the new landscape of post-Congo Liberia. In the pitch-black night, Eunice and Bro. Henry hauled her bags to his car, filling up the trunk and the backseat. Bro. Henry locked the house up behind them; the triumph of hope over experience. Rogues came to Sugar Beach regularly when the family was there; there was no way the house would be unviolated now that it was empty of the family, with Doe's soldiers patrolling the countryside.

Eunice looked behind her as they drove away, but without any lights left on; it was hard to see the house in the dark. It disappeared quickly from view.

Bro. Henry drove the eleven miles to Sinkor, dropped Eunice off at her mother's house, and headed back to his own house nearby. He had no intention of leaving Liberia. He'd be damned if any Country People were gonna run him out of his country. He was Captain Dennis's son, after all.

After six years of living with the Coopers, Eunice was back to being Bassa, living again with her mother and five other cousins and adopted kids in her mother's small house in Sinkor.

How do you rebecome what you were six years before? Can you erase six years?

Mrs. Bull tiptoed around Eunice like she was a fragile flower. Her daughter was used to the best after living with the Coopers; Mrs. Bull felt she was under pressure to keep Eunice in the style she believed she had become accustomed to. She put aside the plumpest and juiciest crawfish from the Cassava Leaf in the afternoons for Eunice, because, she told the brood of stray children who hung around the house looking for handouts, there was now a VIP living there: Mrs. Cooper's Daughter.

She called Eunice "Mrs. Cooper's Daughter."

Eunice's mother told the other kids in the house to make sure they left the good rice for "Mrs. Cooper's daughter." She spent her scarce money on shampoo and conditioner, because, she told one and all, she knew "Mrs. Cooper's daughter" was used to using real shampoo, not the rough caustic soda soap many Liberians used to wash.

In December 1980, seven months after moving back to her mother's house, Eunice graduated from high school at Haywood. Graduation day was steamy, especially under the black cap and gown she had to wear. Sitting among her classmates at Haywood, she spotted two familiar faces in the crowd of proud relatives watching the graduates. One was her mother. The other was Bro. Henry.

"Bro. Henry came to my graduation," Eunice wrote me. She added, proudly: "He gave me $40."

I read the letter enviously. Eunice had graduated from high school. Freedom lay ahead. Nobody could tell her what to do anymore. Nobody could force her to live in Knoxville, hundreds and hundreds of miles from the ocean.

Being in Knoxville felt like straddling two worlds. There was my physical world, with the monotony of going to a school every day where no one talked to me, and coming home to watch *General Hospital* with Marlene, and occasional trips to Sizzlin' Steakhouse with Mommee. At night, Daddy called from North Carolina with updates about his new job—as an accountant with a company in Durham. We could never talk long on the phone, though, because it was long-distance and cost ten cents a minute, unless you called after eleven p.m. When we lived at Sugar Beach, if we wanted to talk to someone, we went to their house.

Then there was the world in my head, the one in Liberia, pre–April 12, 1980. That was the world I cared about, the world that I missed so much. That was the world filled with beautiful ripe smells—of dried fish and tropical flowers. That world was filled with people I knew and people who knew me. It was filled with a deep-to-the-bone knowledge that I was somebody and I came from somewhere, a world that Elijah Johnson and Randolph Cooper and my ancestors had built from scratch through blood and sweat.

Would we ever get to go back? What was Eunice doing? How was Eunice doing? What about Jack and Bolabo and Old Man Charlie and Tommy? Who was in my pink room at Sugar Beach?

I didn't think about the post–April 12, 1980, Liberia, the one that we'd lived in for a month before running away. In my head, Liberia was the Liberia that I'd known before the coup.

Every night at six-thirty, Marlene and Mommee and I turned on *ABC World News Tonight.* Frank Reynolds, Peter Jennings, Brit Hume, and the cast of newscasters were the most spectacular people ever. I liked watching *World News* (not to be confused with local news) because I was sure that Frank Reynolds and Peter Jennings knew about Liberia. Surely they cared? Watching them lessened my homesickness. The program mostly focused on the American hostages in Iran, but it still made me feel comfortable, knowing that Frank Reynolds and Peter Jennings were undoubtedly keeping an eye on Liberia.

My favorite ABC News reporter was Brit Hume at the State Department. He could talk without moving his lips. He stood in front of all these flags and sometimes I thought I could see the Liberian flag, with its eleven red and white stripes, and its one Lone Star.

The Lone Star Forever! The Lone Star Forever!
Oh long may it float over land and o'er sea . . .

Desert it, no never! Uphold it, forever!
Oh fight for the Lone Star Banner, All Hail!

But we had deserted it. At the first sign of trouble, we'd run away. We were refugees.

"Mommee, are we refugees?" I asked one evening.

"Absolutely not."

"What makes us not refugees?"

"Because we paid for our own plane tickets."

In October, Mommee started dating. I'll call him Raymond Jackson. He was tall and beefy, and he wore his hair in a permed comb-over to cover his bald spot. He was the principal of an elementary school in Knoxville and drove a brown Cadillac.

Mr. Jackson took one look at Mommee during services at the Methodist Church in Knoxville and sidled over to Aunt Jeanette to ask who she was. Then he started calling and showing up at our apartment to take Mommee to the movies.

One afternoon, about four months after he first started showing up, Marlene and I were watching *General Hospital* after school while Mommee was out at the supermarket. There was a knock on the door. I peeped into the keyhole and groaned. "It's that nasty Mr. Jackson." Marlene immediately disappeared into Mommee's room, closing the door.

I opened the door. "Hi, Mommee's not here, sorry," I said.

He came in anyway. I ignored him and went and sat back on the couch, where I tried to focus on Luke and Laura.

"How much do you want a stereo?" he asked suddenly, coming to stand near the couch.

I had been begging Mommee to buy me a stereo for weeks. I wanted to play the record albums I'd brought from Liberia— Michael Jackson's *Off the Wall* and GQ's *Disco Nights*. Mommee said we couldn't afford it.

"I really want one," I told Mr. Jackson.

He was standing too close to me. I shifted away from him, but he sat on the edge of the couch. He kept talking, in a low, soothing voice, while he reached over and started to rub my shoulder, and then my breast.

I sat frozen for about thirty seconds. His hand started to slip under my pink tube top. "I could get you a really nice stereo," he said.

I jumped out of my chair and ran out of the living room and into Mommee's bedroom, where Marlene was lying on the bed reading a comic book. I locked the bedroom door. "Get up!" I yelled at Marlene.

"That man still here?" she asked.

"Just get up!" When she didn't move, I just started pushing Mommee's bed, with Marlene in it, to block the door.

Then I heard the front door closing. He had left.

I fretted about whether to tell Mommee. I felt I couldn't tell her after what had just happened in Liberia.

But when she came home, and I followed her into the kitchen where she was unpacking groceries.

"Mr. Jackson touched my breasts."

Pulling out a packet of chicken, her hand stilled. She carefully put the chicken down on the counter, then turned to me, bracing her hands behind her. "What happened?" she asked, slowly.

"He came here and he asked me if I wanted a record player and while he was asking me he touched my breasts."

Mommee eyed me up and down.

"Didn't I tell you to stop wearing those short shorts?" she finally said.

I stalked out of the kitchen, slamming the door to the bedroom behind me. Marlene crept in after me and got into her bed. Neither of us said anything. The silence in the room stretched between us. Tears were running down my cheeks but I tried to be quiet so Marlene couldn't see or hear. She knew what had happened. But she was nine years old.

The next afternoon, when I arrived home from school, Mr. Jackson was sitting in the living room with Mommee. He was on the love seat, and she was on the sofa, where I had been when he touched me the day before. I started to head straight for my bedroom, but Mommee stopped me.

"Raymond has something to say to you," she said.

Mr. Jackson was looking down at his feet. "Uh, I'm sorry I touched you," he said. "It was wrong of me."

"Okay," I said. Then I left and went into the bedroom. Minutes later, I heard the front door closing, and he was gone. I never saw him again.

In August 1981, Mommee decided it was safe for her to go back to Liberia. Relative peace had returned temporarily, and the Congo People who had run away were all trickling back to restart their businesses. Mommee wanted to try to collect rent on some of our remaining properties to help put me through college. She would move in with Bro. Henry in his house in Sinkor, where Mama Grand was living, too. She couldn't go back to Sugar Beach because President Doe had seized it to use for executions.

Marlene and I begged to go back with her. "Mommee, I hold your foot," I said. "Please don't leave us here."

But Mommee was adamant. "No way," she said. "That place is not safe. You all are going to your daddy in North Carolina."

Before Mommee left for Liberia, I made a cassette tape for Eunice with all the latest songs from America on it. Marlene and I talked on the tape, too. "Hi Eunice!" we said, putting on our best okra-infused American accents. Then we dissolved into raw Liberian English. "Eunice, I sendin' you de latest musique!" I yelled on the tape. "I sendin' 'She Used to Be My Girl' by the O'Jays and Cameo and Stacy Lattisaw. You won't believe it when you hear; that girl just fourteen years old, but she can sing so!" I had spent a whole weekend at Bridget and Gabriel's house in Knoxville recording songs to send Eunice.

"Eunice, Eunice how you doin?" Marlene broke in. "You da go to Sugar Beach?"

"Shut up!" I yelled at Marlene. "Wha' wron w'you? You know she can't go to no Sugar Beach!"

Marlene started to tear up.

Then she wiped her face. "You da still go to Relda Cinema?" she said into the tape recorder. "You da see Palma?"

Mommee packed our cassette in her hand luggage. In her checked suitcase, she packed a plastic bag from Eckerd's drugstore filled with the bath and shower products that Eunice had always used to ask us to bring back for her whenever we went on vacation abroad: shampoo and conditioner, Jergens body lotion, lavender-scented bath gel.

Daddy came from North Carolina to pick us up. He drove up in his new car, a used burgundy Lincoln Continental, and put Mommee's suitcases in the trunk. We all piled in, Mommee in the front seat and me and Marlene in the back, and reversed out of the apartment parking lot, and on to Magnolia Boulevard. We drove by the strip mall and K-Mart and onto the highway to the airport.

Mommee wore a brown knit pantsuit and long sleeves even though it was hot in Knoxville in August and it would be even hotter at Robertsfield when she arrived.

"Who meetin' you at Robertsfield?" I asked her at the airport. She was standing in the check-in line, rummaging through her brown bag. I could see Maalox, two big cans of Finesse hairspray, a big jar of Tylenol sticking out. The tape for

Eunice was poking out of the side of her bag, with my hand-writing on the side: FOR EUNICE FROM HELENE AND MARLENE.

"Stop worrying," Mommee said. "Bro. Henry coming to meet me."

She took her leather wallet out. Her wrist, long and white, looked impossibly tiny against the bag, like it could snap at any second. She was wearing the gold bracelet she had gotten made for me by the Mandingo gold man in Liberia when I was seven. It had intricate carvings of circles and diamond shapes on it, and my initials "HCC" in the middle. From the day Mommee first put it on my wrist, I never took it off, until one afternoon in Knoxville when Mommee realized I couldn't take it off because I had "big bones." Then she pried the bracelet off my arm and said she would get the Mandingo gold man to make me another, bigger one, when she went home.

So now she was wearing my bracelet, which was huge against her skinny wrist. I wondered how her small bones would survive going back to that place.

"But s'pose he not 'deah?" I was terrified she would have to go through Robertsfield airport, with all those soldiers there, by herself.

"He will be there."

She zipped up her bag and stood up. Then she looked at me.

"I not scared of those people."

But I was. I was scared enough for both of us. I would never not be scared of those people again.

She hugged us quickly, and whispered something to Daddy. Then she was gone, through the gate, to the Eastern Airlines plane that would take her to JFK, to the Pan Am that would take her back to Monrovia. "Bye, Mommee!" Marlene and I yelled, hoping maybe she'd hear us and reappear back through the gate. We ran to the window and looked at the plane, but you couldn't see anyone through the plane windows. Still we stayed till the plane backed away from the gate. Marlene was crying. She kept saying "Bye Mommee bye Mommee bye Mommee."

Finally Daddy took her hand and turned her away. Mommee's plane was gone now. I followed the two of them through the airport, to the parking lot, back to Daddy's car. We got in and headed down I-70 to North Carolina.

We could only get country music stations between Knoxville and North Carolina. Juice Newton came on the radio, singing "Angel of the Morning." I looked out the window as the billboards whizzed by.

Shoney's. PoFolks. Biscuitville. WELCOME TO NORTH CAROLINA, the sign said. THE TAR HEEL STATE.

Another new school, another new library.

16

GREENSBORO, NORTH CAROLINA, 1981

*O*n the first day of school in Greensboro, North Carolina, I decided to wear the purple pants that Eunice had stitched up for me. It was my best outfit, and reminded me of leaning against the railing outside school with Eunice in the hot Monrovia sunshine, waiting for Fedeles to pick us up.

I wore them with a multicolored striped shirt with a baby collar. I'd gotten that outfit two whole years before, back when we were on vacation in America, at "5-7-9," named after the

Mommee, in a photo she sent me from Liberia

sizes on hand. Eunice had hemmed the pants for me because they were too long when I got them. When the pants got a hole in the seam because I wore them so much, she sewed it up, with black thread. The black thread showed a little but I didn't care. They were my favorite pants. I'd worn them at least once a week that last year in Liberia.

I got dressed carefully that morning, because I knew that unlike the last two schools I had been to in America, I would be staying at this school in Greensboro for two years, long enough to graduate. It was our third first-day-of-school since we left Liberia.

After Holston High School in Knoxville came Jordan Senior High School in Durham, where I was a junior for twenty-seven whole days.

After Mommee moved back to Liberia, Marlene and I moved into Daddy's apartment in Durham, another one of those dreadful 1970s-style complexes. This one was called "The Mews" but bore no resemblance to the cozy British mews Eunice and I had read about in our Barbara Cartland romance novels. Our mews looked like dental offices, and were right next to a Food Town.

It was September 1981. Almost immediately, Daddy announced that he had gotten a job in Greensboro with another accounting practice. He looked around the apartment, with its rented furniture, all matchey-matchey, with distaste. "I've bought a house in Greensboro," he announced. "You can both have your own rooms again."

"How did you pay for it?" I asked, worriedly.

A laugh. "We're not in Liberia anymore," he said. "This is America! Land of the free, home of house notes! I sold the house in Spain for the down payment. The mortgage is going to be pretty high since I don't have credit here, but we'll manage."

I fretted about how Daddy would make ends meet on $15,000 a year and a $900 monthly mortgage payment. But I also had other things to worry about.

"If we're moving to Greensboro, then why do I have to go to this stupid high school here in Durham?" I asked.

He grinned. "We don't move for a month. You expect to just sit around doing nothing for a month?"

So I spent a month of hiding in the library at my new school in Durham, before we moved to Greensboro.

The sign in front of James B. Dudley Senior High School, Population, 626, Demographic: 85 percent black, read: THE BEST HIGH SCHOOL IN THE CITY.

"You two are going to be taking the school bus," Daddy told me and Marlene. We were both appalled. Daddy had a burgundy Lincoln Continental that he had bought—Ford Motor Credit had already started calling asking about late car payments—so why couldn't he just drive us to our schools? We'd seen the scary-looking school kids getting off the buses in our neighborhood. We didn't want to go anywhere near them.

"Daddy, I hold your foot," I begged.

"You'll make friends, Helene," he promised. "Not as fast as Marlene will, but you'll make friends."

I got ready with extreme care that morning. As I applied my black eyeliner, I thought back to that last year in Liberia, when Mommee let Eunice and me buy eyeshadow kits at Evans drugstore on Broad Street. We both got green, which we plastered all over our top lids, then paraded out to show Mommee. She burst out laughing. "No way!" she said, then dragged us into her bathroom and handed us Kleenexes. "Take off your glasses." She called out for reinforcements. "Vickie! Come help me show these two how to put on makeup!"

Vickie took Eunice and Mommee took me. We both took off our huge eyeglasses and squinted at them. I had 20/450 vision but Eunice had progressed to 20/800! "Blind as a bat," I whispered at her. "Shut up!" she whispered back.

"None of you can see so shut up," Mommee said.

All of Mommee's pretty makeup and perfume jars were lined up on the bathroom vanity, next to the sink. She had Chanel and Christian Dior and Elizabeth Arden. She had a bunch of compacts with powder, but they all looked too light for me and definitely too light for Eunice. Vickie had a couple of her own jars with her, and she went back and forth between hers' and Mommee's, mixing them up in a puddle in her hand, then applying them under Eunice's eyes. Soon, all of Eunice's dark circles were gone.

Meanwhile, Mommee dabbed a light brown shadow around my eyelids, then smudged it in. When she turned away to get something else, I peeked into the mirror, putting my face right up against it so I could see without my glasses. I looked exactly the same. "But I can't see it!" I wailed.

Mommee smacked me back around. "Just keep quiet." She had a black pencil in her hand. She leaned close to my face and slowly lined my lids. It was hard to keep still because the eyeliner tickled. I could smell Mommee's perfume, she was so close to me: Joy, by Jean Patou, flowery and Frenchy. As usual when she concentrated, she bit her tongue.

"Okay, you can look now," Vickie told Eunice. "You, too," Mommee told me.

We looked at each other, just saw shapes, so we put our glasses back on. "A ya, you fine, oh!" Eunice said to me. "You, too!" I laughed. It was true. Vickie had made Eunice look exotic. Her eyes stood out like Bette Davis's.

I thought I looked spectacular. The eyeliner made my eyes look huge and dramatic. Though I had been unable to duplicate that look, I dutifully applied my green eyeshadow that morning in Greensboro. I had to try.

I missed Mommee. It seemed out of place that she wasn't around for so seminal an event as my first day at school. As I tried to fluff my hair, I thought about my first day at school in Knoxville, a year before, when she had turned the heat on too high and made muffins and soup to try to make the house seem cozy. If she were here now, she would have plenty to say about my outfit—I could just hear her: "Helene, the time for those purple pants have come and gone. Don't you have anything else to wear?" She'd probably even try to get me to wear a dress or skirt.

She had been gone for two months now. The night before I had written her a long letter, which I left on the kitchen counter for Daddy to mail. Getting mail to Liberia was getting harder and harder. The country wasn't paying its international postal dues, a point of much shame to Daddy, who used to be deputy postmaster general. In order to get a letter to Liberia, you had to find someone in the United States who was going there, and send them your mail. A friend of Daddy's was going home in a few days, so Daddy collected letters in a big package on the kitchen counter.

Mommee was spending most of her time in Liberia "running around." It was a well-known Liberian pastime. "Wha' you doin t'day?" you'd say to a Liberian acquaintance when you ran into them on the street in Monrovia. "Oh, nothing ya. Jes runnin 'round." Running around, from going to the Ministry of Public Works to try to pay your light bill to bribing the people at the Ministry of Foreign Affairs to give you an exit permit to chasing Lebanese merchants for your rent money, can take up a whole day.

Mommee's running around focused mostly on chasing after Lebanese merchants. She also spent a lot of time trying to lease whatever property we had that hadn't been seized by the Doe regime.

On that first day at Dudley—it was in October, so the school year was well in gear—Marlene and I trudged down to the end of the block to catch our buses. Her bus came first, to take her to Vandalia Elementary. She gave me a scared wave as she boarded, and was gone.

I stood on the corner, holding my notebook in my arm, shifting from foot to foot. We had moved into a leafy middle-class neighborhood that used to be all white, but blacks were slowly taking over, and the white people were leaving. The houses were a mismash of colonials, ranches, and even bungalows. It was called Woodlea.

I had spent thirty minutes curling my hair that morning, before pulling up one side in the front. It was the same hairstyle I had worn that day in 1980, just a couple of months before April 12, when Philip Parker walked me to the car and carried my books. Just thinking about that day made me happy. I was primed, I thought, with all of my good-luck charms for a good first day of school in Greensboro: makeup, favorite pants mended by Eunice, lucky hairstyle. When I closed my eyes, I could hear Eunice talking to me.

"What you scared of, you girl? De children won't do nutting to you."

I had on my new contact lenses, which Daddy had gotten me, but they were scratching my eyes and I kept blinking and snapping my head when I turned, because I couldn't roll my eyes from one side to another without it hurting.

I was looking the wrong way when the bus rumbled up, on the other side of the street. I ran across the street and boarded. "Um, are you going to Dudley?" I asked the driver. She just nodded. The kids on the bus were all staring at me with that look I was becoming so familiar with.

"Oh, I see, you can talk big mouth when you in Liberia, but when you get to America, that de time butter can't melt in your mouth, eh?"

Head down, eyes down, I stumbled to the back of the bus and sat next to the window. I stared intently at my blue binder. The kids had started talking again. Everybody was talking at once. I looked out the window.

Then, suddenly, this guy in front yelled, at the top of his lungs: "SHUT UP, HELENE!!!!!"

Everybody on the bus started laughing. I looked up, alarmed. But none of them were looking at me.

Then he did it again. "SHUT UP, HELENE!!!"

Now he was clutching his stomach, doubled over, laughing.

The lump in my throat was huge as I peered out the window, staring at suburban Greensboro flashed by, with its 7-Eleven stores in uniform strip malls. If I were riding into downtown Monrovia from Sugar Beach, I would see ten people I knew before we got to Sinkor. But here, no one even seemed to walk around outside.

"SHUT UP, HELENE!!!"

Finally, we arrived at Dudley.

I went through the motions of homeroom, and first, second, and third periods. I was used to not talking to anyone during class, after my year in Knoxville and month at Jordan, and those weird chair-desks were old hat to me by now. But what I was really dreading was lunchtime, where I knew I'd have to avoid the cafeteria and find the library again.

When the school bell rang, ending Algebra II, and signaling lunch, I dragged myself out of the class and started to wander. In the hallway, students slammed locker doors and called out to one another, en route to the cafeteria.

I decided that before I looked for the library, I'd scout around for my chemistry classroom, the one after lunchtime. That way I'd make sure I could find it, the better to avoid those dreaded scenes when I walked in late and everyone stared.

There were about eight kids in the classroom already when I poked my head in, even though it was still lunchtime. They were chatting, some just sat reading. I was about to dart back into the hall, when one of the boys, who had been in my Algebra II class saw me.

"Hey!" he said.

Everybody looked up at me. I froze, hovering at the door.

"You're following me," the boy said. He was tall and cute, but looked too smart to be cool. His "you're following me" was said in a friendly way, like he wanted me to keep following him.

From some place I'd forgotten still existed, my voice shot back: "Looks to me like you're the one who's been following me, boy-o."

Everyone in the class started laughing. He was laughing, too. "My name is Lee McLaughlin," he said.

I smiled at him, thinking: *I love you, Lee McLaughlin.*

"Where do you live?" Lee asked me.

"Woodlea."

"Hey, Helene Cameron lives over there," he said. "She's got the biggest mouth in the world, but she's okay."

That afternoon, on the bus going home, I felt light and happy. The kids on the bus didn't seem so bad after all. They were loud as hell, but when someone shouted "SHUT UP, HE-LENE!" I finally noticed that it wasn't me everyone was looking at when they were laughing, it was Helene Cameron, who, in the middle of talking to the girl next to her, just rolled her eyes and kept talking.

So I laughed, too. I could hear Eunice's voice, from another world and another place.

"Ehn you see? Now wha' you wa so scared of?"

17

GREENSBORO, NORTH CAROLINA, 1982

$\mathcal{T}$he new President Doe quickly discovered that running a country wasn't the simple thing it seemed from the vantage point of an enlisted soldier watching fat-cat government officials speeding around town in their big cars. Doe tried to collect revenue from a tax base where the vast majority didn't have a pot to piss in, let alone income to tax. He had run off most of the wealthy people who had been the tax base, and the

Helene, senior class yearbook

property seizures he could perform there, like Sugar Beach, were tapped.

Doe decided to start minting five-dollar coins. Liberians mocked them as "Doe dollars," and they were useless on the international market. He also started printing Liberian dollar bills, bearing his rapidly fattening face. When he took over the government in 1980, he had been a lean, wiry army master sergeant. By 1982, he was the fat-cat government official he had so despised, with newly minted currency at his disposal.

The Liberian dollar, which had been pegged to the U.S. dollar since 1847, took a nosedive. It dipped from 1–1 to 10–1 to 15–1 to 25–1, with nowhere to go but down.

Doe was sanguine. He gave government workers and public school teachers and even the enlisted soldiers from whose ranks he came the virtually worthless scraps of paper for their monthly salaries. He supplemented the soldiers' pay with sacks of rice and jugs of palm oil, and gave them blanket leave to supplement the rest of their income by fleecing citizens. The rest of the government workers, including those who didn't have army-issued M-16 guns, followed suit anyway, using whatever little driplet of power they had to hold up the public. You want electricity? You better make sure you grease the palms of the people at Liberia Electric Company. Government ministers ran up a $78,000 tab at Salvatore's Restaurant in one year, and wouldn't pay until the owner paid exorbitant taxes. In U.S.D.

U.S.D., for U.S. dollars, became a new phrase in Liberia. The Congo People who remained in Liberia, and the ones who went back, like Mommee, went and studied the leases they had for rents on their properties that hadn't been seized by the government. Mama Grand looked at her numerous leases with various Lebanese merchants and grinned, her gold tooth reflecting in the sunlight. Hee hee. "Fifteen thousand dollars

(U.S.) per annum," one said. "Three thousand five hundred dollars (U.S.) per annum," another one said.

Mommee looked at her leases. Only one of them—for the Mobil Oil property left to myriad Dennis descendants—said "U.S." The rest just said "dollars."

She tried to renegotiate with the Lebanese merchants, and managed to get a couple to pay her half in U.S. dollars and half in Liberian dollars. She sent the U.S. dollars to us in North Carolina, where Daddy had already fallen far behind on our bills.

She gave some of the U.S. dollars to Eunice, who came to visit her at Bro. Henry's house, where Mommee was staying. Eunice's mother was still tiptoeing around "Mrs. Cooper's daughter."

Except Eunice wasn't Mrs. Cooper's daughter anymore. And Mrs. Cooper wasn't quite the grand dame she used to be anymore. And Monrovia wasn't the same now that the Country People were in charge.

Mommee found an American couple at the U.S. embassy who sent her letters through the American Army post office. When we wrote her letters from Greensboro, we addressed them to Maj. David Underwood, A.P.O. New York.

Early one morning I was asleep in my bedroom in Greensboro when I heard Daddy shouting over the phone. I snapped awake in an instant. It was around four a.m.; it could only be Mommee, calling from Liberia. She had to go to the telecom office in Monrovia and book a specific time to call, and then go back and place the call.

I jumped out of bed and went running, out the door of my bedroom, around the corner into Daddy's room, jumping onto his bed. I beat Marlene to Daddy's phone so she hurled herself downstairs to get on the phone in the kitchen.

"Mommee!" I yelled, after Daddy gave me the phone.

"How's the joy of my heart?" Mommee said.

"I on the phone, too!" Marlene yelled from downstairs.

"How's my lovely Marlene?"

"Mommee we miss you!" Marlene said. "You will come here soon?"

"I don't know, sweetheart. Money's tight." It had been seven months since we'd said good-bye in Knoxville. It felt so strange to hear her familiar voice, with the Liberian lilt, suddenly, right there, across the wire in the same room as me.

"Aye Mommee, please come," Marlene said. I wanted to echo that but I didn't want to seem like a baby. Marlene's voice was dissolving into a whimper as she pleaded. I felt a lump growing in my throat as I silently egged her on.

After a while, Mommee started to sound like she was getting upset.

I changed the subject. "Mommee, guess what!" I said. "I na decide what I will be when I finish w' school."

Her voice caught, but she sounded relieved, too. "Oh yeah?"

"I'm not going to be a Hollywood movie star no more," I told her. "Or a lawyer. I'm gonna be a journalist."

A week before, I had had my come-to-Jesus moment, courtesy of my American history class, taught by a fat short woman named Mrs. Johnson. She was completely uninspiring in all aspects of the class save when she talked about Watergate. Watergate got Mrs. Johnson animated.

She assigned us *All the President's Men* to read. Daddy took me and Marlene to Waldenbooks at Carolina Circle Mall in Greensboro, where he bought me two Harlequin romance novels and *All the President's Men*.

That afternoon, I opened it up, and my life changed. Every minute I had spent devouring the nightly news on ABC had been leading to this.

"June 17, 1972. Nine o'clock Saturday morning. Early for the telephone. Woodward fumbled for the receiver and snapped awake. The city editor of *The Washington Post* was on the line. Five men had been arrested earlier that morning in a burglary at Democratic headquarters, carrying photographic equipment and electronic gear. Could he come in?"

I finished *All the President's Men* in one go. Lying on my bed at three-thirty in the morning, I closed the book and rolled over. This was it. Woodward and Bernstein put Brit Hume to shame. The TV news at night was just a pale imitation of the real thing, I decided. It was all about newspaper reporting. Woodward and Bernstein had overturned a presidency! They had single-handedly—well, Deep Throat helped—brought down the American government.

Lying in my bed that early morning, I plotted my life. I would work for *The Washington Post.* I would write first about politics and corruption and bring down a few governments, like Woodward and Bernstein did. Then, after that, I would move on to cover the State Department, except I would be way better than Brit Hume. Eventually, my reporting would force the United States Army to invade Liberia and get rid of Doe. I would then return to Liberia a conquering hero, a famous journalist, a truth-teller extraordinaire.

In Mrs. Johnson's class that day, I asked obscure questions from the book, practicing my interviewing skills and showing off the fact that I had already finished it.

"Mrs. Johnson, do you think the first story that Woodward and Bernstein wrote implicating H. R. Haldeman was correctible?"

"What?"

"Do you think it was correctible? Should *The Washington Post* have corrected the fact that Sloan didn't implicate Haldeman specifically in his grand jury testimony, like the *Post* said, but rather implicated him later?"

Mrs. Johnson was as much of a press freak as I was becoming. After Watergate, we dove into the Pentagon Papers (Mrs. Johnson was not wedded to chronology) and the bravery of the *New York Times* in publishing these secret documents about the Vietnam War. I looked at her in wonder. "You mean the government told the *Times* they couldn't publish the secret papers, and they did so anyway?" I asked. Was the American press so powerful?

"They took the case to the Supreme Court," Mrs. Johnson said, practically licking her lips in satisfaction. "The press won."

I wanted to be part of that powerful press. I realized that I needed to start getting experience as a reporter, so the next year, my senior year, I signed up for Journalism as one of my electives. My other elective was Typing (because journalists had to know how to type). I took French 4 (for when I went to cover the State Department), AP English, and AP European History (also for future State Department coverage). Science was nowhere on my schedule. I certainly did not need to understand physics in order to bring down the government.

I loved my journalism class. The teacher was Ms. Mundy, and our sole job was to put out Dudley's school newspaper, *The Panther's Claw*. A quiet, cute boy sat behind me—Ollie Haywood Taylor, although everyone called him Haywood. He was the only other person in the class who actually wanted to be a journalist, and we quickly became competitive.

"I wanna do a sports column," he announced on the first day of class.

I rolled my eyes. "Oh please, how parochial. Who wants to read about Dudley's stupid track meets?" Haywood was on the track team, so I knew that's what he wanted to write about.

"My sports column will make your reviews look like bird droppings."

Since I had no interest in writing about the local goings-on at Dudley—that was not why I had become a journalist—I had asked Ms. Mundy if I could write about national politics, and she said no. Then I asked if I could write about foreign policy, and she again said no. "You have to write about things the school cares about," she said. "How about the school bus program?"

Was she kidding? "Okay, can I do TV reviews then?" I asked, figuring that was kind of national.

She agreed, and I dove into my first bylined piece: a review of *Remington Steele,* the TV show with Pierce Brosnan as a private detective. "Pierce Brosnan is absolutely, breathtakingly gorgeous!" I gushed in the newspaper. "And he's British!"

My aspiring journalism got me on Dudley's High IQ Team. It was not a debate team but rather a quiz-show-type team; there were five of us and we each had a specialty area in which we were supposed to excel. My specialty was "current events."

I trained for our team matches at night with Daddy, sitting at the table in the kitchen while he made dinner. He had imaginative menus that combined Liberian food and American food and European food into tasty glop-type dishes. His best creation was spinach and salmon stew over rice. We had already learned that American spinach could be substituted for Liberian potato greens, but Daddy didn't cook it the Liberian way, sautéed with chicken, dried fish, smoked fish, beef, ham hocks, and pepper. Instead, he sautéed the spinach with onions and pepper, and then added tinned salmon.

Sometimes he made corned beef and rice, another Liberian specialty, but again, with his own twist, where he added a packet of frozen peas and carrots to the corned beef stew.

That night, as he threw High I.Q. questions at me, he was working on an egg custard for dessert. We were focusing on obscure capitals.

"Bolivia," Daddy said, whisking egg yolks with a fork.

"La Paz."

Silence. I started laughing. "I just wanted to see if you knew! La Paz and Sucre. It has two."

Daddy went into the cupboard and fished out a few packets of Sweet'N Low. Daddy had been a diabetic for about ten years, and it was a disease the rest of the family always figured was bound to hit one of his children. As it turned out, I had recently drawn the unlucky card. A few months before, I had started eating like a horse—sometimes six times a day, and raiding the refrigerator at night. I was always hungry, and stopped weighing myself, convinced that I was gaining weight with all that I was eating, yet unable to stop myself from always feeling starved.

Then, one day in chemistry class, someone came in with a note that I was to report to the principal's office. Once there, the principal told me that my father was coming to pick me up from school early. Curious, I went out to the front of the school, just as Daddy's burgundy Lincoln Continental was pulling up. It stopped, and the passenger door opened, and out stepped Mommee.

"Mommee!" I screamed, dropping my books and running across the lawn to fling myself at her. She hugged me, laughing, while Daddy looked at us from the driver's side, grinning. I felt like the joy was bursting out of me. I hadn't seen her in nine months, and here she was, tall, thin, tanned, and beautiful, standing right in front of me at James B. Dudley Senior High School.

"Daddy, how you'nt tell people!" I berated Daddy, as Mommee hugged me hard.

He laughed. "I wanted to surprise you."

Finally, Mommee stepped back. "Let me look at the Joy of my Heart," she said, holding me by the shoulders. And then, "How you skinny so?"

It was inconceivable to me—or, for that matter, Daddy and Marlene—that I could be skinny, since in the past few months I had been eating everything in sight. "I not no skinny, you know I na get fat," I said, sheepishly.

That afternoon, we went home, and I got on the scale in Daddy's bathroom, which I had been avoiding since I had convinced myself I was gaining weight because of all I was eating. Shocked, I read the result: 107 pounds. My normal weight was 140.

The next day, Mommee, angry, and Daddy, hangdog, took me to the doctor, who pronounced my blood sugar dangerously high. I was a juvenile diabetic, he said. I ended up in the hospital for a week—in pediatrics, much to my chagrin. They taught me how to give myself insulin injections.

Mommee was furious with Daddy for not noticing my weight loss, but she eventually got over it when she saw how much he blamed himself personally. The night I went home from the hospital, I was prowling around downstairs when I overheard Daddy on the telephone, sounding distraught. "Of all the things to pass on to my child," he said, "I gave her that."

A month later, Mommee left us again and went back to Liberia. And from then on, Daddy put Sweet'N Low in our egg custards.

After dumping six packets of Sweet'N Low in, he went back to the cabinet for nutmeg and cinnamon.

"Upper Volta."

"Why you keep trying to trip me up? You know it's not Upper Volta no more!"

He grinned. "Well?"

"The capital of Burkina Faso is Ouagadougou," I said, enunciating carefully to show off proper. I said it again, because I loved pronouncing it: "Ooh-Wa-Ga-Doo-Goo."

The telephone rang. I raced to answer it, hoping it was maybe my latest crush at school, Chris Fuller.

"Hello?"

"Hello, this is Mr. Bennett calling. Is John Cooper there?"

My heart sank as I handed the phone to Daddy. "That's that man again," I whispered worriedly. It was the same bill collector from the bank who had been calling several times a day for the last month. Daddy wiped his hands on his jeans and took the phone.

"Hello, Mr. Bennett!" he said, his voice full of forced cheer.

I slipped out of the kitchen so I wouldn't hear Daddy on the phone, telling the bank guy that he would soon, very soon, be sending the mortgage check that was two months late. He had been doing extra accounting jobs but had left his accounting firm because he said the pay was too low. Now there was no regular pay at all. He spent a lot of time on the phone with his Liberian friends concocting deals. We always were on the verge of getting a $100,000 windfall that never seemed to materialize.

What did materialize were the monthly bills.

I crept upstairs to my room and lay on my bed in the dark.

The next Saturday, my High I.Q. Team went to the city tournament, and made it all the way to the All-States Round, which was televised.

Dudley was paired against Grimsley High, which was richer, smarter, and whiter than Dudley. There was a German guy on the Grimsley team who looked old enough to be in grad school. His name was Carl-Henry and he had a Groucho Marx mustache. The Dudley team was convinced that the Grimsley kids looked down on us, so we were determined to whip their butts on television.

On the afternoon of the big match, Daddy drove me to the Channel 5 TV studios. My stomach was churning when I took my seat behind the dais onstage, the camera lights heating up my face. The host began by introducing the teams, and then the first questions came.

"What woman in the Reagan administ—" the announcer said and I slammed my hand on the buzzer.

Buzzzzzzzzzzzzzz.

"Miss Cooper?"

"Rita Lavelle," I announced.

"That is incorrect. Minus five points for interrupting. Grimsley, here is the entire question. What woman in the Reagan administration recently caused controversy when she was forced to fire Rita Lavelle, her assistant administrator for solid waste at the Environmental Protection Agency?"

Carl-Henry buzzed, although he totally didn't have to because Grimsley got to answer the question anyway since I'd missed it. "Anne Gorsuch," he said, smirking at me.

"That is correct. Next question. England recently attacked what country . . ."

Buzzzzzzzzzzzzzzzzzzzz.

"Miss Cooper?"

"The Falkland Islands."

"That is incorrect. Minus five points for interrupting. Grimsley, here is the question. "England recently attacked what country for invading the Falkland Islands?"

Carl-Henry buzzed again. Another smirk. "Argentina."

It went on like that for thirty excruciating minutes, all televised on Channel 5. I was crying like a baby when I walked off the stage and scanned the studio audience for Daddy. He was leaning against the pillar, talking to someone. "Come on, genius," he said, grinning when he saw me. He put his arm around me and we walked to the car.

18

MONROVIA, LIBERIA, 1982–1983

$\mathcal{M}$rs. Cooper's daughter had gone missing.

It took Mommee a few months to realize that she hadn't seen Eunice in a while. Eunice usually came by Bro. Henry's house to visit every two weeks or so. Mommee and Eunice would sit on the porch outside. Mommee would send the houseboy to get Coca-Colas at the little shop down the street while she regaled Eunice with stories about what Marlene and I were up to in North Carolina.

Sometimes she had letters from us to give to Eunice, and Eunice always brought letters for her to put in the pouch that Mommee sent to us via her contact at the American embassy. The two of them usually tried to avoid Mama Grand, who was also living at Bro. Henry's house, but that was often hard to do, so their afternoons were sometimes spent getting cussed out by the old lady.

One afternoon, Eunice came by and told Mommee that now that she was out of high school she wanted to take business classes at a small technical school in Monrovia. Eunice didn't ask for money—she never asked for money. But Mommee started fretting, doing calculations in her head. She was already strapped because she was sending almost every cent she had to us in North Carolina to try to stave off the inevitable: the bank was going to foreclose on our house in Greensboro. We would need security deposits and rent to move to an apartment. I was soon going to graduate from high school and would need college money. The windfall deals that Daddy continued to cook up on the phone with his Liberian pals had yet to come through.

"How much for your tuition?" Mommee asked Eunice.

Eunice demurred. She knew what the situation was in Greensboro. She also knew that with Mommee, there were some things that would always come first. Keeping a roof over her daughters' heads, and sending me to college, for Mommee, outweighed all else.

"Don't worry about it, Aunt Lah."

"Oh man, just tell me how much," Mommee said, impatiently.

Eunice started to stutter. "I-i-i-it's two hundred dollars."

Mommee sighed. Two days later, she got Bro. Henry's driver to take her for a rare visit to Eunice's mother's house. As soon as the car pulled up outside the house, the kids who were all living there came tumbling outside, jumping up and down with excitement.

"Mrs. Cooper here! Mrs. Cooper here!"

Eunice and her mother hurried outside. Eunice's mother took Mommee's hands.

"A-ya, Mrs. Cooper, thank you oh."

Mommee smiled, the picture of gracious beneficence. "Aye, you'nt gotta thank me. She ma daughter."

"But Mrs. Cooper, thank you for Eunice oh. Thank you thank you."

Mommee turned to Eunice and handed her an envelope. In the scheme of things, $200 for Eunice to take a business course versus the $4,000 I needed for my first year of college was a small thing. Still, Mommee had had to swallow her pride and go to her least favorite source for the money: Mama Grand. She'd gotten the $200, but had had to endure an hour-long tongue-lashing about Daddy's uselessness and Mommee's poor business acumen and inability to stop "those damn Lebanese assholes from cheating you out of your rent money."

Eunice took the envelope and, quietly, thanked Mommee, who got back in the car and left, unaware that for Eunice, the need for the business course had just been overtaken by something far, far more important.

She had met him a few months before, while playing kickball at the field in Sinkor. His name was Babouchar Jack, and he was from the Gambia. He noticed Eunice, her long lean legs in short gym shorts, straight away, and made his move.

"What's your name?" he asked her.

"E-e-e-eunice Bull."

"My name is Jack."

Within three months, Jack had returned to the Gambia, leaving behind a heartbroken, and pregnant, Eunice.

And Eunice stopped going to visit Mommee.

She stayed away from Mommee for several months, trying to work up the courage to tell her. She remembered all those lectures in the car on the way to First United Methodist Church, Ashmun Street, established 1822, about not getting yourself knocked up before getting a ring on your finger. Save yourself for marriage, Mommee had preached.

Mommee sent Bro. Henry's houseboy to Eunice's mother's house to find out what had happened to her. Why hadn't she seen her? Eunice hid from the houseboy, who returned to Mommee with a shrug.

Finally, Eunice showed up, one Sunday afternoon at Bro. Henry's house. Mommee was lying down in her bedroom with the door closed, trying to stay out of Mama Grand's way, when there was a knock on her door.

"Who is it?" Mommee said.

"That's Eunice, Aunt Lah."

"Eunice! Where the hell you been? Come in."

The door opened, and Eunice walked in. Mommee looked at her silently for several minutes.

"You seacrab," she said. "Is this why you haven't been to see me?"

Christmastime, my senior year in Greensboro. Daddy, Marlene, and I had all moved to our new apartment—the complex was just across Elm Street from our foreclosed house. I had told my friends at school that we "just decided to move," knowing they didn't believe me but too ashamed to admit that our house had been foreclosed upon.

One night the three of us were watching *Jeopardy* when the phone rang. Daddy went into the kitchenette to answer it. He was on the phone, talking quietly, about twenty minutes. I couldn't hear him, which was strange because Daddy usually had a booming voice on the phone.

Something was wrong. A shiver of unease went through me. I strained to hear Daddy, but couldn't make out his words over the sound of Alex Trebek's asking the final Jeopardy question. Finally, Daddy hung up, came into the living room, and turned off the TV, just as the Final Jeopardy jingle was playing.

"Wha' wrong?" I said, alarmed.

He told me that a childhood friend of mine had just had a baby girl. She hadn't told anyone that she was pregnant until right before she gave birth to the baby. Like Eunice, my friend had hidden her pregnancy, scared to tell her parents. Coming so soon after the news that Eunice had gotten pregnant and hidden it from Mommee because she was ashamed at first, the news had shaken Daddy.

"Can you imagine the burden of trying to keep a secret like that, too scared to tell anyone?" Daddy said. He was pacing up and down the living room floor. He disappeared down the hall, then reappeared a few minutes later, still looking agitated. Finally, he walked over to me, lifted me from the armchair. Then he went over and took Marlene's arm and lifted her up. He stood both of us before him.

He took my cheeks into both his hands and looked at me in the eyes.

"Listen, Helene," he said. "Do you know how much your mommee and I love you?"

"Yes, Daddy."

He turned to Marlene. She nodded, silently. She was twelve years old; we were finally both the same height.

"Don't you two ever think that you've ever done something so horrible that you can't tell me, you hear me? Don't you ever ever go holding something like that inside you."

The tears were running down his face as he pulled us to him and hugged us, hard and fierce. I inhaled his scent, English Leather mixed with his hair tonic. He had never spoken the words outright like that before. I felt, for the first time since before the coup, safe and treasured.

19

CHAPEL HILL, NORTH CAROLINA, 1983–1987

$\mathcal{T}$he University of North Carolina at Chapel Hill had the
best journalism program in the South. It also had the added
benefit of in-state tuition, so it was only four thousand dollars
a year. Ford Motor Credit had repossessed our burgundy Lincoln Continental, and Daddy was now driving a fifteen-year-
old green Ford Tempo—there was never really any doubt that

Daddy, Helene, and Marlene

UNC-Chapel Hill, one hour down the highway from Greensboro, was where I would go to college.

We were the Carolina Tar Heels. I didn't play a single sport, but I threw myself into the ethos of college rivalries (Go to hell, State! And take Duke with you!) with abandon. Becoming a Carolina Tar Heel meant I could identify myself as something other than being Liberian.

Unlike the kids at my high schools in Knoxville and Durham and Greensboro, the kids at Carolina, at least, had heard of Liberia. They had a few questions, beyond the "Where's that?" that I was used to.

Like, "Why did your family leave?"

"We just left."

"Isn't it that place that was founded by slaves?"

"Uh-hmm." Luckily for me, their Liberia expertise was limited, so I could turn the conversation before it got to things that now suddenly didn't seem acceptable when viewed through the politically correct lens of an American college campus.

At Carolina, the issue du jour was apartheid and divestiture. To the shock of many of my classmates, blacks were being oppressed in South Africa. The white people were in charge and they said the black people couldn't vote. And our university was doing nothing to stop it! We were still investing in companies that did business in South Africa!

I had been trying to get on the staff of the college newspaper, *The Daily Tar Heel,* since the first day I arrived on campus. They'd already rejected me as a staff writer, telling me to get in line behind everyone else since I was just a freshman, so I assaulted them with editorials. I tried one about what an awful senator Jesse Helms was. They rejected that. I tried another one about how overcrowded the North Carolina prison system was. They rejected that, too.

I decided to try the issue du jour. I wrote a scathing diatribe called "An Atrocity Named Apartheid." It was pious and overwritten, filled with self-righteous indignation, over-wrought phrases, and a lot of words I didn't understand until two days before, when Daddy had sent me a Thesaurus to help me launch my assault on the *DTH*. "In our failure to actively oppose South Africa's apartheid policies, we are condoning a corrosive injustice," I wrote. "A rejection of a people as equal and thinking members of the human race."

I dropped my editorial off at the *Daily Tar Heel* in the afternoon. An hour later, the phone in my dorm room rang, with the editorial page editor on the line to say he wanted to run my piece. My stomach was knotted in anticipation all night; I only managed about two hours of sleep. I was out of bed at seven the next morning, hurriedly showering and dressing before hustling out to the *Daily Tar Heel* honor box near the pit, next to the Student Union building. Would it be there? Ignoring the front page, with its photos of the Carolina basketball game the night before, I turned quickly to the back page, Editorials and Letters.

It was there. Right at the top. "An Atrocity Named Apartheid." They had even gotten a cartoonist to do a drawing of a white guy sitting at the front of a bus, with a bunch of black people in the back, behind a sign that said "colored."

Standing by the honor box, I read the entire editorial, feeling exhilarated and euphoric.

The paper identified me as a freshman journalism major from Liberia.

A white South African student wrote a letter to the editor arguing that I had no business criticizing his country when mine had racial troubles of its own. The *Daily Tar Heel* published that, too.

"So what's the whole deal with Liberia?" Janet, my roommate, asked me.

I tried to explain. "It's not apartheid!" I said. "Nobody was banned from anything."

"But what's the deal with the upper class? Why was there a coup?"

"It's too complicated to explain."

The truth was that the few Congo People left in Liberia were still better off than the Country People. Mommee was still living at Bro. Henry's house, with Mama Grand and Bro. Henry's new wife, Alice. Both of her cars had been seized by the soldiers. She depended on ever-dwindling rent payments from Lebanese merchants to send to us in North Carolina, to keep me at college and to help Daddy with Marlene. But she always knew where her next meal was coming from. She had family in America. She was still Congo.

Members of President Doe's Krahn ethnic group were now the de facto Congo People, with all of the trappings that that implied: the best new cars, the best government jobs, big houses on the beach. And the unrelenting jealousy and bitterness of the rest of the population.

The rest of Liberia's people—the twenty-seven other ethnic groups—were all in the exact same boat they had been in before the coup. The gro-na boys were still hanging around Relda Cinema, unemployed. Five-year-old children were still forced to take to the streets as professional beggars. And the market women were still the only source of any real economy in Liberia, selling their oranges on the side of Tubman Boulevard.

Eunice sent me a birthday card that April. There was no letter in it, just "Love, Eunice." I retaliated by not writing back at all and ignoring her birthday. Mommee had written and told me that Eunice had a baby boy at JFK's Maternity Center in Monrovia. His name was Ishmael.

Eunice was supposed to be attending college here in

America, not living in a corrugated shack in Liberia giving birth out of wedlock, only slightly older than she would have if she hadn't lived with us. I had to ignore it. Focusing on the increasing disconnect between Eunice and me was more than I could handle. So I did what I always did when something seismic happened that I couldn't deal with. I concentrated on the superficial.

I was eighteen years old and becoming more and more American. How was I supposed to keep in touch with someone I never saw, four years older, living in another hemisphere, a place where you could barely contact by mail or telephone? I had new friends. I went to all the Tar Heel basketball games and black fraternity parties. I continued my antiapartheid rants, demanding that Carolina divest from companies doing business in South Africa. I even chained myself to a shanty that a bunch of us constructed on the south lawn in front of the administration building. Then, eschewing all principles of journalism, I unchained myself and headed back to the typewriter in the library to write about it for the *DTH*. This time, I made sure the newspaper identified me as a journalism major from Greensboro.

At the beginning of my sophomore year, Daddy announced that he was fed up with trying to make ends meet in America, and that he was moving back to Liberia, taking Marlene with him. He still drank like a fish, though he managed not to get drunk in front of me and Marlene. Whenever I was home from college on weekends or breaks, he woke up early to cook us breakfast: new things that we never had before in Liberia like hot apples-n-cinnamon oatmeal from the packet and blueberry muffins.

But the money Mommee sent us, for my school fees, and to help with the rent at the new apartment in Greensboro, wasn't enough. His deals hadn't come through. Even though

Liberia was becoming more and more of a mess under Doe, Daddy could still be a bigger fish in the small pond of Liberia than trying to swim upstream in the United States. The man who had lost a million dollars by the time he was thirty was not given to taking any menial jobs to make ends meet in the U.S.A.

I hitched a ride with some friends going to Greensboro for the weekend so that I could help Marlene and Daddy pack. Daddy wasn't bothering to box up things to take home, the two of them were just taking their suitcases and clothes. The apartment was crowded with Liberian friends of Daddy's who lived in Greensboro, and who came by to take our furniture.

I was so angry I barely talked to Daddy that weekend. He was leaving me again. And this time, he wasn't just leaving alone, like he did when he left us at Sugar Beach. He was taking Marlene away from me.

Marlene and Daddy were scheduled to leave for Liberia that Monday. On Sunday night, my ride back to Carolina showed up around seven to take me back to school. I was in Marlene's room as she sifted through which trousers were worthy of going home with her when the car horn blew outside. The lump that had hovered in my throat all afternoon grew, and my face tightened. Marlene was red-eyed as she gave me a fierce hug.

I walked out of her room and into the kitchenette, where Daddy stood leaning against the counter.

"I gone," I said.

"Come here," he said, opening his arms.

I gave him a stiff hug. The tears were pouring now. Quickly, I turned and walked out of the kitchenette and out the front door. As the car pulled out of the lot, I saw Marlene standing in her bedroom window, watching me leave.

The next day, I went to my classes, then to the *Daily Tar*

Heel offices. After that, instead of going back to my room, I went to dinner with some friends. It was ten-thirty p.m. before I finally got back to my dorm room.

My roommate, Janet, was sitting on the bed waiting for me when I walked in. "Your dad's been calling all afternoon," she told me, quietly, her voice full of reproach.

"He's gone now," she said. "He kept calling from the airport, and I felt so bad, and I kept saying, 'I'm sorry, Mr. Cooper, she's still not here,' and he would say, 'she knows we're leaving tonight so I'll call back,' and I didn't know what to tell him."

"Did he say he would call back?" I asked, suddenly feeling sick to my stomach.

She shook her head. "No, the last time he called he said they were getting on the plane."

That night, I cried myself to sleep.

Daddy went to live at Ma Gene's house when he and Marlene got home, and Marlene moved in with Mommee, sharing her bedroom at Bro. Henry's house. Marlene, now in the ninth grade, went back to ACS.

My life had split again. I had the here and now at UNC, with my friends and my journalism classes and newspaper articles and basketball games. But everything and everyone close to me was in Liberia.

A couple of months later, Mommee and Marlene telephoned me in my dorm room at Carolina. It was so strange to hear Marlene's disembodied voice over the line. From the time she was born, when I was five, she'd been by my side. Now she was the exact same age as I was when the coup happened. She had my same teachers at ACS, including Mrs. Perena, my social studies teacher. She had a locker on the high school side, and a crush on a boy, Ahmed, who played on the basketball team. She had lost her baby fat.

Over the phone line, her voice sounded more Liberian.

"What's it like there?" I asked her.

Marlene giggled. "You can come back here and do de' news in siiiiiiiimple English."

The ELBC evening television news shows were still state-run, coming on every night. But since the state was run by Doe, it had to be made accessible to the "we are people." That's what the Congo People were calling the Country People who supported Doe—"we are People"—or, sometimes, simply, "we are," a reference to the revolutionary speeches at the time of the coup about taking power out of the hands of the Congo elites and putting it in the hands of the People with a capital *P*.

Doe, seeking to appease his constituency, had mandated that the evening TV news should be translated from regular English into Liberian English so everyone could understand. Toward the end of the broadcast, a news reader would announce: "And now for the news in siiiiiiimple English." Then a Country man came on and read the news in Liberian English.

That sent Congo People into peals of laughter. I laughed when Marlene explained it to me over the phone, but my laughter was nervous and tinged with a little guilt. The politically correct lens of my American college campus dictated that I not make fun of people for not having the means to acquire an education. That lens said I was partly to blame. What kind of place had my ancestors built, that we took it for granted that so many people weren't educated enough to understand proper English, the national language?

Marlene changed the subject. "Eunice came by yesterday with her son, Ishmael," she said.

"Wha' he like?"

"He got fat cheeks."

I laughed. "Maybe Eunice became a Cooper through osmosis."

Ishmael's father had come back to Liberia after he was born, and Ishmael spent as much time with him as he did with Eunice, who had gotten a job at Firestone Plantations, the massive rubber farm about an hour outside Monrovia. Every morning Eunice had to take a Mammy bus from her mother's house to get to her job in the pension office at Firestone. She was getting paid about $150 a month, good money for Liberia. But she had to work to support herself and to help out her mother, and so she was happy to have help from Ishmael's father in looking after him.

Right after Marlene and Daddy arrived, a man named Thomas Quiwonkpa, a former cohort of President Doe, got a handful of men to take over the national radio station and announce that they were orchestrating a bloodless coup. All of President Doe's ministers were to turn themselves in. They announced the names of a handful of army officials who would be promoted.

But Quiwonkpa didn't do what he needed to do to get control—namely drive a stake through Doe's heart—and Doe escaped within hours, after promising the rebel soldier holding him that he would give him money if he let him go.

Then Doe had Quiwonkpa executed. Quiwonkpa was chopped up while alive. The list of promotions that Quiwonkpa announced on the radio turned into a death list for those unfortunate enough to be named. Doe's soldiers ran around the streets of Monrovia with Quiwonkpa's organs, including his penis and heart. People were invited to walk right up and touch them. The rest of his body was sliced up, too, like hamburger meat, and displayed near the gas station at the Paynesville junction.

I watched the news of the attempted coup on television

with my friends at school. We were crowded around my small thirteen-inch black-and-white television in my dorm room. My friends were shocked at what Doe did to Quiwonkpa and bombarded me with questions. "What kind of place do you come from?"

I shrugged. I could feel my face heating up with embarrassment. How could I explain? Where would I even start?

"You gonna write an article about that for the *DTH*?"

I shook my head. "No way," I said.

That place ain't my country.

20

1985

Liberian funeral is something like an Indian wedding, an Irish wake, and a British coronation rolled into one. Entire churchloads of people holler, bawl, and sing for hours on end, wailing at the passing of the dearly departed. Long-winded sermons are punctuated by piercing screams from designated mourners scattered throughout the church.

The procession to the grave is a long march—on foot, the

strong men in black suits sometimes literally dragging the bereaved, kicking and screaming—through the streets of Monrovia, all the way to Center Street and Palm Grove Cemetery, the final resting home of dearly departed Congo People, at least those who weren't executed by the state during the coup. Those killed by Doe were dumped in the rice rioters grave President Tolbert had had dug following the April 14 demonstrations.

A typical Liberian graveside ceremony is almost always accompanied by a woman, usually not even a member of the immediate family, who throws herself on top of the coffin in the grave, begging to be buried, too, so great is her grief.

"You'all leamme here, oh!" she yells, as weary pallbearers climb in to extract her. "My people, jes leave me!"

The festivities usually start about a week after the death, because it takes that long just to plan everything, from the average two days of wake-keeping to the eight-hour funeral service itself, to the actual burial, followed, finally, by the big party, at the end of the day. Like Liberian wedding receptions, the repasts are the best attended of all the events—you could have two hundred people at your actual funeral, but eight hundred will show up at the repast afterward to eat your palm butter and rice.

Every Liberian funeral includes the hymn "It Is Well with My Soul."

When Ma Gene died in 1985, we tried to plan a simple funeral. None of the close family wanted an elaborate Liberian affair, and Janice, who was in charge, eliminated the wake. We had brought the frail and dying Ma Gene to Minneapolis to stay with Janice and John Bull's mother, Toulia Dennis, during her last months. Janice was working for the state of Minnesota, as a policy adviser on children's mental health issues; John Bull was a financial analyst at General Mills.

"What? You trying to tell me you all not going to have a wake for your grandmother?" one of Ma Gene's friends hollered at us over the phone.

"No, we are not," Janice said firmly.

Our hopes for a simple funeral were dashed on the morning of the service, when car after car started showing up at the church.

"But look at people, oh!" Janice marveled as we peeked out of the pastor's door to watch the congregation assembling. One after another they showed up, decked out in traditional Liberian funeral attire: black hat, black dress, black tights, black shoes, black bag. It was a heavily female contingent from Ma Gene's Bible study classes and her various church activities. They all were furious at us, because they believed we were not giving our grandmother the kind of true, days-long Liberian funeral that a woman of her stature deserved.

As far as I was concerned, Ma Gene was getting more than she deserved, considering that she never went to funerals herself, deeming them too trying on her nerves. She hadn't stepped her big toe into the funeral of her own husband, Radio Cooper.

We planned a short service. Two prayers, two readings, a short life sketch, a short sermon. The old biddies looked at the program and then looked at us, the grieving grandchildren, in astonishment. Finally, as we neared the recessional hymn with no plans for long tributes, one woman jumped up, agitated and clearly unable to take it anymore. Her black hat had a veil attachment that dipped just over her forehead. I had never seen her before that day, but she had greeted us earlier before the service as if she'd known all of us all our lives.

She marched to the front of the church. "Everybody," she yelled, then glared at us pointedly. "Stand up!"

Janice looked at me and sighed. "This woman coming

make all these people here cry," she muttered. We all knew what was coming.

As if guided by some unseen choral director, the biddies started to sing as one:

"When peace like a river, attendeth my way,
When sorrow like sea billows roll,
Whatever my lot, Thou has taught me to say
It is well, it is well with my soul."

On cue, the tears started flowing and the hollering began. The funeral got away from us at that point, never to return.

On July 3, 1985, Daddy fell ill in his bedroom in Liberia. I was in Minneapolis, where I was spending the summer after my sophomore year at the University of North Carolina with John Bull and his new wife, Pieta. Daddy and Marlene were back in Liberia, as was Mommee, so Vicki, now living in Toledo, Ohio, with her new husband, and John Bull were my homes away from college on school breaks.

I had two jobs that summer. One was an unpaid internship at the *St. Paul Skyway News,* a free downtown tabloid that was distributed in supermarkets. I'd tried to get an internship with both the *Minneapolis Star-Tribune* and the *St. Paul Pioneer Press,* but they'd turned me down due to inexperience. Apparently my editorials on apartheid in South Africa weren't enough.

So I cold-called every alternative newspaper, magazine, and supermarket circular in the area asking if they needed a "reporter." *Skyway News* said that as long as I didn't expect them to pay me, they were willing to publish whatever I came up with. My first article for them was a profile of a police artist.

I was also working as a temp downtown for an insurance

company. In the mornings I rode to work with Pieta, who could paint lipstick on her mouth and brush rouge on her cheeks in the time it took for a light to change.

On Wednesday, July 3, I called in sick. I wasn't really sick, but I didn't feel like going to work. I didn't know it at the time, but in Liberia, that was the same day that Uncle Mac found Daddy on the bathroom floor and rushed him to Coopers Clinic.

In Minnesota, it was the day before the Fourth of July, and the temp agency said we could pick up our paychecks after two that afternoon. I knew I'd run out of insulin for my diabetes and would have trouble finding a pharmacy open on the holiday, so I figured I had to pick up my paycheck before the bank closed so I could cash my check and buy insulin.

I didn't make it. A late bus led to a missed connection, which led to me not getting my check until 3:07, and the bank closed at 3:00. So while Uncle Mac was finding my father collapsed on the bathroom floor at Ma Gene's house thousands of miles away in Liberia, I was riding the bus back to John Bull's apartment wondering how I was going to get through the Fourth of July holiday with no insulin. I had taken the last of my supply that morning.

John Bull would have given me money if I told him, but I didn't want to explain to him that my goofing off calling in sick had led to this. So I kept my mouth shut.

In Liberia, the doctors at Coopers Clinic pronounced Daddy in a coma. Marlene and Janice, who had moved back to Liberia six months earlier, took root in his hospital room, monitoring his breathing.

In Minnesota, I decided I would deal with the lack of insulin by starving myself. I spent the holiday on the verge of a diabetic coma myself, queasy and lethargic as my sugar level spiraled higher.

The Liberian in me—the part of me that believes in heart-men, neegee, witch doctors, and that we are all joined spiritually and that there's no way my Daddy could die thousands of miles away from me without me somehow sensing it—still believes that my illness that day was Daddy's way of saying good-bye to me. Nobody in Liberia called John Bull and me to tell us Daddy was in a coma, but I know that while his body lay dying in his hospital bed at Cooper's Clinic, his spirit came to Minnesota to tell me good-bye.

His spirit stayed with me through that entire day and night, as I wrestled with my own insulin-deprivation. I went with John Bull and Pieta to Pieta's family's house for a July 4 barbecue, and stared, nauseous, at the grilled chicken, macaroni and cheese, and baked beans that Pieta's father made. I put some on a paper plate, pushed the food around, and then snuck out to the garbage bin outside and scraped the food off my plate when no one was looking.

Daddy's spirit stayed with me to make sure that I wasn't going to die, too. That night, I lay in my bed, eyes glazed, feeling hollow. I drifted in and out of fractured dreams, overcome by nausea every hour or so. But nothing came up.

On Friday, July 5, Pieta took the day off. I was dizzy as I walked to the bus stop two blocks away, and stopped several times as the nausea swept through me. Finally, I got to the bus stop and waited . . . for what seemed like forever for the bus to arrive. We rode pass strip malls, and then crossed the river and rumbled into the city. I got off at the stop in front of the bank, where there was a line to get to the lone teller.

Twenty minutes later, I had finally cashed my paycheck, and I stumbled, close to fainting now, to the pharmacy to buy my insulin. In the women's restroom at the drugstore, I huddled in a stall, tearing open the wrapper of my insulin with shaking hands. Injecting 25 units of air into the syringe. Extracting 25 units of insulin. Rolling up my sleeve. With shaking hands, injecting the insulin into my arm.

And that is when Daddy said good-bye. His spirit, secure that I would be okay, left me and returned to Liberia to Marlene and Janice, sitting by his hospital bedside.

When I came home from work around six-thirty p.m., Pieta opened the door for me.

I could tell instantly; something was wrong. John Bull was sitting at the dining table, with his back to me, looking at an old photo album.

"Hiya," I said, trying to will whatever was wrong to go away.

She took my hand and led me to the living room. I became even more alarmed. With the exception of John Bull and Vicky, my entire family was in Liberia. I knew right then and there that something had happened to one of them. Liberia was increasingly becoming a place, in my mind, where people died.

"What's wrong?" I asked Pieta.

She spoke slowly. "Your father"—oh thank God not Mommee—"died today."

The relief that it wasn't Mommee stayed with me for several hours, from my initial nodding, quiet and wide-eyed, as Pieta rubbed my arm, as if to lessen the blow. It stayed with me when John Bull got up from the dining table and moved toward me, standing over me, dragging me up from the couch, hugging me. It stayed with me while we telephoned Liberia and talked to Mommee, then Marlene and Janice and Bro. Henry. All the way to that night, back in my bedroom, back in bed, eyes glazed, feeling hollow.

Then I saw Daddy, sitting downstairs in the recreation room at Sugar Beach, in the purple velvet chair that bugs loved to hide in. I saw him driving me and my high school friends to the movies in Greensboro, cracking jokes from the front seat.

I saw him that awful night at Sugar Beach, when we had the family conference with me and Marlene because he and Mommee were divorcing. I saw his back walking down the kitchen steps, getting into his car and driving away. I saw the taillights disappearing up the dirt road.

Lying that night on the bottom bunk of the bunk bed in the room I shared with John Bull and Pieta's daughter, my mind swam with images of Daddy and Uncle Julius drinking their gin and tonics, talking about the Sino-Soviet pact.

In the back of my mind, a thought flared, and I stamped it down. But it came back, impatient and loud. Daddy knew he was going to die. So he went home to Liberia. He wanted to die in Liberia.

At the same time that I was lying in my bunk, Eunice was at work at the Firestone Rubber Plantation. Our cousin came driving to the plant and asked Eunice to get in his car. Bewildered, she left work and got in.

"Look," said the cousin, after the car came to a stop in front of his house. "If I tell you something, don't cry."

Eunice started laughing nervously. "Just tell me," she said.

"John Cooper is dead," the cousin said.

Eunice did what she was told and didn't cry. She just asked the cousin to please take her to Monrovia. She packed a small bag of clothes, and they drove the hour into Monrovia, to the bungalow where Mommee was living with Marlene. Marlene was curled up on the couch in the corner, ignoring the people gathered around. When she saw Eunice, she ran to her.

"Don't cry, baby, don't cry," Eunice said, once again consoling Marlene as she rocked her back and forth. After five years of drifting apart, with Marlene moving from school to school in Knoxville and Durham and Greensboro and finally back to ACS, while Eunice shuttled to the Firestone Plantation and back with her toddler son, a full woman now, suddenly, it was as if time spun back. "Don't cry, ya," Eunice said.

Marlene, Janice, and Eunice sat in the primary rows of official family grievers at Daddy's funeral.

Eunice watched from the pew as Janice read the prayer sent by John Bull. We were stuck in Minneapolis, unable to attend our father's funeral; Mommee, Bro. Henry, and John Bull's mother, Toulia Dennis, had come up with reasons—which I considered spurious—to keep me and John Bull out of Liberia. They said it was too dangerous, and reminded me that I was still technically in the United States illegally, on a visitor's visa. If I left the country, they said, I wouldn't be able to come back.

Eunice listened as Marlene read Daddy's life sketch. She sang along with the choir as they serenaded Daddy with "It Is Well with My Soul." During the middle of a croaking solo by some woman who couldn't sing but inexplicably showed up at the service to warble a tune, the microphone started to wheeze, then screech. In the family pews, the primary grievers began twittering.

"John's tired of listening to that woman butcher that song," Mommee whispered to Marlene.

Mommee blamed Daddy for dying; this was just the kind of thing she'd come to expect from him. She sat in the pew next to Marlene, fuming.

Bro. Henry sat close by, keeping a watchful eye on Marlene. The family was all afraid that Marlene would lose her composure.

On the way to the grave, Eunice marched alongside Marlene and Janice, behind the coffin in the funeral procession, all the way to Palm Grove Cemetery on Center Street.

At the grave, she kept a close eye on a teary Marlene. She hid whatever feeling of grief she herself may have had at the time, because she wasn't one of the true daughters of Sugar Beach. Her role was a complex one at Daddy's funeral: part of the family when it came to memories and feelings and times shared, but an outsider still.

"Have my sympathy," the mourners said as they filed by Marlene and Janice, one by one. "I sorry for you, ya," they said to Mommee. "Oh Toulia, na mind ya," they said to Janice's mother.

A handful of people patted Eunice on the arm, or gave her a quick hug. But mostly, they left her alone.

Eunice stood slightly behind Marlene when Bro. Henry and the other pallbearers lowered Daddy's casket into the ground. A sobbing Marlene stood over the grave, clutching a letter in her hand.

The letter was from me. It was written on three sheets of yellow lined paper. Marlene had read it aloud in church, straight through, without crying.

St. Paul, Minnesota

July 9, 1985

Dear Daddy,

I can't believe this is the last time I can begin a letter with the words dear daddy. There are so many things I want to say to you. There are so many things left for us to do together. I want to show you the newspaper article I just had published. I want to talk to you about the 95 I made on my psychology exam. I want to laugh at your nacho cheese joke one more time. I want to hear you complain about how I never cook, and then watch your face as you struggle to digest my attempts. Just one more time, I want to hear you complain, "Helene, when are you going to clean up that messy room? You need a map to get across." I can't believe I'll never hear you laugh at me again when my school loses a basketball game, or grumble when I ask you to use the car. I can't believe you're gone, Daddy. I don't want to believe you're gone. We didn't get to say good-bye.

I love you so much, Daddy. You've been there for me so many times when I needed you. Any man can be a father but only a special man can be a Daddy. I'm thankful that for 19 years I had you for a daddy.

Death is more universal than life. Everyone dies, but not everyone lives. You did live, Daddy, and you will always live in my heart. Good-bye, Daddy. May your soul rest in peace.

Love, Helene

Marlene threw the letter on top of the coffin, to be buried with Daddy. But she continued to stand there. Bro. Henry grabbed her arm and pulled her away.

"Don't even think about jumping into that grave," he said.

21

Final Break

PROVIDENCE, RHODE ISLAND, 1987–1992

*O*n a bright, crisp, clear two days—May 14 and 15, 1987, I drove my new (used) Renault Fuego from Minneapolis to Providence, Rhode Island, to begin the rest of my life. My senior year at North Carolina had passed in a blur, during which I'd spent most of my time at my part-time job at the

Janice, on **Providence Journal** *Magazine cover*

Raleigh News and Observer on the night cops shift reserved especially for journalism majors from UNC. I sent letters and clips to about fifteen newspapers, but the second I got a nibble of interest back from the *Providence Journal* in Rhode Island, I knew that was where I would go.

Rhode Island was called the Ocean State. I had my life planned out: I would work for a couple of years at a good metro-daily newspaper where I would so dazzle everyone with my reporting that I would get hired by a major paper and become either a Washington correspondent à la Woodward, Bernstein, and Brit Hume, or a foreign correspondent.

I knew one more thing. I would never allow myself to be far away from the ocean again.

John Bull taught me the basics of stick-shift driving in a high school parking lot in Minneapolis. "Just think in increments of ten," he said. "When you get to ten miles per hour, put it in second gear. When you get to twenty, put it in third. When you get to thirty, put it in fourth." For an hour, I jerked my way through the gear shift in the used Renault Fuego John Bull had given me, as the two of us circled the parking lot, before John Bull deemed me ready to take the car onto the street.

The next morning at around five, John Bull and Pieta followed me out to the driveway to wave good-bye. The Fuego was packed with all of my belongings from college: a thirteen-inch television, three suitcases, two boxes of books, my Michael Jackson *Off the Wall* album, and my teddy bear, Gentle Ben. I hugged them both, got in the car, then broke into a grin and jumped back out, clutching two bumper stickers, which I took to the back and carefully taped to the bumper of the car. "Carolina Tarheels" one said. "Go to hell, State," said the other. "And take Duke with you."

"Take that stupidness off people car!" John Bull yelled at me, laughing.

I grinned at him. "That's na your car no more."

I hopped back into the front and peeled away—peeling was one of those things I had always longed to be able to do, and now that I had my own stick shift, I could. I headed east, picking up I-94 to Wisconsin, then I-90 to Chicago, Indiana, Ohio, then that awful I-80 through Pennsylvania, before finally hitting what I considered to be my gateway to the world: Interstate 95, to New York City. I crossed the George Washington Bridge with the radio going full blast and the Fuego's sunroof, which took up the whole top of the car, pulled back for maximum exposure to the sea breezes that I knew were soon coming my way.

A quarter of the way into Connecticut, I caught my first whiff of the tangy Atlantic air, and I broke into a huge smile. It connected me with home, and with Sugar Beach, even as I mentally was putting a distance between myself and Liberia.

And finally, Rhode Island, and the start of my plan to launch myself onto the world. Getting out of my car in front of the Biltmore Hotel, where the *Providence Journal* was putting me up for two weeks while I found a place to live, I surveyed my new domain smugly: it was quintessential New England but in an urban way, with Victorian houses and a run-down charm. And everywhere, there was some kind of access to the water, from Narragansett Bay to the Providence River to the Atlantic beaches off Watch Hill, Misquamicut, and Newport.

It would do, for a few years, I thought.

I had to "get clips." One of my first beats was covering North Providence, a typically Rhode Island town—parochial and Italian. As the *ProJo*'s North Providence reporter, I covered school board meetings, zoning board meetings, city council meetings, and sewer district commission meetings.

North Providence was run by Italian Democrats. The

mayor was Salvatore A. Mancini, a white-haired, old-style Italian-American who everybody called Sal. He wore a giant pinky ring and always greeted me with a toothy grin. In North Providence, everyone called me "that colored [pronounced Kul-led] girl [pronounced ge-el] from the *Journal*."

The *Providence Journal* had an A team and a B team, and I was definitely B team. It also had an I team, made up of the superstar A team reporters who only did investigative stories digging up political corruption, which in Rhode Island was like shooting fish in a barrel. City officials, governors, mayors were routinely being rounded up for taking kickbacks.

But I hadn't proven myself to be a fisherman. The B team players all worked in the *Journal*'s various satellite bureaus, in places like Pawtucket, Westerly, and Woonsocket. I worked in them all: Warwick, West Warwick, Johnston, Greenville, Scituate, Foster-Glocester, Cumberland, Central Falls, Pawtucket, Woonsocket.

To get to the A team in Providence, I had to uncover some corruption.

So far, there had been plenty of corruption to write about. The opening paragraphs of my clips read like a police log. But mostly they were reporting on corruption already uncovered by the police. My biggest breaks were exposing Sal Mancini, the mayor of North Providence, for using town workers to mow his lawn.

I was furious when neither that article nor its follow-ups landed me on A-1. What was it going to take?

As it turned out, it took Liberia.

On December 24, 1989, Charles Taylor invaded Liberia and decimated what little was left of the country after eight years of slaughter and mismanagement under Samuel K. Doe.

The Congo People in Liberia, and a growing majority of the Country People, thought they had it bad under Doe. Then they met Taylor and discovered that bad had depths yet to be plumbed.

Many Liberians, especially those who had been targeted by the Doe regime—like the Coopers, Dennises, and Tolberts—initially welcomed the invasion by Taylor and his ragtag group of rebels. Under the blackest of West African nights, Taylor and a hundred recently recruited disaffected Gio and Mano rebels crossed into Liberian territory from the bush of Ivory Coast. Taylor was a disgraced half-Congo, half-Country fugitive who had worked in the Doe regime. He was accused of embezzling almost $900,000. He fled to the United States, where he was arrested, at Doe's request, in Boston. Then, in a feat so extraordinary that not a single Liberian believed he accomplished this without some covert help from the U.S. government, which had grown disenchanted with Doe, Taylor cut his way out of a Massachusetts jail with a hacksaw blade and slipped out of the window using a rope made of bedsheets.

He ended up in Libya at one point, as a guest of Muammar Qaddafi, before he returned to Liberia at the head of his own rebel army, which he called the National Patriotic Front of Liberia. He enlisted boys and teenagers, drugged them, and gave them assault rifles. He declared himself president. Government soldiers representing President Doe fought back. But slowly, then with increasing speed, Taylor and his army of amphetamine-fueled boys advanced on Monrovia.

On May 22, 1990, Mommee packed two suitcases, and sat in the living room of her bungalow to wait for Bro. Henry. He drove up into her yard, loaded the suitcases into the trunk of his car, and drove her to Robertsfield, where he helped her bribe her way through Liberian passport control and into the departure lounge. Outside on the tarmac, the Sabena flight to Brussels sat, preparing to depart.

Bro. Henry accompanied Mommee onto the tarmac, then

kissed her on each cheek, and turned and walked back into the terminal. Again, he made a choice. No damn Country People were going to run him out of his country.

Mommee walked up the steps and onto the plane.

After the hour-long drive from Providence to Boston's Logan Airport to meet her, I stood in the international arrivals hall for three hours. Where was she? I'd checked with the airline and knew her flight (from Europe, there were no more Pan Am flights between Monrovia and New York) had arrived.

I was fretting about what lay ahead—my mother was moving in with me and would live in my one-bedroom apartment on Waterman Street in Providence. I thought about all my friends who were always visiting, hanging out in my living room, playing my new stereo.

But I had missed her. I had seen her a few times since she moved back to Liberia, when she came to visit for a month or two. She had brought Marlene back to the United States a month after Daddy died, deeming Liberia not safe enough for her daughter. Mommee left Marlene with Vicky in Toledo, where Marlene finished high school before heading to Purdue University, where she was now a junior.

And then Mommee had returned, again, to Liberia, to chase after Lebanese merchants for rent money to keep Marlene in college.

But now, she was here to stay. I could show her off to everyone in Providence! "Hi, here's my mother, see, I have one! I didn't come from nowhere."

Passengers trailed through the double doors connecting the Arrivals Hall with Customs, looking tired and scared. An Indian family. A bunch of Americans. A school group. A pair of African men, their skin almost purple against the paleness of the people at Logan, wearing flannel plaid shirts, polyester long pants, and unfashionable glasses, the frames almost as monstrously big as the ones Eunice and I first got years ago in Liberia.

And then, suddenly, she was walking toward me, looking small—had she shrunk?—and weary and older. She was wearing long pants and a sweater, and a huge gold necklace that Mama Grand had given her years before. Her hair was pulled back into a bun and her glasses—I'd somehow forgotten she wore glasses—were propped low against her nose. Her face was squinched up as she squinted and peered, trying to find me.

She had gotten out of Liberia before Charles Taylor's rebel forces had reached Monrovia, and she hadn't been raped or tortured or killed or any one of the countless other acts of violence that were being visited on women in Liberia in 1990.

"Mommee!" I yelled, pushing my way forward.

After a deep hug, she pulled back and peered at me for about ten seconds. She broke into a huge smile, then hugged me again.

Then, she said: "Those seacrabs in Customs took all the palm butter I brought."

In Providence, Mommee refused to take my bed from me, instead sleeping on my twin-size sofa-bed in the living room. She got a job in a nursing home. She bathed the patients, helped them go to the bathroom, sat on their beds and fed them. She worked the three to eleven p.m. shift Thursdays to Mondays, for about six dollars an hour. She sent most of the money she made to Marlene at Purdue. We saw each other in the mornings and in the early evenings, after I came home from work but before I went out with my friends. Mommee cooked potato greens and palm butter for us—the easiest Liberian dishes to make. Having been served by cooks all her life in Liberia, she didn't know how to make cassava leaf, but she was determined to learn, calling her Liberians friends for instructions.

Janice stayed in Liberia for six more months after Mommee left, during which she was kidnapped and held prisoner by rebel soldiers. None of us had any idea where she was. At night, Mommee and I sat in my living room and watched the news dispatches coming from Liberia with terror. All of the major news stations were there. They ran interviews with rebel soldiers, who had taken to wearing wedding gowns and blond wigs, the better to protect them from bullets and artillery, according to the witch doctors they consulted. They carried M-16s and chatted with the TV reporters about their daily kills.

There were interviews with survivors—one woman reported she watched while a group of soldiers wrapped her mother in a gasoline-filled mattress and burned her to death. At one point, one of my cousins showed up on *Nightline* to speak on behalf of the rebels, talking about how much of a butcher President Doe was. A friend showed up two weeks later on CNN doing the same thing—he was dead one month later, gunned down by President Doe's soldiers.

Finally, in December 1990, Janice escaped Liberia with her husband and one-year-old son, Logosou, over the border to the Ivory Coast. She arrived in the United States looking like one of those emaciated refugees we saw on television. The phone call came in the middle of the night, from John Bull, in Minnesota. He sounded exuberant. "Janice is out!" he yelled. "Janice is out!"

I jumped into my new Toyota Celica—I had given John Bull's Renault Fuego to Tello's little brother, Jim, about a year before when Mommee sent me five thousand dollars for a down payment on a new car—and raced down Interstate 95, to New York, to see Janice the day after she arrived in the

States. She was staying in an apartment in Manhattan with a friend. I kissed the fat cheeks of my new nephew Logosou, as he lay on his stomach on the couch, fast asleep.

"Janice, how you manage to keep Logosou fat so?" I asked her. She and her husband clearly hadn't been eating—they were both skin and bones.

Janice looked away. "I breast-fed him," she said, quietly. "And we gave him all our food. Whenever we had food, we gave it to Logosou." She said that sometimes she found green pawpaws, out in the bush, which were not ripe enough to eat. But she chewed the pawpaws to soften them up, and then fed them to Logosou. He was hungry, and ate it, even though the sour green juice burned his mouth. He would eat, and cry as he ate. But he kept eating.

Janice and I rode the A train from 181st Street to the World Trade Center, and back again, as she told me what had happened to her. About seventy-five rebel soldiers, wearing jeans and T-shirts, attacked the house she was living in with her mother, husband, son, and twenty war orphans. The rebels fired rocket-propelled grenades into the house during a three-hour siege. Janice, clutching Logosou close to her, crouched in an upstairs bedroom with her husband and the others.

After three hours, the soldiers overran the house, and ordered everyone outside. They shot and killed two men in the yard—one of them an informant, for giving them bad information about who was hiding in the house, and one a passerby who happened on the scene at the wrong time. They gunned down Kona, a nine-year-old war orphan who had taken refuge in the house; she did not die. In the afternoon they marched Janice and her family, under the scathing equatorial sun, to their army barracks five miles away.

Janice spent that night a prisoner, huddled in a rebel holding cell, while outside the rebels killed one prisoner after another.

She and her family were inexplicably released the next morning, and they tried to get as far away from the rebel holding barracks as possible, but could only make it a few miles under the burden of two old ladies who were with them, neither of whom could walk. They eventually took refuge in an abandoned house, subsisting on potato greens and green papaya from the yard, and cleaning their teeth with tree bark.

She told me about the night five days later, when a rebel soldier came to the house, took her outside, made her walk ten paces from him, cocked his M-16, and made her stand there for a full three minutes waiting for him to shoot her. In the end, he changed his mind—there was no apparent reason. Two weeks later, Janice and her family escaped the Liberian bush in a school bus headed for Ivory Coast.

"Oh my God, Janice," I said, staring at her. The subway car we were in was empty except for one disheveled-looking man at the front of the car, wrapped in a frayed wool coat. We passed the 125th Street Station. No one got into our subway car.

Janice was looking down at her hands, which she kept twisting into these weird positions. She had recited all this without emotion, but now the hiccups and tears started.

"Janice, did he rape you? The soldier who took you out with the M-sixteen?"

We had been dancing around this for three hours.

"No," she said. "He told me to give him 'six feet.' That's what he said, 'Give me six feet.' That's what they say before they execute you, they say 'give me six feet,' and they make you step away from them."

"Why?"

"I don't know, I think so they won't get blood on them or

something. When you're killing someone with a machine gun you need space."

I thought of the spray of bullets over our heads at Sugar Beach, of Uncle Cecil staring back at his executioner as the bullets kept missing him. *I remember,* I wanted to tell her, but it caught in my throat.

"How long did you stand there waiting for him to shoot you?"

"I'n't know. It felt like long time."

"What you wa' thinking?"

I knew, though, before she said it. When you're waiting for someone to shoot you, you pray. *Please God, I hold your foot. Please please please not like this.*

"I was saying the Hail Mary."

"What!"

We both started laughing.

"Wha' else people will do? I said the Hail Mary!"

"But we na' Catholic!"

"I am now."

Chortling, my mind flashed back to one of our favorite games at Sugar Beach. "Wartime come, you become Catholic straight," I said.

Janice disputed that. She had converted to Catholicism before the war and said she believed that becoming Catholic helped her to get through the madness in Liberia.

I was shocked that she was Catholic. "Hail Mary, full of grace," I said, giggling. "The Lord is with thee. Blessed art thou among women. Blessed is the fruit of thy womb, Jesus. Holy Mary, mother of God. . . ."

I knew what I was doing. It was something I'd done for the last eleven years. Whenever the images start to get overwhelming, I do this: stamp it out with something else.

"Wha' bout Eunice? You ever saw her?"

Janice shook her head. "She was still in Firestone when I left."

"It safe there?"

"Helene, I'n't know. It not as bad as Monrovia, but nowhere in that country safe."

We were silent for a while. Then I said: "I'm going to write your story for the *Journal*."

Two months later, the *Providence Journal*'s Sunday Magazine ran my story about Janice on the cover.

I had written the piece while in the middle of my own personal drama. Liam and I had met two years before, when the *Providence Journal* assigned the two of us to "infiltrate" Brown University, where a spate of racist incidents had occurred. The editors wanted a black reporter and a white reporter young enough to look like students, because Brown had been throwing reporters off campus for harassing their students. We were instructed not to lie about who we were, but the hope was that we looked young enough not to raise any suspicions.

On our first day reporting on the Brown Campus, we sat in the grass under a maple tree and discovered a mutual love of travel. We both dreamed of being foreign correspondents. But beyond that, we just wanted to go somewhere, anywhere, everywhere.

"Sri Lanka," he said.

"Yeah, a cool bar in Colombo."

"Or what about Zanzibar?"

"Well, you know the African places are gonna be the most interesting," I said, not above using Liberia when it suited me. "But I still wanna go to Paris."

"I was supposed to go to Paris a coupla years ago but we went to Bruges instead."

"Who goes to Belgium instead of Paris?"

"Yeah, it was a last minute switch. But Bruges was cool."

"I wanna go to Turkey. To Istanbul," I said.

He kept coming back to Sri Lanka. "I just want to sit in that bar in Colombo, drinking an ice cold local beer, at the beginning of a trip, with weeks and weeks ahead of me to travel around, talk to people, see what they're like, that kind of stuff."

I looked into his face and he looked right back at me, his brown eyes sharp and clear. By the end of the afternoon, I was hooked, suddenly and intensely. He was a tall, clean-cut Irish-American, and very very shy; I knew from the start it would take him a long time to make the first move. We went out every night after work, to Leo's bar in Providence, where we talked about where we had been, and where we wanted to go.

He found a huge poster-size map of Liberia, framed it, and gave it to me. "I wish I could have met your father," he said.

He took me home for Thanksgiving, to his family's vacation house on Nantucket, where I was warmly welcomed by his parents, cousins, priest, aunts, and uncle. A month later, his family invited me back, for Christmas in New Jersey. "Bring your sister," his mom told me.

Marlene was spending her Christmas break from Purdue with me in Rhode Island. At the time, Mommee was still living in Liberia. Marlene and I drove to New Jersey and I played Billy Joel cassettes all the way, until she erupted. "I hold your foot, pleeeeeeeese! Let people listen to something else!"

That Christmas Day, his mom took a photo of me and Marlene, and gave it to me later. "Send it to your mother," she said. "She needs to see how her babies are doing." Months later, when Mommee left Liberia and moved in with me, she brought that picture, now framed, with her, keeping it on the shelf next to the sofa bed where she slept.

He built me a bookcase for my apartment, with compartments for my stereo set, and a coffee table. For Christmas, he gave me a Canon AE 1 camera, for the upcoming trips we were planning together. I gave him a travel book on Sri Lanka, and a pair of jeans. I had been shocked to discover he didn't own a single pair of jeans, and wore only khakis and baggy corduroys.

Just after New Year's, at about three a.m. one Saturday morning, we were sitting on his twin bed in his apartment when he finally leaned over, touched my face, and kissed me. We were clumsy and fumbling and I was ecstatic. He was lying on his bed when I left a while later. He turned away from me, looked at the wall, and said, "I love you."

We took trips to Martha's Vineyard and to New York and to Boston, where I taught him to dance to Public Enemy's "Fight the Power." We biked to Colt State Park in Bristol, hiked to the top of Mount Wachusett in Massachusetts, and sailed to Block Island.

When Mommee arrived to live with me, a refugee from Liberia, Liam stopped staying over at my apartment; I just stayed most nights at his. At first, Mommee looked at me askance. "Be good to yourself," she said on the first evening that I left the house with my overnight bag. I said nothing, and closed the door quietly behind me, feeling guilty.

We went to Paris. We ate fondue in Chamonix in the French Alps, and got so drunk together on the Cote d'Azur that all I can remember of Nice is Liam propping me up by our rental car and saying, "Listen, you have to just put the car in reverse. Can you please just do that?"

Our rental was a Renault, as Satanic as the used Renault that John Bull had given me years before. It was a stick shift, and worked fine, except for when it came time to shift into reverse. Liam couldn't do it; I could, but only because of the blood, sweat, and tears I had spent on John Bull's old Renault.

So there I was, too drunk to drive, in Nice. I put my hand on the stick shift and started giggling.

"Helenie, please," Liam begged. "Just get the damn thing into reverse and I think I can get us back to the hotel."

I couldn't stop laughing.

Exasperated, Liam tried to manhandle the stick shift, but it wouldn't go into reverse for him.

"I can do it," I said, hiccupping from laughing. "Are you pressing the clutch?"

"Yeah."

"Okay." I concentrated, and, gently, shifted into reverse.

And then I started laughing again. Too much rosé wine, too much sun, too much fun.

"I love you, Liam."

He glared at me. "I love you, too, but right now you are really getting on my nerves."

And then we came home, back to Providence, and he told me that we had to break up because his parents didn't want him dating a black woman. He was an only child and had never gone against his parents before. His father was angry because he had lied to them for months, telling them that we were just friends. His priest told him that he was tearing his parents apart, and for what?

"I love you," he said, "but . . ."

But you don't love me enough.

He said, "Sometimes, I hate myself for having so much trouble standing up to them. But I also wonder, if we had children, could I really deal with that? Because, you know, you always dream of having children who look like you."

A heart really can shatter. It's amazing. I looked at his mouth moving but I couldn't hear any more of what he said.

I am Elijah Johnson's great-great-great-great-granddaughter. But that meant nothing to an Irish-Catholic family who wanted their children and grandchildren to look like them.

A week later, on December 28, 1990, Janice arrived, a refugee from Liberia by way of the Ivory Coast. I poured all of my emotion and anger and hurt into the story about Janice's escape from those Charles Taylor maniacs. "The Shadow of Death" was the headline on the cover of the *Providence Journal Magazine* on Sunday, April 21, 1991. "A passage through the world's most horrifying war." Janice's face, staring into the camera, somber and devoid of makeup, dominated the page-length cover photo.

The story got picked up by *The Washington Post*. I got calls from all over after it ran. I didn't start out writing Janice's story thinking that it would be my big break. I wrote it partly because I needed something to throw myself into while I dealt with my Liam issue.

But once the story ran, I knew that if anything would free me from North Providence City Council meetings, this was it. I xeroxed copies and sent them to twenty-five newspapers.

A few months later, as I sat at my desk in the Pawtucket office, my phone rang.

"*Providence Journal*," I answered.

"Helene Cooper please," a woman said over the phone.

"This is Helene."

"Helene, this is Betsy Morris with the *Wall Street Journal*," she said.

Sitting at my desk, I squeezed my eyes shut. Screw the A team. I was about to leapfrog from B team to big leagues. I was on my way.

But you always leave behind something when you move on. As I packed up my apartment in Providence to move to the world of national journalism that I had craved for so long, I left Liberia for good. Final break. I would never be moving back. Mommee was here now, in America, as was Marlene and Janice and Vickie and John Bull. Twelve years earlier, when we'd run away from Liberia after 1980, I believed maybe things would one day go back to normal, and I would go back and reclaim the fourteen-year-old life I had lost. Now I knew that would never happen.

As I left Providence for the *Wall Street Journal*, I detached from my family who didn't make it out. Some of them made that easy to do: Daddy had died. Uncle Julius followed him not long after. Then Bro. Henry died suddenly, of cancer that was discovered too late to do anything about it. I'd stood at the doorway of my living room in Providence, watching Mommee crying on the sofa bed after she found out. I tried to focus on something else, but all I could think of was that day at Caesar's Beach when Bro. Henry tried to teach me and Eunice how to swim.

Liberia wasn't a place where you lived, it was a place where you died.

All 170 years of my history going back to Elijah Johnson and Randolph Cooper and those two ships that took them to West Africa had led me to this. Liberia or America?

It wasn't even close. If you got out, you lived; if you stayed, you died. Mommee, Marlene, Vicky, Janice, John Bull, Tello 'them—all got out.

Uncle Cecil, Daddy, Uncle Julius, Bro Henry, Mama Grand, Uncle Waldron—stayed.

And one other person stayed, too. I thought about her, trying to teach me how to fight that night before the big Relda Cinema showdown with Nyemale; I thought about her smirking next to me at church as we sang our doctored-up words to "Blessed Assurance"; I thought about her dragging Marlene onto her lap and rocking her back and forth on the night of the rape.

I thought about her, and then I moved her into a place deep inside where I kept Daddy and Bro. Henry. It was a place where I could visit when I needed the solace of my family. But it was not a place that would be allowed to interfere any more with my daily living.

I was severing the last link I had—the one in my head and in my heart—with the girl who had been my sister since I was seven.

Good-bye, Eunice.

22

MONROVIA, LIBERIA, 1988–1994

$\mathcal{I}$n 1988, Eunice surveyed the landscape of Liberia, already deeply scarred by Doe, now about to be eviscerated by Charles Taylor and the forces he would unleash in the next thirteen years, and she made a choice.

Her son, Ishmael, was five years old, terrifyingly close to recruiting age for West Africa's legions of child soldiers. If these boys even survived their kidnapping and drugging and enlistment under Liberia's various rebel generals, they would

Child soldier wearing a teddy bear backpack, Monrovia

never get back the childhoods that were stolen from them when they were dragooned to fight a pointless war.

So Eunice did what African women had been doing for centuries, what her own mother had done fifteen years before, what Mommee did in 1981 when she handed us over to Daddy and went back to Liberia.

Eunice gave away her child.

When Charles Taylor invaded in December 1989, launching a spree of revenge killings and slaughter, Ishmael was not there to bear witness, take part, or serve as a statistic. His mother had sent him away, all the way to Gambia, to live with his father, Babouchar Jack, and his father's people. With Liberia's rapidly vanishing infrastructure, nonexistent mail service, and about-to-be-destroyed telephone lines, the distance would also destroy the relationship between Eunice and her son.

Eunice knew that, and she sent him away anyway.

Meanwhile, she remained in Liberia, working her $279-a-month job at Firestone. She was there when Taylor rebels hit the area in 1990. Made up mostly of members of the Gio and Mano tribes, the rebels were after anyone associated with President Doe's Krahn tribe, which itself had used Doe's time in power to visit death upon the Gio and Mano.

On June 10, 1990, Eunice was at Firestone when the rebels arrived. She ran outside in time to see around twenty men, wearing a colorful array of attire, from fatigues to women's dresses, grabbing Harris Brown, a coworker who happened to be Krahn. Brown's ten-year-old son stood in the crowd, crying.

The rebels stripped Brown down to his underwear and sat him on the ground. They shot him from behind, then took a knife and stabbed him in the stomach, and then dragged it all the way up his chest.

After that, the man who killed Harris Brown walked up to his little son, and patted him on the head and said, "Don't cry."

Firestone largely shut down after that, and Eunice joined the legions of African women doing what they do when their world falls apart: she began making cassava bread to sell on the side of the road to make a living. Each day she rose around six a.m., hauled a bucket of water from the well into her bungalow, and washed herself, using a small plastic cup as a makeshift shower nozzle. She and other women around Firestone gathered together to grate and strain the cassava, squeezing it until all the water came out, before using it as flour to bake the bread. Sometimes supplies were skimpy, but they did the best they could. A few months later, Firestone began running as an enterprise again, and Eunice went back to work.

Doe, meanwhile, was killed—shot on September 9, 1990—the first time he set foot outside the fortified Executive Mansion to visit peacekeeping forces sent from Nigeria and other West African countries. Ironically, it wasn't Taylor who got Doe, but a rival rebel lord, Prince Johnson, who had broken away from Taylor to form his own rebel group, beating Taylor to Monrovia.

Prince Johnson's rebels made sure that Doe's death was slow, and videotaped it for posterity, including a section that shows Prince Johnson supervising the proceedings from a chair, sipping a Budweiser, as his men held Doe down, his body squirming. He watched as his men cut Doe's ear off before killing him.

Doe's death was anticlimactic. By the time he died there were so many different groups of armed deranged lunatics raining terror on the country's civilian population that it almost didn't matter that Doe was dead.

Two years later, in October 1992, Eunice was home at her bungalow in Firestone when she heard the first bombs. She dropped to the floor and covered her head, crawling on her hands and knees from the living room to the bedroom.

The contingent of West African peacekeeping forces, called ECOMOG and made up of soldiers from neighboring West African countries, under the auspices of a regional West African alliance of countries, were hitting rebels with a counteroffensive they called Octopus. Believing that Charles Taylor rebels were hiding at the Firestone plantation, they launched an airplane raid, dropping bombs on the houses in Firestone.

Eunice stayed under the bed and survived the night. The next day, she crawled out of her house to survey the damage. Houses had been leveled. Hundreds of Firestone employees— her friends, coworkers—and their families were dead. Eunice fled, as far up-country as she could get. She hitchhiked, along with thousands of other refugees, in cars and Mammy buses until she ended up deep in Grand Bassa County, in a remote area known only as Territory 3C.

She stayed there for two years.

In Territory 3C, Eunice ran into a teenager named Matthew, who she had once allowed to take refuge in her house in Firestone during a bombing. His family agreed to let Eunice stay with them in their mud, thatched-roof hut. Eunice continued making cassava bread and now soap made of caustic soda, which she sold on the side of the road, and gave the money to the family for her room and board.

She had virtually no one to talk to. The villagers in Territory 3C were Bassa, but they had nothing in common with Eunice, whom they called a "Congo woman."

After about a year and a half, the villagers started acting funny. Eunice, ever stoic, had remained a loner. People stopped sharing food, instead hiding it from her. Matthew's family accused her of carrying on with their son, even though he was only seventeen to her thirty-two.

So Eunice left, beginning the 230-mile trek by foot to see what had become of Monrovia.

23

THE WORLD, 1994–2003

 *T*housands of miles and an ocean away, while Eunice traveled on foot through Liberia's war zone, sleeping on the floors of families willing to give her room for the night, I was staying in hotels and inns, delivered by airplanes, taxicabs, trains, and boats.

All major newspapers keep a list that tracks the whereabouts of their reporters at any given time. At the *Wall Street Journal* that list was called Wandering Reporters. Any reporter leaving home base had to send an e-mail to the Wandering Reporters list, detailing where they were going, when they were coming home, and how they could be reached. The Wandering Reporters list went out every morning to bureau chiefs and department heads.

I arrived at the *Wall Street Journal* determined that I would become a fixture on the Wandering Reporters list.

I started my career at the *Journal* as close to the bottom of the paper's hierarchy as you can get and still call yourself a reporter. That meant putting in time in that most hated of places, as far as I was concerned, the Deep South. I was mired in the Atlanta bureau faking business reporting like I knew and liked it. I had no intention of sticking with business reporting. My plan was to prove myself so inept at it that the *Journal* editors would quickly assign me to what I actually wanted to do, cover the State Department in Washington, or become a foreign correspondent.

The Coca-Cola earnings stories I wrote were particularly impenetrable. My first story carried the life-or-death news that the major U.S. beverage companies were expected to report mostly higher second-quarter earnings in July 1992, as "the industry slowly emerges from the price competition and consumer skittishness that hurt growth last year."

I followed that up with Coke's actual second-quarter earnings report, writing that "the soft-drink giant said net income rose to $581 million, or 44 cents a share, from $482.4 million, or 36 cents a share, a year earlier."

The plan worked. "I think we need to use your vivid eye for detail to look for colorful stories around the region," my boss, Atlanta bureau chief Betsy Morris, told me. Except "the region" as defined by the *Wall Street Journal* bureau coverage map, was my vision of Hell: Mississippi, Alabama, Tennessee, Florida, Georgia, South Carolina, and North Carolina. On my first work traveling assignment, Betsy sent me to Mississippi to interview the surviving members of the all-white jury that had refused to convict Byron De La Beckwith back in 1964 for killing the civil rights leader Medgar Evers.

"Oh wow, that sounds like such a great assignment!" I said, smile frozen, all the while thinking, "Is she crazy? She wants me to go knock on doors of Ku Klux Klan members in rural Mississippi?"

Thankfully, that mission proved fruitless and no KKK members opened their doors to me.

But if I wasn't willing to write business stories, then I had to do more human interest, and in the Atlanta bureau, human interest meant race. That's all they ate, drank, and talked about in the South.

I went to Winston-Salem, North Carolina, to write about "the breakdown of the peaceful co-existence between blacks and whites in this once placid Southern town," after the town's paternalistic corporate benefactor, Reynolds-Nabisco, was taken over by New Yorkers. I went to Hemingway, South Carolina, to write about "this all-white town" that was trying to secede from the mostly black county in which it was stuck. I went to Tunica, Mississippi, to write about how riverboat gambling had brought $140 million to Tunica in one year, but the ruling white town fathers were spending the windfall to "build beautiful 'boulevards' to the dockside casinos" and not putting any money into the mostly black public school system, which ranked lowest in the state.

Tunica's hotel was called the Delta Plantation Inn, so I stayed in Memphis, an hour and a half away, and drove into Tunica every morning, down Highway 61, through flat swampland. The drive was worth it because it gave me just the lede I needed. "TUNICA, Miss.—Driving south on Highway 61 from Memphis, visitors are greeted by ubiquitous cotton fields, ramshackle farmhouses, corrugated shacks and an incongruous parade of billboards. 'Shake,' says the first, 'Rattle,' says the second. 'And roll. At Harrah's.' "

Arriving in Tunica, I quickly took off to interview the requisite poor black people for my story. They weren't hard to find in Sugar Ditch Alley, the town's big slum. I followed a dirt road off Highway 61, navigating my rental car through potholes that seemed at once familiar. The air was humid and sticky in the Mississippi Delta, with kudzu vines clamoring for attention, wrapping around trees, bushes, and everything else. The sky was engorged with water but unable to burst. I had the air conditioner in my rental car on high, blasting into my face.

I finally rounded a bend and saw a shack in that shotgun style so prevalent throughout Mississippi. A rusty 1970s era Buick, missing three tires, was parked in a lean-to that was once a carport. There was a pile of car parts scattered around the yard, including two sets of stacked tires that served as outdoor patio furniture.

My contact with the family was a young woman who worked as a cleaning lady at the casino. I'd met her the day before, and asked to visit her at home to continue our interview—she'd been too nervous to talk to me at the casino anyway. She wouldn't let me use her name in the paper because she didn't want to anger her boss. I sat in the darkness of her living room—a dilapidated love seat propped against the wall—and tried to take notes from the light of the lone window. It was hard to see; the house was dark even though it was daylight.

I was just about to ask her to turn a light on when I stopped myself. *They don't have electricity, stupid.*

She told me about what it was like to grow up on the wrong side of the tracks in a world of plenty. "Those white people, they don't give a damn about us," she said. "They don't even see us. They drive around in their air-conditioned cars, and it's like we don't exist."

I was outraged, outraged by the injustice of Mississippi! Imagine that: rich, privileged people going about their lives, pocketing their gambling riches and ignoring the plight of the people around them! I fired up my laptop and launched my *Wall Street Journal* front-page assault on Tunica.

"Mired in a segregated agrarian society, the county embodies many of the images the rest of the South has been trying to dispel. Its cotton fields are filled with black laborers, many of whom live in corrugated-tin housing on the outskirts of town. Of the county's 9,400 residents, 76% are black. Its white upper-class residents tend to live in Tunica, the city proper, while black residents tend to live in the county. Big decisions are made by the county board of supervisors, which is 60% white. Schools are effectively segregated: Public schools are mostly black, while most white students attend the private Tunica Institute of Learning."

Meanwhile, in Liberia, my school, the American Cooperative School, was shuttering. It's hard to keep a private school open, charging $6,500 a year, when Charles Taylor rebels, wearing wedding gowns, blond wigs, and masks, are running around the country killing people.

The Liberian population didn't only have the rebel soldiers to contend with; they also found themselves under attack from the peacekeepers sent by West African countries. "Keeping the peace" meant raiding villages, bombing residential and commercial compounds, and raping young girls.

During one bombing campaign in 1992, rebel soldiers hit the hydroelectric plant that powered Monrovia's electrical grid. And with that, the power went out, for good.

While I trawled the southern American states for stories, other reporters trawled Liberia.

November 11, 1992, Reuters: LIBERIA CEASE-
FIRE FAILS; NIGERIAN JETS HIT REBELS

BY JOHN CHIAHEMEN

MONROVIA—Nigerian planes swooped through
the suburbs of Monrovia to hit rebel targets on
Wednesday after a regional ceasefire failed to halt
fighting in Liberia's civil war.

November 12, 1992, The Wall Street Journal:
SCIENTISTS STUDY HOW SOME
CENTENARIANS HAVE MANAGED
TO STAY HALE AND HEARTY

BY HELENE COOPER, STAFF REPORTER
OF THE *WALL STREET JOURNAL*

ATHENS, Ga—Twenty-four hours after Mary Sims
Elliott learned that her 77-year-old daughter Jose-
phine had died, she kept an appointment for a
lengthy interview about how she herself had lived
to be so old.

May 21, 1993, The Guardian: 'WHERE
THERE ARE ANY LITTLE GIRLS
THEY SHOULD BE RAPED.'

BY MARK HUBAND

Liberian rebel fighters have massacred scores of ci-
vilians as they retreat before an offensive by West
Africa's peace enforcement troops.

May 20, 1993, The Wall Street Journal:
MANY DOCTORS WHO TREAT TB FAIL TO FOLLOW GUIDELINES, STUDY FINDS

BY HELENE COOPER, STAFF REPORTER
OF THE *WALL STREET JOURNAL*

ATLANTA—Many doctors are ignorant of recommended guidelines for treating tuberculosis, a new federal study found, a failing of critical concern as the number of TB cases continues to rise.

After two years slogging through Tunica, Tupelo, and points surrounding, on June 2, 1994, Alan Murray, the *Journal*'s Washington bureau chief, offered me a new assignment: international trade. I would be based in the Washington bureau but travel the world. The *Journal* couldn't have custom-made a more dream job for me. I could fulfill my foreign correspondent and my Washington political reporting fantasies at the same time.

Two months after I started the Washington job, Alan sent me on a trip to China with Ron Brown, the commerce secretary. "Focus on all those Democratic donors he's taking with him," Alan said.

"No problem," I chirped gleefully, and trotted out of the bureau to deposit my passport with the Commerce Department people who were organizing the trip. I was part of the traveling press attached to the official delegation, so I would be one of four reporters on the plane with Brown and the corporate CEOs.

The next day, my desk phone rang. On the line was the Commerce "advance" woman, in charge of getting the Chinese visas for the delegation.

"You have a Liberian passport," she announced.

"Yeah, so?"

"Well, it's just, we've never seen one of these before. Is it real?"

I hung up, disgusted. But I made a mental note to speed up my application for U.S. citizenship so I could rid myself of my odious Liberian passport as soon as I could.

That China trip launched my orgy of travel, both on my own dime and, increasingly, armed with the *Wall Street Journal* corporate American Express card. I was off to Haiti next, to cover the U.S. invasion. In the slums of Port-au-Prince, I tut-tutted at the miserable lot of the average Haitian, surviving on $235 a year. Ignoring the fact that Haiti actually outranked Liberia in per capita income, I wrote scathing stories about just how big a mountain there was to climb for Haiti to get on its feet. I wrote about the Haitian currency, called "gourds," which were virtually worthless, and termed the Haitian money system "voodoo economics." I wrote about how removed from the rest of the population was Haiti's Creole upper class, the "elites," in their fancy mansions in Petionville.

After Haiti it was on to Alaska's Inside Passage, where I took a float plane that landed on the water. I gingerly climbed out of the plane and into a small boat that then took me farther out to sea to a Commerce Department ship that was doing God knows what out there with U.S. taxpayer money.

On May 13, 1997, I woke up at six a.m. in my apartment in the Adams Morgan neighborhood of Washington, D.C. I put on a black shift dress and a lavender linen jacket, walked out the door and drove to the U.S. District Courthouse. There, in the shadows of the U.S. Capitol, surrounded by seventy-seven other immigrants, I proudly recited:

"I absolutely and entirely renounce and abjure all allegiance and fidelity to any foreign prince, potentate, state, or sovereignty of whom or which I have heretofore been a subject or citizen."

I swore to protect America against all enemies, "foreign or domestic." I promised to bear arms on behalf of the United States if called upon. I reassured that I was making this promise of my own free will, without any mental reservation or purpose of evasion.

"So help me God," I vowed.

It was a beautiful Washington spring morning when I walked out of the courthouse with my American flag in my hand, surrounded by three friends from the *Wall Street Journal* who came to watch me become a citizen. I posed for photos underneath the statue outside, next to the preamble to the American Constitution. With the brown leather backpack I bought at the Ipanema hippie fair in Rio strapped to my back, I was the picture of jaunty, carefree Americanness.

From the courthouse, I went straight to the passport office on 19th Street, where I applied for an expedited American passport. No more Liberian passport for me, with all those furrowed brows and demands for explanation. *"You have a Liberian passport? You must be so upset about the trouble in your homeland!"*

Enough of that. From here on in, I was a citizen of the U.S.A., baby.

U.S. of A.

On my new American passport, I traveled up the Mekong River in Cambodia on the roof of a rickety ferry for a story on garment factory workers, and cavorted around Derry, Northern Ireland, with naked taxi drivers for a story about how British men were lining up to do strip shows because of the popularity of the movie *The Full Monty*. I sailed the Baltic Sea for a story on booze cruises between Sweden and the Aland Islands in Finland, and flew from Moscow to Riyadh to Cairo to Amman to London—all in about twenty-four hours—with U.S. Secretary of State Madeleine Albright during negotiations in the run-up to the Kosovo war.

I was half-asleep on the flight, in the middle of the night, way back in the press section of the plane, when a State Department official tapped me on the arm. "Huh?" I snapped awake quickly. "What?"

He grinned. "We're refueling midair. Wanna come up and see?"

I followed him down one side of the plane and then up steep circular stairs to a small cubbyhole where we could see the pilots. An American Air Force fuel plane was somehow attaching itself to the bottom of our plane with a long gas hose. We had dropped altitude so the two planes could hook up. The process took about half an hour, and the back of our plane kept dipping, making me want to vomit.

I went back to my seat and looked out into the darkness of the sky—Where were we? Over Syria? The Ukraine?—and shook my head. A thought flashed through my mind. Maybe Neil Armstrong did walk on the moon.

Naaah. He couldn't have.

Oh, white man can lie, oh.

Meanwhile, the death toll in Liberia climbed ever higher.

> February 1, 1995, The Los Angeles Times: WAR, WOE, LAY WASTE TO LIBERIA: Perhaps 15,000 have died in five years of a factional free-for-all so chaotic that much of the bloodshed is carried out by children who have no idea why they are fighting.

BY JOHN BALZAR

The fighters are too weak to win, too strong to be defeated, too maniacal to fathom. So Liberia awakes and greets another day of absurdity; the hope of peace seems as elusive as the war is exhausting in this wrecked nation, America's beachhead in Africa.

But I had other fish to fry.

January 30, 1995, The Wall Street Journal:
SANCTIONS LOOM AS U.S., CHINA BREAK
OFF TALKS

BY HELENE COOPER AND
MARCUS W. BRAUCHLI

The U.S. and China inched closer to a trade war as negotiations in Beijing over protection of intellectual property rights broke down.

In the spring of 1996, I was busy making plans for my big summer vacation trip to Alaska. My friends Alyson, Lee, and I flew to Seattle, rented a Ford Explorer, and then drove to Alaska, camping along the way. Once there, our biggest worry was whether we'd be attacked by grizzly bears.

"This is the best thing I've ever done," I said, as we sipped cabernet wine around our lakeside campfire in Canada's Yukon Territory. "I feel like I'm in another world."

I was as far away, psychologically, as I could get from Liberia. As I "roughed it" sleeping in my tent, sautéing mushrooms over the campfire, and snapping photos of Denali Mountain from my Canon AE1 camera, not once did I think about what was happening in Liberia. I did not think about the artillery shelling in Monrovia. I didn't think about the "peacekeeping" pounding at Firestone. I didn't think about women giving birth on their own in the forest to the children of rebel soldiers who had raped them and left them to die.

I did not think about Eunice, about whether she was managing to survive the madness coming out of Liberia. I did not think about whether soldiers in wedding gowns had raped or killed her, or whether she had food to eat, or clean water to drink.

I did not think about her.

July 24, 1997, Reuters: TAYLOR GETS MAN-
DATE TO REBUILD WRECKED LIBERIA

BY JOHN CHIAHEMEN

MONROVIA—Former warlord Charles Taylor won
a landslide victory in Liberia's post–civil war presidential election, according to final results declared
on Thursday.

July 24, 1997, The Wall Street Journal Europe: ON
YOUR RIGHT IS ST. MARK'S BASILICA; ON
YOUR LEFT . . . RUN!—IT'S SUMMERTIME IN
EUROPE, AND THE TOUR-GUIDE COPS ARE
OUT IN FULL FORCE

BY HELENE COOPER, STAFF REPORTER

VENICE—Douglas Skeggs leads the small group
of tourists to an alley behind St. Mark's Basilica.

He whispers to his assembly from Yorkshire, England. And as he does, Mr. Skeggs, a history lecturer, sneaks wary looks over his shoulder.

November 19, 2001, Insight on the News:
SEVERING LIBERIA'S SINEWS OF WAR

BY KENNETH R. TIMMERMAN

The U.N. is preparing new sanctions against Liberia's strongman Charles Taylor, who seized that African country's profitable international shipping registry and is brokering "conflict diamonds" from guerrillas.

November 15, 2001, The Wall Street Journal:
TOUGH TALKERS; POOR NATIONS WIN
GAINS IN GLOBAL TRADE DEAL,
AS U.S. COMPROMISES

BY HELENE COOPER AND GEOFF WINESTOCK

DOHA, Qatar—After seven years of back-room haggling, the 142 nations of the World Trade Organization finally agreed to launch a new round of trade talks that keep the global economy on track toward freer trade and investment.

Exotic datelines were now my signature at the *Journal*, and I was a regular inhabitant of the Wandering Reporters list. My colleagues joked that I came up with story ideas by poring over maps to find the most obscure places, and then concocted story proposals that would get me there and back with a cool dateline.

They were right. At the *Journal*, the all-important dateline is based on where the "lede" of your story—the opening paragraph—is based. So I made a point to head for the unknown whenever I got somewhere. The more obscure the dateline, the better. For instance, doing a story out of the Indian Ocean island of Mauritius, I purposely avoided factories in the capital, Port Louis, instead traveling to the less well known but more picturesquely named Curepipe, so my dateline could read: CUREPIPE, Mauritius. When I went to Madagascar, I made sure I interviewed people in Antsirabe, which nobody ever heard of, so I wouldn't have to dateline my story out of Antananarivo, the capital.

I went to Walla Walla, Washington, for a story about whether sheep should be allowed to vote in a caucus over how to spend import fees; to Mariehamm, Aland, for the story about how Europe's single currency could mean the end to booze cruises in the Baltic; to Pragtri Farm, Washington, for a story about environmental activists training in rappelling so they could storm an upcoming WTO meeting; Manciano, Italy, for a story about how poor, autistic pecorino cheese-making Tuscan teenagers would be hurt by the U.S. trade fight with the European Union over bananas.

And finally, to Camp Virginia, Kuwait, for a story on the U.S. Army's V Corps, and their preparations for war.

And with that, my relentless pursuit of datelines led to its inevitable conclusion: Iraq.

I had become part of the small group of reporters at the *Journal* who were expected to go anywhere. It was both a badge of honor and a curse; the reason why I was on a flight to Palm Beach, Florida, the day after the November 2000 presidential elections to cover the recount, and on an Amtrak train to New York City two days after September 11, 2001.

In October 2002, a few months before the Iraq war started, my bureau chief in Washington scanned the newsroom looking for volunteers. But even before his eyes alighted on me, it was a foregone conclusion that I would go.

24

IRAQ, FEBRUARY–APRIL 2003

*W*hile Liberia was convulsing one more time in the death throes of one more war, with a new rebel group—called LURD, or Liberians United for Reconciliation and Development—gunning for Taylor and bearing down on Monrovia, I was at military boot camp preparing to embed with the U.S. Army, who were going in to liberate the besieged population of . . . Iraq. While Liberians were crawling on their hands and knees on the floors of what was left of their homes to get away from rockets and grenades, I was hanging out with a five-hundred-strong press corps at the swank Kuwait Hilton Resort, getting anthrax vaccinations and going through training sessions on how to use my gas mask.

"Who are you putting me with?" I demanded, for the hundredth time, of Maj. Mike Birmingham, the press liason for the Army's Third Infantry Division. "I better get a good unit, you hear me? I better be up front."

The luxurious Kuwait Hilton was not a bad place to wait for President Bush to start his war. During the day, I shopped with my colleagues for desert war sundries that we forgot to get when we were in the States: lip balm, canteens, extra batteries for our Thuraya satellite phones. I really wanted some night-vision goggles but they cost $1,800—the same as the expensive French-made flak jacket recently purchased for me by the *Wall Street Journal*, and I knew there was no way the *Wall Street Journal* beancounters would turn a blind eye to the additional expense.

WSJ reporters Michael Phillips, Nick Kulish, and Yaroslav Trofimov were in Kuwait with me, and the four of us were our own band of brothers (and sister) in arms. We commandeered Mohammad, a hip, cool, Beatles-loving Lebanese taxidriver who traveled with $5,000 getaway cash in his socks. Mohammad took us to the mall during the day and to the pool hall or Go-Kart tracks at night. He took us to Kuwait City's only outdoor gear store, where a tailor measured us for khaki multi-pocket vests and cool cargo pants.

"I only want pockets around my knees," I ordered the tailor, standing with my arms outstretched as he measured my surprisingly shrinking waist. "No pockets around my hips—they'll make my butt look fat."

We were all four rapidly losing weight in the time we had

been waiting around for the war to start, because there was no alcohol to be had in Kuwait City, at least none we could find. We had long finished the scotch that a friendly marine had smuggled in for me in a Listerine bottle (minty scotch is best if you use 7Up as a mixer). Every night we hung out with the other reporters and bemoaned the lack of liquor. One night a group of CNN reporters spread the word that they had smuggled in a case of wine, and we all rushed to their chalet at the Hilton. It turned out to be altar wine. We drank it anyway.

When we weren't out shopping, we spent our time searching for a Thuraya satellite. The *Journal* had issued us both Thuraya and Iridium satellite phones, along with laptop computers that would allow us to file our war stories from the desert. But the Thurayas and Iridiums were both finicky in completely different ways. The Thuraya could hold a signal for days on end, and you could hear someone ten thousand miles away as clear as if they were right next to you. But first you had to actually find and lock onto a Thuraya signal, which we discovered we could only do from the rooftop of the Marriott Hotel in downtown Kuwait City.

"We are so screwed," I said, after Michael and I blew an entire day on the Marriott roof trying uselessly to lock into a satellite. "What's the point of getting ourselves practically killed in a war if we can't call home and say we're getting killed?"

On other days, we watched war movie DVDs on our laptops: the *Dirty Dozen, Three Kings.* As the days spread to weeks, and then a month, I found myself actually praying for the war to hurry up and start. "Screw the U.N.!" I muttered at another alcohol-free journalists party. "I can't take this waiting anymore."

The next day, Mohammad took us back to the mall. He

had to drive at exactly sixty-four miles an hour, because all cars in Kuwait are wired so that when the driver hits sixty-five an annoying beep-beep sounds to alert you that you're driving too fast. We listened to the radio, and Nick started chatting to Mohammad about music. I stared out the window at Kuwait City, as we passed a Fuddruckers restaurant.

I heard a familiar intro: the beginning of Michael Jackson's song "Liberian Girl," from his 1987 LP *Bad.* A woman whispered seductively in Swahili, since Michael Jackson apparently didn't bother to find out that we don't speak Swahili in Liberia.

The gloved one started to croon: "Liberian girl . . . you came and you changed my world, just like in the movies . . ."

Nick, laughing, asked Mohammad to crank up the volume.

"Oh, gimme a break!" I protested. But Mohammad and Nick were both laughing now and singing, so I gave up and joined in with them. We howled: "I love you, Liberian Girl!!!!!"

Of course, I was now the least Liberian girl a Liberian girl could be. I hadn't stepped foot in Liberia in years. I was now an American citizen. I still spoke Liberian English to my family, but my cullor was now impeccable, and I dreamed in American. The only way someone I met for the first time had any clue I was from Liberia was if they happened to ask me where I grew up, or overheard me talking to my family. Otherwise, I was just a nondescript black chick with an accent that could be from Chicago or New York or Philadelphia.

I lived the American dream, with my bungalow outside Washington, D.C., and my convertible and my trips to Bruce Springsteen concerts. When an immigration officer in Honolulu told me "welcome home" as I transited through on my way back to mainland U.S. from Singapore, I burst into tears and thanked him profusely. When September 11 happened, I was outraged and teary at the attack on "my" country.

I knew, even as we frittered away the days awaiting word on the invasion, that Liberia had descended into the ninth circle of hell, where ten-year-olds were taken from their parents and forced to fight in the country's never-ending civil wars. But my concern, at this moment, was whither America? The great United States of America was invading Iraq, and I was there to record it for posterity as a war reporter.

Finally, we got our unit assignments for the war. They placed me with a unit of ground combat engineers, in the Third Brigade of the Third Infantry Division. We weren't told what our assignments were until, late one night, we were taken on a three-hour bus ride through the Kuwaiti desert to the makeshift camps where the army units were preparing for war.

I had a hundred pounds of gear when I staggered off the bus. It was pitch-black outside, and I could barely make out the soldier in front of me as we were led into a tent where our names were called out. "Cooper!" the major in charge of the reporters said, looking up from his notebook.

I wobbled forward, weighed down by my twenty-five-pound flak jacket and heavy backpack. I took off my helmet. The soldiers all stared. Apparently, Major Birmingham hadn't told them that I was a girl.

The major in charge of reporters looked at me for what seemed like an eternity. Then he turned to a good-looking black guy standing in the corner. "Well, don't just stand there, Lieutenant Bryson," he said. "She's your reporter."

Lieutenant Bryson walked up to me, avoiding eye contact. He was one of those clean-cut, upright, boy-next-door guys with an overdeveloped respect for authority. I followed him out of the tent and we walked into the desert night. It took my eyes forever to adjust to the darkness, and my matchlight wasn't helping at all. I could barely see my own feet, let alone what was in front of me. I also wasn't used to carrying so much gear. I slowed my pace, picking my way carefully.

When Lieutenant Bryson noticed I was having trouble keeping up with him, he reached over, unbuckled the strap of my backpack from around my waist, and hoisted the pack onto his shoulders.

"Thanks," I said. "So, where are we going?"

"Well, we were supposed to be going to my tent, because that's where you were going to be sleeping. But we can't go there, um, uh, because, um . . . well, you know."

After conferring with other members of his unit, Lieutenant Bryson finally put me in a tent with Capt. Carmen May, a twenty-two-year-old blond logistics supervisor and one of the few women in the brigade. We shared a tiny two-person tent, with just enough space for our two cots and our backpacks. The space under our cots was reserved for boxes of MREs— the army's Meals Ready to Eat concoction, which, if you're hungry enough, can be surprisingly tasty. Especially with Tabasco.

After a week out in the Kuwaiti desert making war preparations, the day of the invasion came, and I was sent off to join my actual invasion partners: three combat engineers in an armored tracked vehicle that was to be part of the westernmost convoy leading the invasion. Our mission: sweep into Iraq to seize Tallil airfield, secure or lay bridges over the Euphrates River for the advance on Baghdad, and clear the route of land mines so that the troops behind us can safely pass.

"Excuse me, what?" I shouted, when informed of the assignment. I was sitting on top of my tracked armored vehicle, straddling the little turret that the gunner—Sgt. Anthony Dobynes, the vehicle commander—used to see who he needed to shoot. We were part of a massive miles-long convoy plowing its way to the Iraqi border in a slow-moving, stop-and-go formation. Before me, I could see a bristling array of big guns amid a flickering line of taillights stretching far north toward the border.

"When you say, 'clear the route of land mines,' how exactly is that going to be done?" I yelled at Sergeant Dobynes.

He grinned. "We blow them up, baby girl."

All around me, explosive devices known as "miclics"—army parlance for Mine Clearing Line Charges—sat parked in the desert, waiting to detonate land mines. The miclic was a trailer-mounted 5-inch rocket attached to a 350-foot hoselike line containing about 1,750 pounds of C4 explosives. When launched at the edge of a minefield, the device whistles as it snakes through the air for up to 100 yards and lands innocuously on the ground. Then the line is detonated by remote control from a nearby tank, exploding most mines in an area 9 yards wide by up to 100 yards long. And just about everything else unfortunate enough to be in its path.

On and on through the desert we rode, steadily northwest toward the border, and Iraq. It felt like we would never get there. It felt like we would get there too soon. I was scared; I was ready. I wanted this war to start so that it could be over.

Something was wrong with me. I felt so antsy, surrounded by strangers, wrapped in a chemsuit, dirty, filthy, confused. I was in the desert when I should have been in the rain forest. I felt out of place, stupid, empty. For the first time in a long time, I felt clearly that I didn't belong. I didn't belong in Kuwait. I sure as hell didn't belong in Iraq.

My career choices had led me, inexorably, to this point. And now I was in the wrong country for the wrong war.

The next night, my brigade rolled over the final berm in Kuwait, and into Iraq, the first of George Bush's massive invasion force to do so. Forty-five minutes later, the vehicle I was in broke down in the sand. The miles-long convoy swept around us while Pfc. Sergio Banuelos, the driver, struggled to restart the engine. Nothing. The convoy's last tank passed, and the roar of engines faded until the night was quiet.

"Shit! Shit!" yelled Pfc. Juanita Santana. From the gunner's seat, Sergeant Dobynes, the tank commander, jumped through the roof hatch onto the sand. He and Private First Class Banuelos tried to get the sixteen-ton vehicle going again. Inside, Private First Class Santana kept yelling: "Shit! Shit!"

I huddled in the corner of the cramped vehicle, my heart pounding. What kind of fly-by-night unit had I hooked up with? I couldn't believe we had actually broken down as soon as we crossed the border. And the convoy just left us?

"Shit! Shit!" Private Santana yelled again.

Private Santana was a little thing from the Dominican Republic, and she had a heavy accent. She was usually calm and quiet, but clearly could become excitable. She threw open the back hatch door, grabbed her M-16, and jumped out into the sand. Then she turned and looked at me. "You don't have a weapon?" she demanded.

I shook my head, "no."

She was disgusted. "I can't believe you don't have a weapon," she said. With that, she locked and loaded her gun and began pacing in front of our vehicle.

The night was eerily quiet. And cold as hell. I took out my notepad, and got out of the vehicle. Around the front, Sergeant Dobynes and Private Banuelos continued to work on the engine. There were intermittent grunts, followed by "Fuck!" and "Shit."

I wandered a few steps from the vehicle, then remembered there were supposed to be land mines around and quickly turned around, went back to the vehicle, and leaned against the side, where I propped my notebook in my hand. I dug out my matchlight and started to write.

"Forty-five minutes into this invasion and we're already in trouble," I wrote.

Suddenly, Private Santana started screaming again. "The enemy is behind you!!! The enemy is behind you!!!"

Oh. My. God.

Sergeant Dobynes and Private Banuelos jumped up. I dove into the back hatch of the vehicle for my flak jacket—why the hell had I taken it off? My hands were shaking as I tried to do up the flap. Now I could hear the sound of the approaching engine, as what looked to be a huge tank pulled up behind us.

I couldn't believe I was about to be taken prisoner, or worse, just forty-five minutes into this stupid invasion. I checked the front of my flak jacket to make sure the word *PRESS* showed clearly. Would it help me or hurt me?

The gigantic tank rumbled to a stop right behind our vehicle. Out emerged four young whippersnappers—American Army, sent to rescue us. The big tank they were driving was actually a fifty-six-ton, armored recovery vehicle called the M88. What Private Santana had been yelling was actually "the M-eighty-eight is behind you!"

It took a good thirty minutes for my heart to stop pounding. And this was only the first night of the war!

The M88 had to tow our broken-down vehicle for twelve hours, some sixty miles, through the desert before we caught up with the main convoy, which had assembled in a spot the Pentagon war planners picked out for them. They called it Attack Area Barrow. As we drove into the security perimeter, a land mine exploded, tearing the back off the Humvee unfortunate enough to be driving over it.

My training course had devoted an entire week to learning

how to get out of tricky situations. Unfortunately, Lesson #1, according to the ex–Royal Marines who taught the course, was "Minefields: Stay Outta Them."

As that was no longer possible, I quickly zeroed in on the other lesson I learned in my training course for getting out of minefields alive. I froze, and refused to take a single step. I even tried not to breathe.

"Baby girl, what you so scared of?" Sergeant Dobynes laughed at me. "We're gonna be retracing our steps out of this minefield soon."

Actually, the army made us stay in the minefield for six of the longest hours of my life. From where I crouched in my vehicle, I could see two land mines poking out of the sand.

I took out my Thuraya satellite phone and dialed. Mommee picked up the phone on the first ring. "Y'all now cross the border into Iraq?" she said.

"How you knew it wa' me?"

I could see her rolling her eyes, all the way across the Atlantic, where I knew she had been waiting by the phone for me to call. She had stayed in Providence for four years after I left for the *Wall Street Journal*, moving to a small studio apartment just down the street from my old place. For several years, she had continued working as a nurse's aide, sending money to Marlene until she graduated from college. I sent her postcards from Istanbul, Beijing, and Stockholm, and called every few days. When I sent out my Wandering Reporter dispatches, I always cc'd Marlene, since Mommee didn't have e-mail. When Marlene moved to the Washington, D.C., area a few years after graduating, Mommee followed. Now we all lived in the same neighborhood, within two miles of each other. It was as close to a Cooper compound as we could get in America.

"Sweetheart, it better have been you, or I would kill you for taking so long to call."

I laughed. "I alright, everything alright," I said, deciding not to mention the two land mines staring at me from a few feet away. "We taking a lil rest, then we going to one airbase tonight, but I can't tell you where it is cos I can't divulge our secret battle plan!"

I promised Mommee I would call her in a day, and said good-bye.

I reached Marlene on her cell phone at the tidal basin in Washington, where she was fishing with her boyfriend, Aleks. She sounded serene, calm. I decided to tell her so.

"You sound calm," I said.

She started yelling at me. "Calm? Calm? How people will be calm you over there in Iraq?"

I hurriedly got off the phone.

Finally, we began to move out of the minefield, right back out the way we came. When we cleared the field, our convoy stopped, and I finally, gingerly, stepped out. All around, soldiers were walking around their tanks and Humvees, preparing for the night's assault on Al-Nasiriyah, the first town on the road to Baghdad.

My vehicle was still being towed by the M88. I collected my backpack, laptop, and the rest of my paraphernalia. "I am not going to Baghdad behind no tow truck," I announced.

In about fifteen minutes, I had installed myself in the backseat of a Humvee, riding with the unit's chaplain, David Trogdon, and his driver, Spec. Kyle Miller. We were at the back of the convoy, which began moving north, slowly, preparing to confront Iraq's Eleventh Infantry Division, which was protecting Nasiriyah, Tallil airfield, and a bridge over the Euphrates River.

It was dark, and we were "traveling black"—without headlights, so the Iraqis couldn't see us. Everyone put on night-vision goggles, which make it much easier to see, although they give the air a greenish cast. I'd never before seen up close the actual bombing of a town, and the sight had my heart pounding. An explosion in the distance created a huge fireball. "Who did that?" I yelled at Chaplain Trogdon. "Us or them?"

"We're doing it to them," he said.

Nearby, U.S. soldiers lobbed a torrent of 155mm shells at Iraqi troops about nine miles away. There was frantic chatter over the radio. "Do not stop! Do not stop! The convoy must keep moving!" The message was clear: if the convoy stopped while bombing Iraqi positions, it would become a line of sitting ducks.

Then the convoy stopped.

For about fifteen minutes we just sat in line in the sand. In the Humvee, no one talked. On the radio, the screaming chatter continued: "You must keep moving!"

Finally we started moving again. A series of seven deafening soniclike booms went off just to the left. At the wheel, Specialist Miller started cheering. "The MLRS!" he yelled, clapping his hands. We had just used the Multiple Launch Rocket System to fire twelve rockets containing cluster bombs on the Iraqis. As they landed, fireball after fireball exploded.

I tried to drown out Specialist Miller's cheering, and the sound of the shelling. My palms were sweating and I was getting overwrought. What must it feel like to be on the receiving end of all of this TNT?

No sooner did that thought enter my head, then our Humvee burst open in a thundering, violent crash.

We were hit.

My first thought was no thought, it was pain. A sudden, searing explosive pain in my back so intense I knew I was mortally hurt. My head was crushed into my spine. I couldn't breathe. There was yelling outside; it took me several moments to realize I was the only one in what was left of the

Humvee; somehow both the Chaplain and Specialist Miller were gone. I had been sitting in the backseat, but now my head was pinned to the steering wheel. There was a crushing weight on my back.

Outside, shouting. "Get her out of there!"

The only part of my body I could move were my fingers, which were pinned against my trousers. I felt a warm liquid oozing through my chemsuit. Then someone was reaching into the Humvee to touch me. Then another yell.

"MED-EVAC! MED-EVAC! She's bleeding out! She's bleeding out!"

"I can't move!" I yelled. I was slowly realizing I wasn't dead yet. We hadn't been hit by an Iraqi bomb. A tank, one of ours, had run over my Humvee, crushing the vehicle and pinning me to the wheel. Chaplain Trogdon and Specialist Miller, in the front seats, both got pushed out either side of the Humvee as it crumpled. I was not so lucky.

Or was I? After what seemed like hours but was more like just five minutes or so, somebody figured out that since the tank hadn't been so much as scratched, they could just back it up from on top of me. A huge weight lifted off my back as the tank reversed. They pulled me out of the now-crushed Humvee, and spread me on my back in the sand. Somebody began to examine me.

And at that moment, as I lay in the sand in the desert, my chemsuit soaked with what turned out to be oil, not blood, I thought of Liberia.

I shouldn't die here, I thought. What a stupid place to die. What a stupid war to die in.

If I'm going to die in a war, it should be in my own country. I should die in a war in Liberia.

25

MONROVIA, SEPTEMBER 2003

*L*ooking down from my Ghana Airways flight onto the dense green rain forest that surrounds Robertsfield, all I could see was bush.

In the 2003 edition of *The World's Most Dangerous Places*, Robert Young Pelton ranked twenty-four countries and regions he deemed to be the world's most unsafe. The highest

Bullet casings, Monrovia

score—five stars—were reserved for three places bad enough to secure the label Apocalypse Now.

Chechnya, Colombia, and Liberia.

Pelton's chapter on Liberia is a quick CliffsNotes synopsis of the low points of Liberian history with special emphasis on the years since the Congo People were thrown from power. He included the ubiquitous mention of Liberia's picturesquely named rebel "generals" like General Butt Naked, General Fuck-Me-Quick, and General No-Mother-No-Father. General Butt Naked led the Butt Naked Brigade of child soldiers, many of them children he kidnapped and later killed. His battle attire included sneakers, a gun, and sometimes a lady's purse. Other than that he was naked, although his soldiers often wore women's clothes, bridal gowns, and blond wigs. He told journalists that he sometimes swam into lagoons where children were playing, dived under the water, grabbed one, and took them away and broke their necks.

"Calling what happened in Liberia in the 90s a 'civil war' is crediting it with too much organization and purpose," Pelton said. "The reality was the villagers were slaughtered by tribal-based militias that marked, like dogs pissing on a tree, their territory with the skulls of their victims."

In September 2003, Charles Taylor, the most recent strongman to butcher Liberia; the architect of three civil wars in Ivory Coast, Sierra Leone, and Guinea; the man who campaigned during the Liberian presidential elections in 1997 using the slogan "He killed my ma, he killed my pa, but I will vote for him anyway," had just been driven out of the country by his overwhelming desire to stay alive. Rebel soldiers had reached Monrovia, an anemic (yet, in the eyes of Liberians, fearsome) force of thirty-two U.S. Marines had landed at Mamba Point, and just under five thousand West African peacekeeping troops had been deployed. Nigeria offered Taylor safe passage out of town; on August 11, he took it and left. Liberia was beginning its twenty-first ceasefire since Taylor started his war in 1989.

The only way to get to Robertsfield airport was through one of the neighboring West African countries. I flew from Washington to Accra, Ghana, and spent the night there before going back to the airport a full three hours before my flight to Robertsfield was supposed to leave that morning, because that's what you had to do in Accra if you expect to get on the plane. There was a huge crowd of Liberians around the Ghana Airways counter, clamoring for attention. It was ninety degrees, but a woman in line behind me was wearing a fur coat. Another one was in full churchgoing attire, from her purple feathered hat, with a veil across her forehead, to her black patent leather high-heel pumps. Everyone except me was dressed to the nines. High-heeled strappy sandals, tight pencil skirts made of colorful "country cloth," a handful of lapas.

Most of them were displaced people from the refugee camps in Ghana who were returning to Liberia.

I was immediately engulfed by pushing, shoving, and a racket of raw Liberian English. I tried to disappear into my reporter mode, where I observe and listen but don't speak. But it was hard not to engage when the achingly familiar sound of Liberian English surrounded me.

The flight was delayed, although the Ghana Airways ticket woman was inexplicably telling people that it had already left. I soon spotted someone I knew. Aumuo Abdallah, the baby sister of Cherif Abdallah, Eunice's old crush. "I can't believe how grown you are," I marveled, then immediately felt like an idiot.

We chatted in line, I admired her shoes; she was more casually dressed than the rest of the passengers, in designer jeans and high-heeled sandals, but still had me beat by a mile in my heavy Timberland hiking boots and cargo pants.

Finally, Aumuo and I got up to the ticket counter. "The plane has left," the Ghana Airways woman announced, eyeing us sourly. One man from the group of displaced refugee people pushed up against me. "The plane ain't na no leave, yah," he said. "That woman just talking yenkenh."

After about ten minutes of arguing with the ticket woman, she finally conceded that the plane had, indeed, not left, gave me and Aumuo boarding passes, and took our baggage to check. I dreaded handing her my duffel bag; it held some things that were suddenly near and dear to me. It also held my flak jacket from the Iraq war. Ceasefire or no ceasefire, Liberia was still a war zone, so I had brought my Kevlar with me.

"This is insane," I muttered to Aumuo.

Aumuo laughed and gestured at the chaos around us. "You see all this? Multiply it by ten when you get to Robertsfield."

Everyone knew Robertsfield was manned by marauding gangs of rebels and government soldiers out to extort money from arriving passengers. Nobody in their right mind went through without some sort of protection. The *Washington Post* had just the week before described it as a "tornado of aggression."

The plane finally showed up, four hours late, at around three-thirty p.m.; we had now been at the airport for seven hours. Aumuo and I were positioning ourselves near the front of the line when another acquaintance, Rose Tolbert, walked up, followed by a curious-looking man. He introduced himself, in an American accent, as Alex St. James. He wore a dark blue two-piece expensive-cut business suit, which looked incongruous amid the sea of colorful Liberian attire that surrounded us in the departure lounge. "What do you do?" I asked him.

"I can't tell you," he replied. "I know you're a journalist."

Aumuo looked like she was trying hard not to laugh. It didn't take long to figure out that he was a Liberian who left in 1979, and had returned as part of the political team of Nat Barnes, Charles Taylor's former minister of finance, who was now running for president of Liberia.

Unlike me, Alex St. James had lost, or appeared to have lost, all of his Liberian English. He looked totally out of place, speaking cullor, dressed like an American investment banker. Not that I could criticize; I looked American, too, with my Iraq attire, but at least I could still speak Liberian English.

"He'd better drop that cullor," I muttered to Aumuo.

On the plane, Alex St. James was in first class, and, in typical Liberian male fashion, sent the flight attendant back to us in economy to offer us some wine. "No thank you," I enunciated carefully, then immediately regretted it when I saw the flight attendant pouring a glass of white wine for Rose, who had accepted.

The returning refugees were loud. And the plane kept making a noise that sounded like the horn of a car.

"Beep beep."

Across the aisle, a man erupted. "I Say! Ya'll blowing horn in the air?" Midflight, he yelled: "Good-bye Ghana! Take your hard country. We g'wen home!"

The flight took less than an hour. I kept my face glued to the window as we descended into Liberia. It looked green, lush, and completely uninhabited. Fierce white waves from the Atlantic hurled at the shoreline. "There are no houses down there, just trees," muttered the woman behind me.

It was exactly what I was thinking. The descent to Robertsfield seemed to have gone backward in time instead of forward. There were no new buildings, houses, or the normal signs of progress you get when you return somewhere after a long time away. Just dense green jungle and white waves from the ocean.

My heart was in my mouth. I was finally doing something I knew I should have done a thousand different times. Every time I got on a plane to fly to Geneva to cover trade talks for the *Wall Street Journal*, or boarded a flight to London to visit friends for the weekend, or organized trips for myself up the Amazon River in Brazil, I should have instead been coming here, to Liberia.

I should have been coming here, to Liberia, to find Eunice.

The remnants of Robertsfield finally surfaced, barely visible in the now torrential rainstorm. It didn't look quite as bad as I'd expected. There was one rusting old Soviet-era plane on the tarmac, some corrugated shacks, and several half-finished construction projects. The plane taxied down the runway and finally came to a stop, dinging on the bell that signals you can get up. There was an immediate stampede into the aisle. Then we stood pressed together for fifteen minutes while the airport workers brought the steps to the plane. I could feel my heart race. Finally, the flight attendant opened the door.

My throat caught the scent of burning coal fires mixed with the dampness of the rain. Descending the steps, I took deep breaths, afraid that I'd soon get used to the smell and not notice it anymore. It filled my throat, my whole body, with an aching familiarity.

We ran through the rain to what passed for the arrivals terminal, where a crowd of people, all of them having bribed or bartered their way past airport security, waited to meet those who arranged for "security" to get them through Liberian immigration. There were a handful of soldiers wearing the green fatigues of the West African peacekeepers walking around.

I'd asked a family friend, Marie Parker, to send someone to help me get through Robertsfield. Mr. Green was holding a sign up with my name on it. I ran to him and hugged him—I had never seen him before in my life—thrilled that I wouldn't have to go through immigration alone.

He hustled me into an office, where he'd already given one immigration officer a dollar to stamp my passport. I looked at the stamp. "Why does it say forty-eight hours?" I asked the officer. "I have a six-month visa that I got at the Liberian embassy in Washington."

The officer grinned at me. "That was just your entry visa. Now you need to go to Immigration in Monrovia for your staying visa."

He looked at me. "You're not no American woman," he said.

"So what?" I said.

"So wha' you brought home for your countryman?"

Mr. Green pushed me through the crowd to the door to Customs. A short skinny guy in a button-down shirt with three buttons missing, raggedy shorts, and no shoes ran to the door and slammed it shut in our faces before we could get through, bolting the lock behind him. Mr. Green looked at him. "Don't you remember the tip I gave you?" he asked. The guy grinned and opened the door.

Shockingly, my duffel bags had arrived in the baggage claim room, a small, hot, stuffy holding pen that was packed with passengers, airport workers, and various hangers on, all yelling at one another. I pointed out the blue bag to Mr. Green, who picked it up. I picked up the green bag, filled with its precious contents.

Pantene shampoo and conditioner, Jergens almond lotion,

Optima hair perms, shower and bath gel. They were for Eunice. They were the same things I had always brought home for her when we were growing up and left her at Sugar Beach to go on vacation in Spain; the same things I'd sent home to her through Mommy, when she moved back.

I hoped she would still want them.

A uniformed woman approached. "Prove to me that's your bag," she said.

I showed her my claim ticket.

"That's not a real claim ticket," she said.

We stood at an impasse. If she thought she was getting my bags, she was nuts. I was still awed that they had actually made it through baggage claim in one piece; there was no way I was parting with them now.

"That claim ticket is forged," the woman repeated. She reached over and tried to take my bag. I swatted her hand away.

Then, suddenly, a fight broke out to the left of the Customs woman. As she turned her head to see what was going on, Mr. Green grabbed the green bag from me and ran out. I ran behind him, clutching my laptop case to my side.

"Sacki, let's go, let's go!" Mr. Green yelled to the driver as we sprinted out of the terminal. Sacki jumped from his perch on a jersey barrier and ran to a Mitsubishu Pajero, gunning the engine. We threw my bags inside and peeled away from Robertsfield, leaving a cloud of dust behind us.

Welcome home.

On the drive from Robertsfield to Monrovia, little children ran to the side of the road from small hut villages as we passed. They were dirtier, more desperate-looking, than the Country children from my youth. The bush looked green, impossibly green. There were huge holes, where trees had been cut down during various wars by ravenous people looking for food. After about thirty minutes of bouncing along the road, trying to avoid the giant potholes, we came upon the turnoff to what was once the road to Sugar Beach. It had always been impossible to see the house from the main road; it still was. But with the turnoff overgrown with bush and vines, you could barely tell there had once been a road there. The three-headed palm tree that I had always used as a landmark was gone.

Mr. Greene looked back at me, slumped in the corner of the backseat. "Didn't your family used to have their house back there?" he asked me.

I nodded but said nothing.

Then we were passing Daddy's old gas station, now a pockmarked police station. Then ELWA, the Christian radio station. Around the bend, and to the right, Liberia's football stadium, now an encampment for war refugees. To the left, in front of a zinc house, a fat little girl, her hair wild and her stomach bulging, stood in a small yellow rubber tub. She kept squatting, grabbing a handful of water, and throwing it in the air, shrieking all the while with laughter. Behind her, a young woman sat on a chair, scrubbing the little girl's back with a soapy sponge. The domestic scene was incongruous in the middle of the war wreckage.

The Paynesville junction snuck up on me before I realized where we were. Hadn't there been a traffic light there? Arriving at the Paynesville junction had always been a major milestone in the journey from Sugar Beach to town; a sign that civilization was just around the corner. It had heralded the beginning of Monrovia's population center, with the bustling market across the junction and the two gas stations vying for business across the road from each other.

But now there were no gas stations, just more squatters, sleeping on the cement, sitting on cardboard boxes, standing around, gesticulating at the cars going by.

We turned left at the Paynesville junction and headed toward Congo Town. Where were the palm trees? We hit a crater in the middle of the road and I bounced in my seat, bracing myself against the impact. Then we were in Congo Town. I strained hard to the left, trying to see if I could see our old house, but it was on Congo Town Back Road, and you still couldn't see it from the main road.

And then, finally, we were on Tubman Boulevard headed toward what passed for our capital city.

Even if you ignored the war damage—from the bullet and artillery holes in the buildings and houses to the casings on the side of the road, to the displaced-people camps and the checkpoints of peacekeeping soldiers—Monrovia looked like a hellhole. The country had not had electricity or running water since 1992. The city's streets were jammed with garbage, teeming with people on foot who had run away from fighting up-country to Monrovia. As we passed, skinny war orphans, their eyes huge against sunken cheeks, ran up to the car, their palms outstretched.

I kept flinching, every time a child darted up to our Pajero, which, along with the other cars along the road, was traveling too fast to stop if one of them slipped and fell. None of the stoplights in Monrovia worked, so the only time we stopped was when we got to the military checkpoints. Each time we did so, young men wheeled feeble old women in wheelbarrows, and sometimes supermarket carts, up to our car, their palms outstretched. Both Mr. Greene and Sacki ignored them.

The odors of urine and garbage and rotting animal carcasses filled my nose. But there was also that familiar scent I loved so much, of burned grass and burned coal.

As Sacki drove, I drank in the sights like a starved refugee myself.

There was First United Methodist Church, established 1822, with a hole in the side where a rocket had pierced it. There was the Parker Compound, where Philip and Richard had lived and where I took piano lessons. The four houses had peeling paint and fallen roofs. Three of them had been ripped to their skeletons, as people had pried away any materials that had any usefulness. There was Sophie's Ice Cream Parlor, overgrown with vines.

The blue paint-flecked frame of Relda Cinema was still there, as was the sign that said "relda." But the roof was sunken; still it apparently remained the center of action in Monrovia. The parking lot in front was full of squatters, some of them sifting through garbage, some of them just sitting in the shade of the Relda facade.

I was home, and home was Hell.

And yet.

There was something else there, too. Pride. Not at what Monrovia had become, but at the fact that it was somehow still there, as proof that I came from somewhere.

Mr. Green and Sacki took me to Mamba Point Hotel, where most of the journalists covering the Liberian war stayed. It was near the American embassy, and had a generator so it often had electricity. The owner was Lebanese, and he knew how to attract journalists in war zones: with a reliable bar. There were a bunch of U.N. and relief-worker types clustered on the patio when I arrived.

The receptionist at the front desk called for a porter to help me with my bags. After putting them on the floor of my second-floor room, the porter turned to leave.

"Wait ya," I said, fishing into my wallet for a five-dollar bill. "Ehn, heah something."

The porter looked at me in surprise. I knew what he was thinking. I looked like an American journalist—no self-respecting Liberian woman would wear hiking boots—but I spoke Liberian English?

"Ma, wha' your name?" he said.

"Helene Cooper."

He smiled, and turned and walked out of the room, closing the door quietly behind him.

I sat on the bed, finally alone, and took a deep breath.

For the past few weeks I had taken refuge in the formalities: arranging my flight, finding a place to stay, getting a Liberian visa, organizing a car, setting up my satellite telephone so it would work with my new laptop—the old one had been crushed in my Humvee accident in Iraq—even paying the bellhop just now. But now, there were fewer and fewer errands standing between my here and now, and what I had to do.

I procrastinated for one more day, using the excuse of finding a car and driver for my stay in Liberia. I spent the day doing what everyone does in Monrovia: running around. First to find someone willing to rent me their car (forty dollars a day). Then to Immigration to get my staying visa. To the cell phone company to get a sim card for my newly purchased cell phone, usable only in Liberia. Liberia had no land lines, so cell service was the only way to communicate by telephone. Charging your cell phone meant finding someone with a generator.

After a full day of this, I was exhausted when I got back to the hotel, where the lobby attendant handed me a pink slip. "That Parker fella came to see you," he said.

I broke into a grin, for a moment feeling like that thirteen-year-old again. Philip and I had kept track of each other through the years; and Richard, Philip's brother, who lived in Ghana, was still one of my best friends. Indeed, I had stayed with Richard during my one night in Accra on my way to Liberia.

I called Philip. "Cooper!" he yelled into the phone.

We arranged to go to dinner that night. In my room, I dug out my makeup case and frowned. What had I been thinking when I packed? All I had was eyeliner and lipstick. Carefully, I applied both, and curled my hair with my curling iron. Then I went down to the hotel bar, where I waited for Philip to arrive. I couldn't rival most of the Liberian women in the bar, who wore high heels and tight skirts. My twenty-three years in the United States had made me forget a fundamental tenet of being a Liberian woman: dressing up.

But I had, at least, exchanged my hiking boots for my Teva sandals. And thankfully I'd had a pedicure before leaving the States, I thought, looking down at my red toenails.

Suddenly, Philip was standing in front of me, grinning. He looked exactly the same. He wore jeans and a burgundy ox-ford shirt, and his eyes smiled as he took my hands and kissed both my cheeks.

"Hello, Cooper."

"Hello, P.C."

I felt the smile start deep in my stomach, and soon, I was grinning back at him.

That night at dinner, we had our first real conversation, not as a hero-worshipping teen to her crush, but as one adult to another.

Philip hadn't turned his back on Liberia, even though his father was executed. He and Richard left Liberia soon after we did, and he'd gone on to get his engineering degree at the University of Massachusetts at Amherst. After he graduated, he moved back to Liberia. There was never any question in his mind that Liberia was where he belonged.

"But how can you live here knowing what they did to your pa?" I asked him.

Philip lost his animation and was quiet. I was afraid that I had pushed too far—I'd seen him several times over the years on his visits to the States, but I'd never talked to him about the execution.

Finally, slowly, he started to talk. He said that in 1984, after he returned to Liberia, he went to church with his mom. Then-President Doe, who had executed his father on the beach, walked in with his entourage, and sat four rows in front of him. For about an hour, Philip sat paralyzed, consumed with rage. A twenty-one-year-old man, he wanted to jump over the pews and rip Doe apart. He was filled with a hatred so intense he couldn't move.

But "at some point during that church service, I realized I had to let it go," he said. "I wanted to live in Liberia badly. I'm not just a social security number here. And I knew I couldn't live here if I let the hatred consume me."

I looked at him in wonder. I hadn't wasted my first crush on someone unworthy.

"So Cooper, wha' finally made you come home?" Philip asked me. "You reporting?"

"I'nt know . . ." I began, then stopped. I didn't know what to say. Finally, I muttered: "Yeah, I reporting."

That night, I went back to my hotel room and sat on the bed again. My insides were churning. Images filled my head, of my thirteen-year-old self, in the months before the coup, before everything changed for good.

I could see Eunice, giggling with me in my room as we picked out what I would wear to the Sadie Hawkins dance and patiently listening to me afterward when I came home busting with excitement about dancing with Philip. We had gone from sharing every single day with each other, sleeping every single night in the same room, to not communicating for fifteen years.

I was scared, so scared that I had squandered fifteen years. I didn't even know if she would want to see me. My stomach convulsed.

No more procrastinating. It was time for me to go find my sister.

From Washington a week earlier, I had called Bridgestone Firestone headquarters in Nashville, and they took my contact details and said they would pass them on to the plantation manager in Liberia. A day later, I was pulling onto Route 1 from the Target parking lot near my house in Virginia when my cell phone rang. It was the plantation manager at Firestone.

I started to shake, and pulled to the side of the road.

"I'm trying to find Eunice Bull," I said.

"Yes," he said slowly. "Eunice isn't here right now."

He used the present-tense. There was so much static on the line it was almost impossible to hear. "I'm her sister!" I yelled. "Tell her her sister's coming home!"

As soon as I hung up the phone with him, I called Marlene. Far more than me, Marlene had anguished about Eunice over the years. A few months earlier, Marlene had called me at work one morning, crying. "I can't stop thinking about Eunice," she said.

Sitting on the shoulder of the road with my cell phone at my ear, I listened to the phone ring. When Marlene answered, I yelled: "She's alive!"

"What?" she said. "I can't hear you."

"Eunice is alive!" I repeated. The traffic screamed by me on Route 1, but on the other end of the phone there was only silence. Then, finally, Marlene said: "For true, Helene, you gotta go home."

My second morning in Liberia, I put the things I'd brought for Eunice in my backpack and met my driver in the hotel parking lot. He was a skinny twenty-eight-year-old named Ishmael Morris. I was determined to show Ishmael that I didn't believe in class differences, and I invited him to have breakfast with me before we struck out. He looked at me, aghast.

"No, Ma, I alright here." He was standing under a palm tree with a bunch of other drivers. All of them were assigned to the various journalists and United Nations workers who had descended on Liberia to cover the war and ceasefire. They looked at me curiously.

Feeling foolish, I walked back into the hotel and had coffee. I stole a plate, with some breakfast rolls, for Ishmael, as though I could single-handedly, and in one morning, make up for the past 175 years.

"We're going to Firestone," I told Ishmael, getting in the front seat of the car, an eighteen-year-old Toyota Corolla with no air-conditioning, radio, or much else. Ishmael nodded and backed out of the parking lot.

I'd been home only one day, but the squalor was starting to look normal. The incongruous political signs: ("Corrupt Liberians must be exposed and severely punished!") next to public service announcements: ("Do not peepee here!") and only-in-Liberia political civics declarations: ("Ghankay says, Electricity is the key to Liberia's future!") as the caption to the ubiquitous photo of Charles Taylor, this time sporting his "Country" name, Ghankay.

A painting of a man standing next to, presumably, his wife, but looking lasciviously at a cutie-pie girl walking by swishing her rear, read: "HIV AIDS is here! Stay with your own!"

We were just entering Sinkor when a pickup truck packed with Charles Taylor "antiterrorism" soldiers pulled up in front of us. The soldiers—all teenagers—carried machine guns; one held a rocket-propelled grenade that he pointed at me and grinned. I asked Ishmael to slow down and let them get a little farther away.

We drove past a shack surrounded by garbage with a sign outside that said "Transcontinental Enterprises," past God First Tire Co., and the Smythe Institute of Management and Technology, down a road lined by shanties. We got to the military checkpoint in Congo Town. A hyper Nigerian soldier told Ishmael to open the car trunk. He asked Ishmael what was in my backpack, which was inside the trunk. Ishmael told him he didn't know, that he should ask me. The Nigerian soldier went ballistic.

"Get out of the car," he screamed at me, then turned his rage on Ishmael. "That's a challenge to me! How dare you tell me to ask your boss lady! *You* are supposed to ask your boss lady!"

I told the soldier that Ishmael really didn't know, but he was having none of it and continued to scream. I bent down to open my backpack, and he stopped me, saying he didn't care what was in it, that Ishmael shouldn't have disrespected him. A guy passed us on a motorcycle and whistled, then yelled out: "You're too fine for that harassment!" Then sped away.

Ishmael and I apologized profusely to the Nigerian soldier, and finally he stomped off.

As we continued on to Firestone, I fumed. All of the Congo pretensions I thought I had lost after twenty-three years of living in the United States came back with a vengeance. Who did that damn Nigerian soldier think he was? Here he was, in *my* country, and talking to us like he owned the place. This was typical aggressive Nigerian behavior, throwing his authority around. Well, we would see about that.

Ishmael, who had remained calm, interrupted my furious plotting and started chatting me up. "Maybe next time when you come home, I won't be your driver, I will be your friend," he said. From the driver's seat, he turned, looked at me, and smiled, his skinny arms relaxed against the wheel. I gave a nervous smile back, and inched away slightly.

"Okay," I said.

We drove for another forty minutes, back along the road to Robertsfield, veering left past the airport toward Firestone. My stomach started to spasm as we turned onto the Firestone Road. Suddenly we were in a lush, manicured otherworld, surrounded by tall majestic rubber trees. The temperature dropped immediately, courtesy of the shade provided by the trees.

As we drove farther into the compound, the sprinkling of tiny bungalows grew, until finally we were on Main Street, Firestone, with its neat manicured one-story office buildings and row after row of residential bungalows for Firestone employees.

"She works in the labor office," I told Ishmael, who slowed down the car and asked a man walking along the side of the road for directions. The man pointed toward a building on the right. We turned and pulled up, parking right in front.

There were about ten people milling around outside the office when I got out of the car, strapping my backpack onto my shoulder. I could feel the pump from the Jergens lotion inside digging into my side.

"Um, I'm looking for Eunice Bull," I said, to no one in particular. A man pointed to the second door.

I stepped inside, and stood in the doorway, hesitantly.

I didn't see her at first.

Then a murmur of voices throughout the room began.

"Eunice your sister here."

"I say, Eunice, ehn that your sister there?"

"Aya, here Eunice sister, oh."

Then I saw her, across the room. Her huge glasses filled

her face . . . was she still wearing the same glasses? And I was engulfed in a huge hug. Tears rushed down my face; she immediately started berating me. "We are not going to do that here. We are not going to do that here," she said. Then we were both laughing, pulling back, then hugging again.

"You're home," she said. "You're home."

All the while holding my hand, she turned to the people in the room, and made a formal presentation.

That stutter.

"T-t-t-his is my sister."

26

MONROVIA, SEPTEMBER 2003

$\mathcal{E}$unice and I went to lunch at Firestone's restaurant, over-looking the plantation's manicured, ridiculously green, golf course, observed by a suddenly intrusive Ishmael.

"Thank you for the shampoo," she said.

"How's your mother?" I said.

"How long you will be in town?" she said.

The first baby steps. There was so much more that we

Eunice, Firestone

had to say. There was so much more that I had to say. I was annoyed at Ishmael, annoyed that he had accepted my insincere invitation to join us for lunch when he had refused my sincere invitation to join me for breakfast. Couldn't he see I needed to talk to Eunice alone?

She was plumper. Her cheeks were fuller and she had lost that gazelle look that she'd had as a teenager. Now she was rounder. I started to laugh.

"Wha' you laughing at?"

"Your face," I said, laughing harder.

"What funny 'bout people face?"

"You look like a Cooper," I said.

Eunice knew immediately what I meant. She sucked her teeth indignantly. "I beg you, ya. Tha' y'all the ones with those Cooper people fat cheeks."

Staring at me, she marveled: "Look at lil' Helene Cooper grown woman now."

I snorted. I was no grown woman by Liberian standards; I looked like a kid, I thought. A few days ago, when I was in Virginia packing to leave for Liberia, Mommee had come to my house to inspect the clothes I was taking with me. She'd never done that before when I traveled.

She was aghast when she looked at my travel wardrobe: there pairs of trousers, three shirts, a pair of hiking boots, and a pair of Teva sandals. "You have to take a dress," she said. "You're going to a war zone, but Liberians dress up, no matter what."

"Aye Mommee, leave people 'lone," I retorted. "Wartime come, when they be evacuating people, you will be glad I not tryin to get on no helicopter in heels."

After lunch, Ishmael and I took Eunice back to work, and made plans for her to stay with me at Mamba Point Hotel when she came to Monrovia that weekend. As Ishmael and I drove back to Monrovia, through the war wreakage of Paynes-ville and the bullet-scarred houses in Congo Town, accosted, again, by children running up to the car with their palms out-stretched, I felt happiness and sorrow at the same time. From the outside, at least, she seemed fine, though a little more re-served. I didn't know what that reserve was hiding. And I couldn't help but think, looking into the vacant eyes of one little boy who walked slowly to the car as we sat waiting to go through a checkpoint, that I could appease my conscience by fishing into my backback and giving him a twenty-dollar bill. I would soon be going back to the United States, where I could, again, put all this behind me.

Eunice lived with it every day.

The next time I saw Eunice, I vowed to myself, Ishmael would not be around to stop me from asking the question that I had traveled twenty-three years back in time to ask.

"Did you hate us for leaving you?"

We were sitting on my bed in my room at Mamba Point Hotel. Two days had passed and Eunice was in Monrovia for the weekend. Ishmael had finally been dispensed with—I had told him to take the rest of the day off.

I was getting the twenty-minute briefing on her life, and giving the twenty-minute briefing on my own.

I was looking for forgiveness.

Eunice laughed. "Is that what you think?" she said, look-ing straight at me as if everything had just clicked for her. She shook her head. "I think God made it for me to stay here so I could be strong."

She said, "Y'all were a good Congo group. My Congo group was a different Congo group than my pa's group."

I flinched at hearing my family being described as a "Congo group," but said nothing. This was the first time I was hearing that Eunice's father, who she had rarely talked about at Sugar Beach, had also been raised by a Congo family.

"They treated him like a slave," she told me. Her father had slept on the floor, eaten outside with the servants, washed his host family's clothes, cleaned their house, and replied "yes ma" whenever called by the lady of the house.

"With Aunt Lah and Uncle John," she said, "I never felt like a stepchild."

Eunice asked about my life, about Iraq—she somehow had heard that I had been in Iraq for the war. She asked about my mom, and most of all, about Marlene.

"How's my baby?" she asked.

I handed her the letter Marlene had sent to her, smiling inwardly. Eunice still thought the sun rose and set on Marlene. "She got one Serbian boyfriend name Aleks."

"Serbian?" Eunice said. She made it sound like I said that Marlene was dating a Martian.

"Yup. He' fro' Serbia. He could be the one."

"Aya, my baby now become big woman," Eunice said, eyes misting. She pumped me for information about Marlene, and I acquiesced, grumbling all the while. "She working for the Kennedy Center," I told Eunice. "She now buy house and all."

"So she alright? She happy?"

"Yeah yeah, let people hear their ear with your Marlene business," I said. "That foolish girl alright."

Eunice sighed, then got up off the bed and walked into the bathroom. "Aya Ma, but the room not bad at all," she called out.

Ma? She'd never called me that subservient title before, why was she starting now? "Don't call me that," I said.

Walking back out of the bathroom, she was laughing. "I duh' call everybody that," she said. "But fine, Helene. You don't want me to call you Ma, I won't call you Ma."

Uncomfortable, I changed the subject. "Guess who I had dinner with last night—Philip Parker!"

Eunice howled, collapsing back onto the bed and rocking back and forth. "Please don't tell me you still like him!"

"He's lovely," I said to Eunice, brightening up as I launched into describing my favorite subject. I knew inside that I was doing it again—papering over a seismic moment in my life by focusing on the superficial.

"Wha' bout you? You na finally get married!" I marveled.

Eunice spent her weekdays at Firestone, and her weekends in Monrovia with her new husband, a lively, gracious man named John Walker, whom Eunice just called "Walker," so I had started calling him that, too. As we'd driven from the Firestone restaurant back to Eunice's office two days before, she'd put me on the phone with him. "I can't wait to finally meet you!" he had boomed. "You'n't know how much my wife da' talk 'bout y'all."

He worked for the United Nations as a civil affairs officer; the two had just gotten married the year before. Eunice said that she had met Walker nine years before, in 1994.

"I had just come back to Monrovia from up-country," she said.

"Wha' you were doing up-country?" I asked.

That's when she told me about the peacekeeper bombing at Firestone, about running away and hiding in Territory 3C for two years, about making and selling caustic soda soap on the side of the road. She told me about how alone she felt, staying with that family who didn't talk to her.

She told me that she hadn't seen her son, Ishmael, since she sent him away from Liberia in 1988. She told me she had heard that he was in London, but that information about him was hard to come by. She told me she worried at night that he didn't know her anymore, that he had forgotten his mother, that she would not ever see her son again.

As she told me the story, it was as if she was recounting the day-to-day maneuverings of a normal life, errands or a shopping list. She told the impossible with a shrug. I kept interrupting her with incredulous questions. "Wha' you mean you'n't seen Ishmael since 1988?" I asked, stunned.

Her replies seemed absurd, delivered without effect. "I not sure Ishmael would still know me," she said, quietly.

I thought about how Ishmael would be almost twenty now, older than his mother was when her adopted family left her and fled to the United States. I thought about the years I had spent without Mommee, how I had missed her every day, how I worried about her in Liberia, how that pain and fear had become my background music. And I wondered if Ishmael felt anything like that for Eunice.

That night, Eunice slept in the spare twin bed in my hotel room. I lay awake, listening to her breathing. I turned my face into my pillow so she wouldn't hear me crying.

"Which branch of the Cooper family you from?"

The question came out of the blue. Two days later, while Eunice was back at work at Firestone, I went to the cemetery on Center Street, where Daddy, Radio Cooper, Mama Grand, Bro. Henry, Uncle Waldron, and Uncle Julius were all buried. The Dennis plot sits right next to the Cooper plot. I had barely stepped my foot out of the car when a grave-worker walked up to me with that question.

"How you know I'm a Cooper?" I asked him.

"All ya'll look de same."

"My father was John L. Cooper Jr," I told him. He hugged me, introducing himself as Mr. Smith Blay. He was barefoot, in shorts and a T-shirt, and he smiled at me happily. "I used to work for your pa at the post office."

Mr. Blay took me to Daddy's grave. Someone had stolen

the headstone. Someone else had written the wrong birth year.

I sat on Daddy's grave, running my hands over the cold cement. The grave was surrounded by weeds. The whitewashed cement was chipped.

"Hello, Daddy," I said.

There was no wind, just the stillness of the humid Liberian air. In my peripheral vision, I saw a group of young men gathering around me. They were closing in when Mr. Smith Blay went to them and shooed them away. "Ya'll can't see de girl needs some privacy? Leave her 'lone."

My mind scanned through all the things I needed to tell Daddy, and somehow, the first thing that came out of my mouth was the bragging of a fifteen-year-old trying to impress her father. "Guess what, Daddy," I said, starting to grin. "I'm a reporter. I did it."

I sat on the grave for an hour, with Mr. Smith Blay keeping watch, talking to Daddy about the places I'd been. "China," I recounted triumphantly, knowing he had always wanted to go there. "I went to a state dinner in China. Deng Xiaoping shook my hand."

Surrounded by the graves of my Cooper and Dennis ancestors, I described the inside of the Forbidden City for Daddy, the vastness of Tiananmen Square, the impossibly wide streets of Beijing. Tears rolled down my face, as eventually I ran out of things to tell him. But still, I sat, silent now, as I thought about the Coopers and the Dennises, and about how far I had come from that day in 1829 when Randolph Cooper and his three brothers walked off the good ship *Harriet* to start my father's line in Liberia, or that day in 1821 when Elijah Johnson walked off the ship *Elizabeth* to start my mother's line.

Had I really thought that I could just turn my back on Liberia? I could never leave. A part of me was buried here, would always be right here in the dirt of Palm Grove Cemetery.

Finally, I ran my hand over the cement of Daddy's grave one more time, stood up, and turned around. Mr. Smith Blay was still guarding me from a distance. I walked over to him, kissed him on the cheek, and left.

A few days later when I was invited to attend a meeting of Prominent Liberian Women with the interim first lady, Mrs. Blah, at the Executive Mansion, my past reared its head again. I was wearing a yellow linen skirt suit borrowed from Philip's Aunt, Marie Parker, who informed me that "you cannot, absolutely not, show up at the Mansion in pants!"

There were sixteen Prominent Women at the meeting. We filed in and sat at the massive oak conference table on the fifth floor, just three floors beneath the family quarters where President Tolbert was killed twenty-three years before. We were waiting for the interim first lady when the door opened, a man walked in, pointed to me, and announced: "You! Come here! I know this face. You're Helene Calista Esmeralda Esdolores Dennis Cooper!"

I was shocked that William C. Dennis, another cousin I hadn't seen in twenty-three years, could remember my ridiculous full name. I laughed, and briefly became the topic of conversation among the Prominent Liberian Women. They talked about me as if I wasn't there.

"Oh, she's Calista and John's daughter!"

"You can see the Cooper people in that face."

"No, no, she look just like Calista."

"For true, oh, that Calista right there."

"I knew her when she was knee high to a pup!"

"Is she the journalist? Or is that Janice?"

I really shouldn't have ignored Mommee's advice to bring

a dress with me. I was starting to feel self-conscious tooling around Monrovia every day in my Iraq attire. On Sunday morning Ishmael came to pick me up for church, and looked at me slack-jawed. He was wearing neat black pants, a white button-down shirt, and a tie, his tall skinny frame suddenly rendered serious and purposeful in his Sunday best. I was in black slacks, a white shirt, and my Tevas.

It was too much for Ishmael. "You will wear trousers?" he asked me.

"Ishmael, lemme lone. What else people got?"

He looked like he wanted to say something more, but I got in the car and slammed the door, fastening my seat belt. "Let's go."

We parked outside on Ashmun Street, and walked in through the side door of First United Methodist Church, Established 1822, and straight to the family pew.

The church had bullet holes in the walls and a huge crater in the back from artillery shelling. But inside, everyone, except me, was in full Sunday attire. One woman wore a green dress with green shoes and a matching green hat with a green feather poking out the top.

There were familiar faces inside—faces I recognized instantly. I smiled and waved at friends of my parents, who motioned to me, pointed, waved, and whispered to the people next to them. Someone slipped a note to the pastor, and she paused in the middle of her announcements.

"One of our own has returned," she said, turning to look at me. Fighting a mixture of embarrassment and pride, I smiled. Joe Richards, an old friend of my parents, walked up to me and pushed me to the front to take a bow. Afterward, during the offering, he asked me for my cell phone to call Mommee. "Your daughter is standing here next to me in church in pants and sandals," he told her.

At the end of the sermon, the pastor said: "I want us all to now raise our voices for 'Blessed Assurance.' "

I stood up as the opening chords began on the organ. The joy started from deep in my stomach, gurgling up through me before bursting wide onto my face. They still sang "Blessed Assurance" every Sunday.

After church, Ishmael drove me to Eunice's house to have lunch with her and her husband, Walker. She had cooked one of my favorite Liberian dishes: fufu and ground pea soup. By Liberian standards, they lived well, sharing a two-bedroom concrete house in a Monrovia suburb, but the house had no running water and was illuminated only by candles and a single, battery-powered lightbulb. On a wooden bookshelf were a handful of books, a wedding photo, and one photo each of Marlene and me. In the second bedroom were two mattresses; Eunice had become a foster mother to four native Liberian children.

I was bracing myself, because I knew that after lunch, I wanted to talk Eunice into going back to Sugar Beach with me. No one in my family had been back there since the coup. Former President Doe had used the property as an "antiterrorist training camp"; in reality it had been used for summary executions. Many Liberians were afraid to go there. Nine bodies had recently been dug up on its grounds, many with their limbs detached.

Eunice didn't really want to go. I knew why; it was the same reason none of us who had been there the day the soldiers came, wanted to go back. I certainly didn't really want to go. Going back to Sugar Beach meant confronting that night, coming face-to-face with the death of my childhood.

But *I* didn't die that night, and neither did my mother or my sisters. By hiding away from Sugar Beach all those years, I felt as though I was allowing the rogues and the rapists to win.

They had successfully hijacked my childhood as I remembered it, so that all I really had left of Sugar Beach was the memory of one night.

My childhood was more than that. It was who I am. And I wanted it back.

"Eunice, I beg you," I said. "Don't make me go by myself."

I knew she would eventually agree. Had she ever denied me or Marlene anything we'd asked of her?

She sighed. "Alright, Helene. I will come wi' you." But she turned to her husband, Walker. "You coming' wi' us, too."

It was Sunday afternoon, and Monrovia was quiet as Ishmael, Walker, Eunice, and I drove from Eunice's house across the bridge to Sugar Beach, taking the same route that Fedeles, Eunice, and I had taken to get away from the April 14 rice riots in 1979. Instead of driving through the city, we circuited through Paynesville, turning left at the junction and then driving past ELWA toward Sugar Beach.

Daddy's old gas station showed up on the right, and Eunice asked Ishmael to slow down. "Helene, Jacob Doboyu duh still live here," she said.

"For true?" I was shocked; I hadn't thought about Daddy's factotum in twenty-three years.

We pulled into the parking lot in front of the gas station, now a police station, got out, and walked over to the house next door. He was sitting on the front steps, still looking exactly like Nelson Mandela, with salt-and-pepper hair and crinkling eyes.

"Hello, Eunice!" Jacob Doboyu said cheerfully, getting up.

Then, looking at me, his jaw dropped. "Calista?" he said, incredulously.

"No, Helene."

"Helene? Baby Helene?" I was swept up in a hug and I

laughed into the air, wondering how a seventy-year-old man could actually lift me up. He put me down and pinched my cheeks.

"Ow!"

"Oh let people hear their ear. I was pinching your cheeks when you were a baby!"

He, too, had heard, somehow, that I was a reporter. He, too, knew somehow that I had been in Iraq. I wondered how everybody in Liberia seemed to know this, and all of them acted as if two months in Iraq for the war was somehow more dangerous than thirteen years of civil war in Liberia.

Finally, we got back into the car and continued the five more minutes to the Sugar Beach turnoff. We had to park on the main road and hike down a mud path to get there. We started down the path, and I noticed that Ishmael wasn't following. I turned to him. He shook his head; he had heard the execution stories. "I staying by the car," he said. "I will be here when ya'll come back."

Down through the bush Eunice, Walker, and I walked, toward the ocean. "Palma 'them house used to be here," Eunice said. I stopped and looked around. There was nothing, just bush and vines.

If this was the spot of Palma 'them house, then . . . I turned west.

And there it was, just beyond that last hill and around that final bend, our house at Sugar Beach still stood, overlooking the Atlantic. Mommee's carpet grass still blanketed the grounds, as did the frame of the boys' house, where Bolabo used to sleep during the day before assuming his "guard" duty to protect us from the rogues at night. Remnants of the butter cream paint still clung to the frame, along with a few specks of roasted red pepper trim.

But that was it. Looters had taken the windows, roof, marble flooring, bathroom fixtures, furniture, and the kitchen sink. I scanned the front yard, wondering where Doe's executions had taken place, then tamped down the thought. It was intolerable, I would lose it if I let myself think about Doe executing people at Sugar Beach.

There were no doors. We climbed up the back stairs. My heart was thumping with trepidation, as a feeling of familiarity swept through me. I had climbed these steps a thousand times before, tripping over the dogs that had slept on the porch outside.

We crept into the kitchen—it was dank and dark—and found several Bassa families of squatters occupying the upstairs quarters. A woman was cooking a pot of rice over coals in the middle of Mommee and Daddy's bedroom—the very spot where Eunice, Marlene, and I had huddled on the night of my mother's rape.

In my old pink bedroom, the walls were now the dull gray of cement. Someone had tacked a piece of lapa cloth where the sliding glass doors used to be to protect from the wind and rain. An old woman was sleeping in my bedroom closet. She rolled over and looked at me when I walked in, then closed her eyes and went back to sleep.

I could hear Eunice talking to Walker in Marlene's room, and I headed down the hallway to them. They were standing in the middle of the room, where Marlene's bed used to sit, surrounded, every night, by the mattresses that Eunice, Vicky, and I dragged in there to sleep on. Walker was shaking his head at Eunice quizzically. "But why y'all all slept in here?"

She shrugged, impatient. "This where we wanted to sleep."

In my mind I could hear Marlene shrieking with laughter as she and John Bull played "Boofair" and swiped purloined candy from each other. I saw Vicky trying to teach Janice how to do the "bus stop" dance, their two Afros bobbing to the beat in front of the mirror. Down the hallway I could hear Daddy imitating Mommee yelling at him to put on his slippers so he could stop sneezing; I could see Mommee rolling her eyes that he was daring to tease her.

I could see Eunice and myself, huddled on our mattresses with our flashlights in the dark, reading Barbara Cartland novels and whispering about whether we should wear the white go-go boots that Daddy had bought us back in the United States to the Relda matinee that Saturday, or wait to premier them later at a bigger event.

One of the squatters joined us in Marlene's room, and Walker started chatting with him. I turned to Eunice, and we exchanged a glance.

Without saying a word, she walked out of the room, down the hallway, around the bend, past the TV lounge and toward the stairwell. I followed her down the stairs and through the tunnel that led to the recreation room.

Where had it actually happened? In the play area, where there was carpet? By the sliding doors, where the marble floor would have been hard and cold? Where had they raped my mother?

I hadn't been downstairs since that day in April 1980. When we'd returned in May 1980 to pack our suitcases to leave Liberia, I hadn't dared. Now, twenty-three years later, here I was. With the windows gone, the recreation room was dank and smelled of the sea. No squatters appeared to sleep downstairs; unlike upstairs, there were no makeshift curtains and sheets tacked to the open doorways. It was just a big empty cavernous room. Still, I could see my favorite purple velvet chair, Daddy's leather sofa where he held forth on the Sino-Soviet pact with his friends, the playroom stacked with Marlene's toys.

Neither Eunice nor I said a word while we drifted around downstairs. There was nothing to see; yet there was everything to see. My mother had made a stand here. She had fought for us. She had fought for her daughters to remain children, and even though that night had seen the end of my childhood, still, somehow, she had won. Weren't Eunice and I standing here as proof?

I heard footfalls—someone was joining us. I turned to Eunice; she was standing, her feet apart, leaning against the wall, staring into the recreation room.

"You ready to go?" she finally spoke.

In a few days I would be packing up and leaving Monrovia. I would bribe my way out of Robertsfield and onto Ghana Airways to Accra, and then onto British Airways to London and then Washington, where Marlene would meet me and take me back to my house in my nice neighborhood with its quaint front porches and picket fences. I would leave Eunice with the new Liberian cell phone that I had purchased, so she would never be unreachable for me again.

But phone or not, I would still be leaving her. Eunice would return to Firestone, to her husband, to her foster children, and Sugar Beach would again be a memory. Still, I knew which memory would prevail—the Sugar Beach of my childhood, a beautiful dancer disrobing as we bounced along the road away from civilization. The Sugar Beach where my mattress sat next to Eunice's mattress on the floor of Marlene's bedroom as my customized pink bedroom sat empty.

I nodded. "Yeah," I said. "I ready."

Eunice and I were silent in the car on the drive back to Monrovia, as Walker chatted quietly with Ishmael. I felt an odd mixture of sorrow and euphoria. Eunice just looked out the car window, saying nothing.

A thought entered my head.

"Hey, Eunice," I said, "they sang 'Blessed Assurance' at church today."

Immediately, we were both laughing, then singing:

"Breakfast this morning, with biscuits and cheese . . ."

The car drove on, past Daddy's old gas station, and the squatter encampment in Paynesville, past bush and swamps, swollen from the rains.

"This is my story," we sang. "This is my song."

AUTHOR'S NOTE

This book is a memoir, but it is also a work of discovery. I interviewed my family members and my friends, as well as participants in the ongoing documentary that is Liberia's evolving political history. I also spent four months during a fellowship at the Woodrow Wilson Institute conducting research into the American Colonization Society and the founding of Liberia. The ACS journals were enormously helpful, as were several books, particularly *Prince Among Slaves* by Terry Alford (Oxford University Press, 1986) and *Liberia: The Quest for Democracy* by J. Gus Liebenow (Indiana University Press, 1987).

Conversations that are recounted in this book in which I was not a participant come from interviews with at least one actual participant. Thoughts that are attributed to specific characters come from the characters themselves, be they through in-person interviews, telephone conversations, letters, emails, or—in the case of my great-great-great-great-grandfather, Elijah Johnson—personal journals.

One thing I've learned from all this: our parents, grandparents, and great-grandparents are the best resources any of us has when it comes to figuring out each of our individual stories. There was a wealth of knowledge waiting for me; all I had to do was shut up and listen.

Helene Cooper
January 14, 2008
Washington, D.C.

ACKNOWLEDGMENTS

If I had known how hard this was going to be, I would have spent my growing-up years reading great literature instead of romance novels. Thankfully, I had an editor who recognized the difference between drivel and good writing, and, more important, had no qualms about telling me when I handed in the former. Marysue Rucci put her own heart and soul into this. She was encouraging and supportive and, best of all, she knew when I needed my rear kicked. The distance between my first draft and my final draft was a marathon, and I never would have reached the finish line without her.

At Simon & Schuster, David Rosenthal supported this book through four years of rewrites and proved his street cred by sweating his way through a fiery Liberian meal filled with Scotch bonnet peppers. Not too many publishers can say that,

Sugar Beach Crew: Vicky, Marlene, Janice, Eunice, and Helene

I'm thinking. Virginia Smith was hugely efficient in the final sprint to publication. My thanks also to Tracey Guest, Lisa Healy, and Linda Dingler.

At William Morris, Suzanne Gluck and Dorian Karchmar held my hand and bucked me up. Their suggestions were invaluable, from my original book proposal, ironed out with Suzanne in the bar at One Aldwych in London, all the way to my final rewrites, which Dorian plowed through while on maternity leave.

The Woodrow Wilson Institute gave me a place to hang my hat when I got sick of writing in my basement, and, more important, provided me with the best assistant around: Amy Brisson, who found me Elijah Johnson's journal.

I have been very lucky to work at the world's two greatest newspapers: the *New York Times* and the *Wall Street Journal*. At the *Times*, Arthur Sulzberger, Jill Abramson, Dean Baquet, Gail Collins, Doug Jehl, Phil Taubman, Bill Keller, and Andy Rosenthal have given me the best sandbox in which to play. At the *Journal*, Alan Murray, Jerry Seib, and David Wessel taught me how to report and write and paid my corporate American Express bills. What more could any aspiring globe-trotter ask for? And Bob Davis gave me the two central tenets of writing to which I will always subscribe: "Go out on a limb, and don't be a wuss."

A long time ago, at the Black Friar in London, Danny Pearl told me that I should one day write this book. My memories of his friendship and courage have sustained me through my worst moments of self-doubt.

Six friends read (and reread and reread) my manuscript. Roe D'Angelo asked for "more Marlene." Bryan Gruley demanded self-reflection. Nicholas Kulish told me to lose the flip tone. Shailagh Murray asked for more of my dad. Michael Phillips told me to add ten pages to the end. Amy Schatz made me spell out what made me so scared in my pink room at night. Together, the six of them helped me figure out what I wanted to write, how I wanted to write it, and how to live with myself after I wrote it.

My thanks also to Sarah Abruzzese, Silvia Ascarelli, Elizabeth Crowley, Anne Gearan, Sarah Herzog, Farhana Hossain, Craig Hunter, Vicki Ingrassia, Tom Jennings, Neil King, Elise Labott, Pam Lilak, Conley McCoy, Wendy Moniz, Laura Nichols, Carla Robbins, Michael Shapiro, Joseph Sozio, Amy Stevens, Caroline VanZoeren, Eliza VanZoeren, and Alyson Young for targeted work during my various meltdowns. David Cloud told me to add descriptive scenes about the sand between my toes. I dismissed his specific suggestion as rubbish, but took his general advice. And thanks to my galley readers—Scott Shane, Jonathan Gordon, Mark Mazzetti, Steve Weisman, Mark Suzman, and Philip Shenon.

My Liberian friends and cousins may never speak to me again. But they gave me such rich material: Veda Simpson, Philip Parker, Richard Parker, Ethello McCritty Miller, Bridget Dennis, Seward Cooper, Jeanine Cooper Heffinck, and Karen Mygil.

My family has always been my rock. My brother, John Lewis Cooper III, gave me his quiet support when he wasn't threatening to consult a lawyer. My stoic Serbian brother-in-law, Aleksandar Vasilic, gave me the ultimate confidence booster of bawling all the way through the manuscript when I gave it to him to read. Two of my sisters, Janice Cooper Kudayah and Victoria Dennis Johnson, corrected my errors and made me remember things I had long buried. One sister, Eunice Bull Walker, let me dig into her head and memories, and, more important, accepted me unhesitatingly, as if twenty-three years apart had never happened. And finally, my sister, Marlene Cooper Vasilic, read the manuscript ten times and each time pushed me to go deeper, to be more tactile, to think about how things smelled, to close my eyes and remember. I could never have written the book without her. Together, those four women are amongst the strongest women I know.

But not the strongest. That title goes to my mother, Calista Dennis Cooper. Thank you, Mommee, for so much more than I could ever put down on paper.

PHOTO CREDITS

1. Cooper Family Collection
2. Cooper Family Collection
3. Public Domain
4. Cooper Family Collection
5. Cooper Family Collection
6. Caesar Harris Historical Art Gallery, Monrovia
7. Cooper Family Collection
8. Cooper Family Collection
9. Cooper Family Collection
10. Cooper Family Collection
11. Jimmy Carter Presidential Library and Museum
12. Cooper Family Collection
13. Cooper Family Collection
14. Cooper Family Collection
15. © Fort Worth Star-Telegram Collection, Special Collections, the University of Texas at Arlington Library, Arlington, Texas
16. Cooper Family Collection
17. Cooper Family Collection
18. Cooper Family Collection
19. Cooper Family Collection
20. Cooper Family Collection
21. Cooper Family Collection

22. Providence Journal
23. © Getty Images
24. Cooper Family Collection
25. Cooper Family Collection
26. © 2003, Los Angeles Times. Used with permission.
27. Cooper Family Collection
28. Cooper Family Collection

ABOUT THE AUTHOR

Helene Calista Cooper is the diplomatic correspondent for the *New York Times*. Before joining the *Times* in 2004, she spent twelve years at the *Wall Street Journal* writing about international economics, trade, and the war in Iraq. Born in Monrovia, Liberia, she now lives in the Washington, D.C., area.